Pio

Naval War
of the Pacific
1879–1884

STRATUS

Published in Poland in 2020
by STRATUS s.j.
Po. Box 123,
27-600 Sandomierz 1, Poland
e-mail: office@mmpbooks.biz
as
MMPBooks,
e-mail: rogerw@mmpbooks.biz
© 2020 MMPBooks.
http://www.mmpbooks.biz

ISBN
978-83-65958-77-8

Editor in chief
Roger Wallsgrove

Editorial Team
Bartłomiej Belcarz
Robert Pęczkowski
Artur Juszczak

Text and research
Piotr Olender

Translated by
Kazimierz Zygadło

Drawings and maps
Robert Panek

Proofreading
Roger Wallsgrove

DTP
Stratus sp. j.

Printed by
Wydawnictwo
Diecezjalne i Drukarnia
w Sandomierzu
www.wds.pl

Table of contents

1. The origin of the conflict

The period of the struggle for the independence of South America and its liberation from Spanish rule was practically over in December 1824, when the army of Gran Colombia under command of General Sucre defeated Spanish forces at the battle of Ayacucho. Thus crumbled the last bastion of the Bourbon dynasty in Peru. Consequently, new countries began to emerge on the ruins of the Spanish dominion. Without going into further details, their borders, at least in the initial period, were defined by those of the former Spanish provinces.

Organizing their colonial possessions in South and Central America, the Spaniards divided them into viceroyalties, headed by viceroys representing the monarch. Initially, there were only two viceroyalties of Mexico and Peru, which were divided into *audiencias*. After the Bourbons seized power in Spain, Philip V undertook the task of reforming the colonial administration in order to make it more effective. As a result, in 1717 he established the Viceroyalty of New Granada, while *audiencias* were replaced by *intendencias* run by intendants who were more closely subordinated to royal authority. In 1776, during the reign of Charles III, another Viceroyalty of the Rio de la Plata was established. It was mainly established in order to more efficiently defend the southeastern shores of the Spanish colonies in South America in case of a conflict with Great Britain. However, since the territories of the new viceroyalty were relatively sparsely populated or developed, the Spanish authorities decided to incorporate into them the terrains of Upper Peru (later Bolivia) with the *intendencia* of Potosi and its rich silver mines in order to strengthen their potential. The latter was incorporated into the new viceroyalty in its previous

The Atacama Desert, one of the driest places on Earth.

Coast of the Atacama Desert, south of the harbour of Tocopilla.

form, i.e. with a strip of land reaching the Pacific Ocean, which divided the Viceroyalty of Peru into two parts: northern (Peru) and southern (Chile).

That quite unusual shape of the Potosi province border had its origins dating back to the 16th century. Following the discovery of rich silver deposits in Potosi, a problem arose concerning their transportation. The logical solution was to deliver the mined ore to a port on the Pacific coast and transport it by sea to the north, to the area of the Isthmus of Panama, through which it was transported by land to Portobello. There, it was loaded on board the *Terra Firme* ships, to be carried to Spain. In order to ensure that the Potosi authorities would be able to freely transport the silver, it was decided to put under their jurisdiction the strip of land reaching up to the coast of the Pacific with a harbour, which would facilitate the export of precious metals. That place was the town of Cobija (founded in 1587, also known by its initial name of Puerto La Mar). The route to that harbour, leading through the Calama oasis, was thus under control of the authorities of the same province in which the silver was mined. However, after the incorporation of Upper Peru into the new Viceroyalty of La Plata, the transport of silver changed direction, heading towards Buenos Aires[1]. Therefore, the access of the Potosi *intendencia* to the

---

1   Due to the harsh conditions in the Atacama desert, the Spaniards had already used the route running from Potosi to the shore of Lake Titicaca (mostly to Aygacha), from where silver, transported by mules, was transshipped onto boats, then transported to the other side of the lake and finally, again transported by mules through the Andean passes to one of the Peruvian ports, mostly Arica. Although this road was much longer, it was also more convenient.

The harbour of Cobija (as seen in 1879), also known as Puerto La Mar. It was the oldest harbour on the Bolivian costa established back in 1587, which used to serve as an export centre for silver mined in the mines of Potosi.

Pacific was no longer necessary. Nonetheless, the old borders remained, which later influenced the territorial shape of the newly created South American states. When, at the turn of the 1830s and 1840s, the borders of Bolivia were finally formed, the country, although located in the centre of the continent, had access to the Pacific through that area of the Atacama desert located within the borders of the former Potosi *intendencia*. In practice, however, from the point of view of the Bolivian government that fact was not significant, because the inaccessibility of the Atacama desert, through which the road to Cobiji ran, made the transport of the majority of goods from the centre of the country to that harbour and back unprofitable.

Located on the west coast of South America, the Atacama desert is one of the driest places on earth. The average annual rainfall is between 10 to 50 mm, but in some areas it has not rained for centuries! The desert itself stretches roughly from Arica in the north to the Copiapó River in the south, for a length of about thousand kilometres, covering a 100 kilometre deep strip from the coast of the Pacific to the foot of the Andes (its area is about 105,000 km²). It is mostly composed of sandy and stony terrain with salt deposits. As a place hostile to both humans and animals, it was mostly uninhabited at the beginning of the nineteenth century[2]. Therefore, as such, it constituted a natural border for the three countries it was located within. Peru was in possession of its northern part down to the lower course of the Loa River. The central section, located south of the Loa River, stretching down to the city of Antofagasta belonged to Bolivia, while the rest of the desert was within the borders of Chile. However, as it soon turned out the Atacama, although inhospitable, was not a useless piece of land as it was full of countless riches.

As a result of the exceptionally dry desert climate, the coast, mainly in the northern part of the desert, had an abundance of guano (large deposits were also found on the coastal islands, the largest

Guano mine.

The anchorage off the Chincha Archipelago, Peru. These islands were known for their extensive guano deposits.

---

2   The desert was inhabited by primitive tribes of *Changos* and *Atacameños* Indians. The size of their population is very difficult to determine, but in the 1860s it probably did not exceed 20,000 people scattered over about 1,000 kilometres of the coastline within the borders of Chile, Bolivia and Peru. R. E. Latcham, Los Changos de la costas de Chile, Santiago de Chile 1910.

THE CHINCHA (GUANO) ISLANDS: MIDDLE ISLAND, AS SEEN FROM NORTH ISLAND.

were on the Chincha Islands archipelago located in the Pacific Ocean, west-northwest of the city of Pisco). Guano is simply dried bird droppings, mainly those of cormorants, pelicans and seagulls. The inhospitable coast of the Pacific, west of the desert, offered favourable living conditions for these species. Numerous schools of fish which appeared off the western coast of the continent served as their feeding grounds. Scarcely any precipitation contributed to the accumulation and conservation of bird droppings, which after centuries in places formed a layer several dozen meters thick.

Guano is characterized by a high content of phosphates and both calcium and magnesium nitrates as well as a number of other compounds, which makes it an excellent natural fertilizer. Its properties had already been known in the Inca Empire period, but were later forgotten. The famous explorer and naturalist Alexander von Humboldt made guano well-known in Europe at the beginning of the 19th century. However, at first, it did not arouse much interest. The value of guano as fertilizer had not been known in the United States until 1824 and since 1840 it became a sought-after commodity on the market. Demand for guano led to its extensive mining, with profits mainly supporting Peru, as three-quarters of its resources were located in that country.

Despite growing production (it is estimated that a total of approximately 13 million tonnes of guano were mined up to the end of the 1870s), demand for that fertiliser increased steadily and along with it rose the price. As farmers got used to the new fertilizer and guano prices rose steadily, the search for a mineral that could replace guano began. An alternative was found in the form of sodium nitrate, which had even more advantages. Containing more than 15 percent of nitrogen, it could serve as an excellent raw material for the production of efficient nitrogen fertilizers, successfully replacing guano. Moreover, it could also be used for processing into potassium nitrate and for producing explosives, not to mention the fact that it was used as a preservative in the food industry. No wonder that after 1872 the demand for guano began to gradually decline (although there were still buyers interested in it), while the demand for nitrate increased. The richest nitrate deposits in the world were also found in the Atacama desert, mostly in its northern area. While guano was mostly found in Peru, saltpetre deposits were distributed more evenly across all three countries which had the desert within their borders. However, its main deposits were located in the north, mainly in the areas under Peruvian and Bolivian control.

The drop in the price of guano, which took place in the early 1870s, hit the Peruvian economy hard. It had already been going through difficulties due to excessive debt and difficulties in paying interest,

The Antofagasta waterfront. The town had become the main saltpetre export harbour on the Bolivian costa in the 1870s.

as well as internal political problems resulting in continual coups and the consequent changes of government. Until the 1860s, guano sale was so profitable that, although Peru's debt had already been alarming at the time, the revenues from the guano monopoly, which accounted for approximately 60% of the budget revenue, made it possible to maintain liquidity and timely payment of all debts, leaving some surplus in the state treasury[3].

Discovery of the advantages of sodium nitrate and the increased demand for it, which took place after 1872, limited the demand for guano and at the same time caused its price to fall. Still worse was the world economic crisis which began after 1873 as it reduced demand for copper, Peru's other major export commodity. All this drastically reduced budget revenues and caused a sharp surge in deficit. However, despite the crisis, in the 1870s nitrate prices remained high, with rich deposits in the Peruvian province of Tarapaca and on the Bolivian *costa* (coast). In 1875, the Peruvian government nationalised the entire saltpetre industry (for compensation in bonds against future income), while simultaneously trying to buy concessions for all possible deposits in Bolivia[4]. Therefore, the Peruvian authorities tried to do exactly the same thing as they had done before with guano, i.e. to secure a monopoly on its extraction and trade in order to maintain budget revenues at the former level without changing the tax system (based primarily on mining concession fees, the guano and then the saltpetre monopoly as well as customs duties).

The Bolivian authorities, which had been bound to Peru by alliance since 1873[5], did not oppose the attempts to create a Peruvian nitrate monopoly, as above all they were afraid of possible Chilean claims concerning the Bolivian *costa*, since ambiguities concerning the delimitation of the borders existed practically from the time both countries had come into being. In order to resolve any contradictions, the Chilean-Bolivian Treaty[6] was concluded in 1866, which regulated the disputes by establishing borders between the two countries on the 24th parallel and creating a common area for the exploitation of minerals between the 23rd and the 25th parallel, with citizens of both countries being free to settle there. That provision increased the influx of Chilean immigrants to the Bolivian *costa*, who were attracted by

---

3   In 1869, guano sales totalled GBP 4 million, compared to only GBP 2.6 million in 1875, B. W. Farcau, *The Ten Cent War. Chile, Peru and Bolivia in the War of Pacific, 1879–1884*, London 2000, p. 19.

4   Initially, in January 1873, the Peruvian government established forced mediation of state agencies for the export of saltpetre in order to control its sale. The new regulations proved ineffective and in May 1875 the entire saltpetre industry was nationalised, C. R. Markham, *The War between Chile and Peru*, London 1882, p. 89.

5   Text of the treaty: *Boletin de la Guerra del Pacifico 1879–1881*, Santiago 1979, pp. 30–31. Argentina was also invited to join the alliance, although this issue was still discussed in the Argentinean Parliament in 1877, the country decided not to join Peru and Bolivia (C. R. Markham, op. cit., p. 80).

6   This treaty was concluded in the face of the Spanish intervention that took place between 1864 and 1866. After the departure of the Spanish fleet from South American waters and the signing of peace in 1871, the old disagreements and disputes began to resurface.

the possibility of earning decent wages in the local saltpetre, silver and copper mines[7]. Consequently, in 1875 they already constituted 90 percent of the population of the Bolivian *costa*, becoming the dominant element in the province of Antofagasta, which encompassed the coast and the desert areas. That fact began to create cause for concern among the authorities in La Paz. If we also take into consideration the fact that these were mostly Chilean companies, and above all, the powerful *Compania de Salitres y Ferrocarril de Antofagasta* (which in turn was controlled by British capital), which was the largest shareholder in the Bolivian saltpetre mines, the concerns of the Bolivian government could hardly be regarded as unfounded.

Meanwhile, in 1874, following another coup in Bolivia, when the dictator Agustína Morales had been overthrown, power was seized by the party of the great landowners known as *hacendados*, who were more pro-Chilean oriented. The new government confirmed the 1866 provisions in a new treaty,

---

7   Those willing to work in the emerging saltpetre mines could also be found in Bolivia, however it was difficult for them to get to their own coast since the communication routes running through the Atacama were inaccessible. Consequently, they found their way into the Peruvian mines located in the province of Tarapaca, where it was much easier for them to reach. The Chileans, however, had no problems getting to the Bolivian *costa* by sea.

finally establishing the border at the 24th parallel. It also gave warranty not to increase tax rates on raw materials extracted in the common exploitation zone for the next 25 years and exempted goods crossing the borders of both countries from customs duty. Consequently, the Bolivian coastal province became practically dependent on supplies of products from Chile. The exports of Chilean goods to Bolivia also increased, which hurt the interests of domestic producers and caused widespread discontent. However, before the new treaty could be ratified, the country was shaken by another coup in 1876, in which the *hacendados* government was overthrown. Power was seized by Hilarion Daza, who proclaimed himself the new president of the country. Daza's government immediately nullified the treaty with Chile, which consequently had to lead to increased tensions between the two countries. In February 1878, Daza's government imposed an export tax of 10 centavos per quintal[8] on Bolivian saltpetre. What was worse, it had to be paid retroactively back to 1874. That was the proverbial last straw. The set price was not too steep in itself[9], but its introduction was in violation of the agreement – the Bolivian government unilaterally changed the tax rates on the raw material, which it had earlier warranted not to do. Consequently, the *Compania de Salitres y Ferrocarril de Antofagasta* refused to pay the new tax and in response to that the Bolivian authorities ordered confiscation and auctioning of its assets. Daza had decided to take such a radical step in order to improve the country's finances, which were ruined by political instability and constant coups (to which he himself contributed by paying his supporters after seizing power), hoping the Chilean authorities would not react in any way. For quite some time Chile had been involved in a conflict with Argentina concerning the territory of Tierra del Fuego, to which both these countries laid claims. It escalated at the beginning of 1878, but on December 6, both countries came to an agreement by signing the Fierro-Sarratea Treaty, which did not resolve the conflict completely, but regulated relations between the two sides on the basis of a compromise and thus averted the danger of war. That agreement, not taken into account by Daza, gave the Chilean authorities free rein in the north, enabling them to take decisive action.

Indeed, for the Chilean government, the step taken by the Bolivian authorities regarding the export tax on saltpetre was unacceptable. Although Chile was one of the most economically developed countries in South America, it was also affected by the global crisis that broke out after 1873. All the more so, since the demand for one of Chile's main export commodities, copper, had significantly decreased. In that situation, the authorities in Santiago counted heavily on the revenues from the saltpetre industry. Meanwhile, the nationalisation of the saltpetre industry in Peru and then the failure to ratify the treaty with Bolivia virtually eliminated any chances of achieving that goal. That could have caused serious economic disruption. The introduction of a 10-cent saltpetre tax by the Bolivian government was the proverbial straw that broke the camel's back. Consequently, an armed intervention or even war had become acceptable solutions. All the more so, as the Chilean side was backed by foreign entrepreneurs, especially British, who had invested considerable amounts of money in the saltpetre industry and did not want to accept the losses that would be caused by the actions of the Bolivian authorities, had they entered into force.

The road between Antofagasta and Calama (present day photo). In 1879, it was the only route connecting the Bolivian coast with the interior of the country.

---

8   The currency of Bolivia was the Bolivian peso (called *boliviano*) divided into 100 centavos – therefore, the tax for the export of one ton of nitrate would amount to one Bolivian peso. Theoretically, it had the value of around 4 British shillings, however, the attempts to repair the financial problems of the country by debasement of the currency and the related inflation resulted in the decrease of its value to about 3 shillings on the eve of the war. *The Statesmen's Year-Book., Statistical and Historical Annual of the States of the Civilised World for the year 1878* (vol. XVI; ed. F. Martin), London 1878, p. 492.

9   After the outbreak of war, the Chilean government imposed a tax on the export of saltpetre, which amounted to 40 centavos (Chilean). It did not prove prohibitive in any way and did not cause a dramatic drop in revenues for the mine owners., B. W. Farcau, op.cit., p. 44.

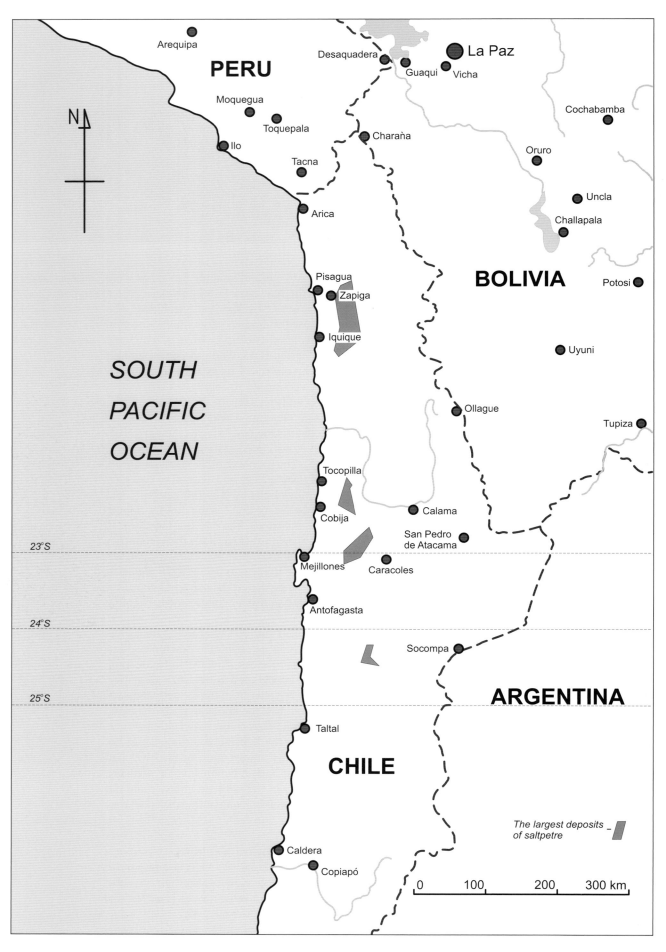

Borders of Chile, Bolivia and Peru before the outbreak of the war

10

2. Opponents

Bolivia

Of the three countries involved in the exploitation of the Atacama's wealth, Bolivia was undoubtedly the one with the least economic and military potential, clearly inferior to its ally – Peru and its potential opponent – Chile.

On the eve of the war, Bolivia was a vast country, with an area of over 2,182,000 km², inhabited by more than 2 million people, including at least 800,000 mostly non-Spanish-speaking Indians. The country itself could be divided into an unexplored Amazon area, inhabited only by uncivilized Indian tribes, the mountainous Andean area and the most densely populated plateau of Altiplano, containing the capital city of La Paz, inhabited by about 26,000 people[1]. There was also a part of the Atacama desert with the harbours of Antofagasta, Cobija and Mejillones, of which the first played the most important role in 1879[2]. That desert province, which was named Antofagasta after its largest town, was connected to the rest of the country only by a relatively poor desert road leading through the oasis of Calama. Consequently, the harbours of the province worked almost exclusively to satisfy the local needs connected with the export of guano, copper, silver and saltpetre which were mined locally, and the import of the essential goods needed by their inhabitants.

Apart from exploitation of minerals on the coast, the Bolivian economy was based on extensive agriculture, which provided a living for the majority of its inhabitants, and on mining, mostly of silver and copper. There was virtually no industry and production was limited to primitive manufacturing. There were only two railroads operating in the entire country. The most important was the one running between La Paz and Aygacha, a harbour on Lake Titicaca, the export centre for the majority of minerals, which were then exported through the Peruvian harbours (transport through Antofagasta, Mejillones or Conija was not feasible due to difficult terrain conditions).

The annual budgetary revenue of Bolivia was under 3 million Bolivian pesos (*boliviano*), which was equivalent to less than 600,000 pounds sterling (according to the official exchange rate, actually it was about 450,000). Nearly every year budgetary expenditures greatly exceeded revenues, which were approximately 4.5 million pesos, that was 900,000 pounds (according to the official exchange

Hilarion Daza Groselle, the President of Bolivia.

---

1 However, in 1869, due to upheavals and coups d'etat, the seat of the authorities was moved to the fortified town of Oruro.

2 At the beginning of the 1860s, the largest settlement on the Bolivian costa was the port of Cobija with 2380 inhabitants, with a population of the entire province of about 5,300 people (*The Statesmen's Year-Book...1870*, vol. VII, op.cit., p. 488). In 1868, however, the city was destroyed by an earthquake and its population dropped below a thousand. The role of Cobija was then taken over by the Changos settlement of Mejillones, which had been founded in the 1840s. It soon became an important centre for the mining of guano, as well as its export. Pursuant to the agreement of 1866, a customs office was established in the town to control the export of guano and metals mined in the Chilean-Bolivian common mining zone. However, shortly afterwards, it was moved to Antofagasta, located about 60 km to the south, which at that time began to rise to the role of the main administrative and economic centre of the Bolivian province (the majority of Bolivian saltpetre was exported through Antofagasta), its population growing to approximately 6,000 people at the end of the 1870s (A. Curtis, *To the Last Cartridge. The story of the War of the Pacific 1879–1884*, vol. I, West Chester 2007, p. 43).

President Daza on the streets of La Paz, following the declaration of war with Chile.

rate, actually it was about 450,000). Nearly every year budgetary expenditures greatly exceeded revenues, which were approximately 4.5 million pesos, that was 900,000 pounds (according to the official exchange rate, actually about 675,000). The difference was covered by loans (in 1875, public debt was the equivalent of 3.4 million pounds, with roughly half of that amount being foreign loans, while the other half constituted domestic debt) and by minting of debased coins (before the outbreak of the war the actual value of *boliviano* was less by roughly 25% from its nominal value)[3].

Bolivian soldier.

The Bolivian army was in the same disastrous situation as the economy and finances of the state. Theoretically, it comprised three infantry regiments (the *Colorados* Regiment served as the presidential guard elite unit[4]), two cavalry and one artillery regiments. However, actually, each of the infantry regiments comprised only one, incomplete battalion. One of the cavalry regiments comprised two squadrons, while the other had only one. The artillery regiment had merely two Blakely mountain guns and 4 mitrailleuses. The army had no engineering units and the Bolivians also had no navy[5]. Moreover, out of the about 2,000 troops, as this was a total of men serving in the aforementioned units, over 500 were commissioned officers (16 in the rank of general), many of whom exceeded the retirement age, which made them incapable of active service[6]. Regular forces were to be supplemented

3   *The Statesmen's Year-Book…*, vol. XVI (1879), op.cit., pp.491–192.

4   The pay of a private in that regiment was equivalent to that of an officer (captain) in other units, B. W. Farcau, op.cit., p. 58.

5   On March 29, 1879, President Daza issued a decree offering letters of marque to each individual willing to equip a warship and operate against Chilean commerce (T. B. M. Mason, The War on the Pacific Coast of South America between Chile and the Allied Republics of Peru and Bolivia, 1879–1881., Washington 1883, p. 26). In response, a few Peruvian officers suggested to Bolivian diplomats, who resided in Lima at that time, to help them equip a suitable vessel. A small steamer *Laura* was purchased and purportedly even armed. A group of Peruvians and Bolivians was going to capture one of the Chilean steamers running off the coast of Peru in a surprise attack (the *Itata* or the *Loa* were considered as targets of this attack). Finally, the privateering effort never happened and the plan was dropped after Peru entered the war.

6   *Boletin…*, op.cit., p. 31; A. Curtis, op.cit., vol. I, pp. 2-3; B. Vicuña Mackenna, *Guerra del Pacifico. Historia de la campaña de Tarapaca*, *vol. I*, Santiago de Chile 1881, pp. 157–159. However, the large number of officers in the Bolivian army

by the National Guards, which in theory should have comprised 28 infantry battalions, the equivalent of 8 cavalry regiments and an artillery battalion[7]. Actually, these units only existed on paper and did not constitute any real power.

Admittedly, following the outbreak of the war, riding on the wave of patriotic effusion numerous volunteers were formed into 16 new infantry battalions (including one in the Peruvian province of Tarapaca, which comprised Bolivians working in the local saltpetre mines) and 5 new cavalry squadrons. However, there were shortages in arms and equipment for those units. The artillery was reinforced by the purchase of a battery of modern Krupp mountain guns (six 60 mm C/72 guns). Three thousand Remington M 1871 riles were also purchased (1,500 such guns had already been in possession of the armed forces, as well as twice as many older Snider-Enfield M 1866 rifles, which had been converted from Enfield Pattern 1853 muzzle loaders) to arm the volunteers. To help, Peru also supplied a number of rifles but it was not enough to satisfy all the needs. Consequently, the new units were armed with various, often obsolete weapons which were at hand[8]. All in all, though, within a year the Bolivian army was finally expanded to about 10,000 troops. However, most of the new units did not achieve combat readiness until 1880.

The majority of common Bolivian soldiers were Mestizo or Aymara Indians. Both combat training and morale of the regular troops were acceptable (in case of the *Colorados* it was even very good), although their discipline left much to be desired. Training of the volunteer units was much worse, although their morale was relatively high (at least at the beginning of the conflict).

Peru

In the coming conflict, Peru was the main ally of Bolivia, although finally it became its major part, which bore the brunt of the military operations against Chile.

Peru was of comparable size to Bolivia. Admittedly, its total area was half the size of the latter, at 1,300,000 km². However, its population was much larger, as it exceeded over 2.7 million people. Peruvian society was multiracial. Out of the total number of its citizens roughly 57% were Indians, at least 20% were of mixed-race, while the whites constituted no more than a dozen or so percent of the entire population[9].

Peruvian territory could be divided into the Spanish-speaking coastal lowlands (*costa*), Indian, Quechua-speaking mountain regions (*sierra*) and the sparsely populated territory of Montana in the Amazon River basin, covered by thick forests and inhabited by wild Indian tribes and all sorts of adventurers[10], which was of little importance. Peasants, who lived off the land, constituted the majority of inhabitants of both coastal and mountain regions. Most of them, especially in the mountain areas, were still farming in communes (although in the 1820s, right after winning their independence, the Peruvian authorities abolished them and granted the farmers their lands). Apart from small farms there were also *haciendas*. Those located in the mountains provided food for coastal towns, while those on the coast produced mainly sugar or alternatively cotton for export. Besides agriculture, Peru's main branch of economy was mining. Copper, iron ore (its large scale mining only began in 1870s) and silver were mined in the mountains. In the 1870s the country began the expansion of its metal industry. In the years 1874–1875, the first blast furnaces were constructed in Huanco. Guano and saltpetre were mined in the coastal areas[11].

Mariano Prado Ochoa, the President of Peru.

proved beneficial when its numbers were beginning to grow. Admittedly, the quality of the newly formed army units differed, but increasing its numbers would have been impossible without such an overblown officer corps.

7   B. Vicuña Mackenna, op.cit., ...*Tarapaca*, vol. I, pp. 160–161.

8   Ibidem., pp. 3-6; G. Esposito, Armies of the War of the Pacific 1879–1880, Chile, Peru & Bolivia, Osprey Publishing Ltd., 2016, p. 38; G. Esposito, A Garcia Pinto, The War of the Pacific, Winged Hussar Publishing 2018, pp. 30–31.

9   *The Statesmen's Year-Book...*, vol. XVI (1879), op.cit., p. 563.

10   The population of Montana was not officially censused, but it was estimated at over 300,000 people. Consequently, in 1879, the entire Peruvian population would exceed 3 million people. *The Statesmen's Year-Book...*, vol. XX (1883), op.cit., p 563. Moreover, due to the rapid industrialization of the *costa* and following the establishment of diplomatic relations with China in 1874, large numbers of Chinese workers were being brought in to work there, as the shortage of labour had become more apparent (by the outbreak of the war, their numbers had risen to approximately 45–50,000).

11   *Dzieje Ameryki Łacińskiej*, vol. II: 1870/1880–1929 (edited by R. Mroziewicz, R. Stemplowski), Warszawa 1979, p. 122.

Lima, the capital of Peru.

Mining industry development, especially in the mountains, stimulated the construction of railroads. A total of over 3,200 km had been built by the outbreak of the war. Over 2,000 km belonged to the state, while 400 km were co-owned.

The largest Peruvian city was the capital Lima. By the end of 1870s its population was over 100,000 people. Other large cities in order of their size were Callao (33,500), Arequipa (over 29,000) and Cuzco (over 18,000 people)[12]. Callao, situated not far from the capital, was arguably the country's largest harbour. Also significant were the harbours of Arica and Iquique, which were the centres of guano and saltpetre export.

The annual budgetary revenues of Peru in 1875 amounted to 10.8 million soles (less then 2.2 million pounds sterling), while the budgetary expenditures were approximately 12.5 million soles (2.5 million pounds sterling)[13]. National debt, which equalled 49 million pounds sterling on the eve of the war, constituted a heavy burden on the country's budget. There were debt servicing difficulties, which pushed the Peruvian government towards the idea of a saltpetre monopoly. These revenues were still insufficient as already since 1879, Peru had had serious difficulties with timely payment of interest.

The main source of revenues for the Peruvian authorities were those from the guano monopoly, as well as duties and mining taxes (these were lowered in the 1870s, but more emphasis was put on legalisation of mining operations and on effectiveness of collecting all the associated fees). The role of guano export was clearly becoming less significant in the structure of income, giving way to saltpetre export. In 1879, saltpetre constituted 37% of the Peruvian export value and sugar 27.6%, while guano was only 7.7% (in the early 1860s it constituted approximately 60% of the export value)[14].

Despite economic problems, Peruvian military strength was significant and the country deserved to be called a local superpower (taking into consideration South American conditions). On the eve of the war the Peruvian peacetime army had a nominal strength of about 5,600 officers and soldiers formed into 7 single battalion regiments and an independent infantry battalion, 3 cavalry regiments and artillery units. However, due to numerous vacancies, effective strength of these units did not exceed 4,500 men[15]. Roughly every fifth Peruvian soldier held an officer's rank and there were as many as 26 generals. Apart from the regular army, the Peruvian authorities also had police units at their

---

12 *The Statesmen's Year-Book…*, vol. XXI, op.cit. pp. 604–605.

13 The currency in Peru was the sol (which was pegged to the French franc – one sol equalled 5 French francs) divided into 100 centesimos. It equalled about 4 shillings (*The Statesmen's Year-Book…*, vol. XVI (1879), op.cit., p. 567). In addition to bullion money, the Peruvian government also issued banknote soles, however, their rate of exchange was determined by the market. At the beginning of the war one banknote sole equalled 40 centesimos, while at the end of 1880, it was only 7 centesimos (T. B. M. Mason, *The War on the Pacific Coast of South America between Chile and the Allied Republics of Peru and Bolivia, 1879–81*, Washington 1883, p. 27).

14 *Dzieje Ameryki Łacińskiej…*, op.cit., p. 123.

15 *Boletin…*, op.cit.; A. Curtis, op.cit., vol. I, p. 26; B. Vicuña Mackenna, op.cit., …*Tarapaca*, vol. I, p. 335.

The ironclad Independencia in the floating dry dock. The Peruvians possessed a well-equipped shipyard infrastructure at their main naval base in Callao, which allowed for their warships to be in better condition than those of their enemy.

disposal: Civil Guards in the towns and Gendarmerie in the countryside (the latter included a few cavalry units). These had a total of about 5,500 men who could reinforce the regular army. There was also the National Guard, which could be called to arms in case of national emergency. Theoretically, it could muster up to 65,000 men, but actually the numbers were much lower. Its members hardly ever trained together and bearing in mind the woeful condition of their armament, they were of no real military value[16]. Some of the guardsmen could easily reinforce the units of the regular army in case the latter were being expanded.

Peruvian army infantry troops were mainly armed with a locally-made model of the French Chassepot M 1866 rifles, known as Castanon, and original French-made ones (a total of over 5,000 items). There were over 2,000 Comblain M 1870 rifles and 3,000 firearms of other manufacturer (including a substantial number of Snider-Enfield M 1866 rifles). Following the outbreak of the war large numbers of rifles were purchased as new units were being equipped: 1,500 Spanish Remington M 1871 rifles (bought through Honduras), about 5,000 Egyptian Remington M 1868 rifles (purchased through Costa Rica) and a few thousands of ex-Turkish Peabody-Martin M1874 rifles captured by the Russians during the war of 1877–1878, then sold to the Americans who in turn delivered them to the Peruvians. Cavalrymen were armed with sabres and partially with short lances and cavalry carbines of assorted designs, mostly Remingtons and various types of Winchesters. Initially, the Peruvian artillery had a total of 28 Blakely rifled mountain muzzle-loaders of various calibres, four 78.5 mm Krupp C/67 field guns,10 Vavasseur field guns and a few single pieces of assorted designs. Even before the outbreak of the war, the mass production of 55 mm White rifled breech-loading bronze guns (based on the Vavasseur M.1871 mountain gun) and 60 mm Grieve rifled steel breech-loaders (based on Krupp C/72 mountain guns) was launched locally. A total of 80 of the former design (31 mountain and 49 field guns with slightly longer

---

16 F. A. Machuca, *Las Cuatro Campañas de La Guerra del Pacifico, vol. I*, Valparaiso 1926, p. 93.

The warships of the Peruvian navy: the seagoing monitor Huascar (centre), the corvette Union (left) and the gunboat Pilcomayo (right).

barrels) were manufactured, as well as 42 of the latter[17]. However, the majority of these guns were delivered after the outbreak of the war (the final batch of 20 White guns was delivered at the end of 1880)[18].

Apart from these, the Peruvians had a significant number of heavy guns in stock, which allowed them to fortify the harbours in the south of the country and up-gun the Callao defences or selected warships. Outside of the artillery which constituted the permanent armament of the Callao defences (10 rifled guns of calibres ranging from 279 to 229 mm), their arsenal housed 72 heavy guns including 20 rifled ones of calibres from 279 to 107 mm and 52 smoothbore Rodman and Dahlgren 1000 to 68-pounders[19].

Following the outbreak of the war the Peruvians began the expansion of the army by creating 17 new infantry battalions (not taking into account a few additional National Guard battalions) and re-organised the artillery into 3 regiments. As events unfolded and losses were suffered new units were being formed. During the war, up to 1881, the Peruvian army ranks saw over 40,000 men in service (not taking into account those who served when the war broke out).

The basic tactical units of the Peruvian army were: infantry battalion, cavalry regiment or squadron and artillery battery. During the war larger units were formed which mostly comprised 3 battalions with assigned units, which were called "divisions". At a later date these "divisions" were formed into corps of various sizes, mostly of 3–5,000 soldiers.

At the outbreak of the war the majority of ordinary soldiers were of Indian descent. They were relatively well-trained and willing to sacrifice, although of poor civic awareness. Their loyalty was directed to their officers rather than to the county they were to defend[20]. At a later time, many inhabitants of the *costa* enlisted in the expanded Peruvian army. The majority of them volunteered, as they were more aware of the cause they had been fighting for. However, they were apparently not as well-trained. The officer corps left much to be desired, since in part its members were those who rose in the ranks only due to their connections and social status and not their actual merits. Making decisions, the high rank

---

17 A Curtis, op.cit., pp. 27–28; G. Esposito, op.cit., pp. 36–37; G. Esposito, A. Garcia Pinto, op.cit., pp. 68–70, According to W. F. Sater (*Andean Tragedy. Fighting the War of the Pacific, 1879–1884*, Lincoln-London 2007, pp. 64–67) White guns were manufactured in mountain and field variants. A total of 31 of the former and 49 of the latter were made.

18 R. Gonzales Amaral, *La artilleria en la Guerra del Pacifico, Academia de Historia Militar,* Santiago de Chile 2013, pp. 8-10.

19 B. Vicuña Mackenna, op.cit., ...*Tarapaca*, vol. I, p. 339; F. A. Machuca, op.cit., pp. 94–94. The arsenal held the following numbers of rifled ordnance: 1x279 mm Blakely, 4x229 mm Vavasseur, as well as 7x203 mm, 4x163 mm, 4x130 mm and 4x107 mm Parrot; The numbers of smoothbore guns (Rodmans and Dahlgrens) was as follows: 2x1000-pdr, 21x450-pdr, 16x166-pdr (According to F. A. Machuca these were 125-pdr guns) and 15x68-pdr.

20 After the fall of Lima, the French Adm. Dupetit-Thouars was supposedly taken by Col. Lynch on a tour of the captured enemy positions. To explain to him the reason why the Chileans were able to defeat their opponents, a Chilean officer took him to a hospital were the wounded of both armies were being treated. When he asked the wounded Peruvian soldiers who they had been fighting for, they had told him they had been fighting for their commanders. When he asked a wounded Chilean soldier the same question, he replied that he had been fighting for his country. This anecdote rather vividly describes the motivation of both sides., A. Curtis, op.cit., p. 29.

officers often took into account not military, but political considerations, in fear of their own position and with distrust towards others who held positions of authority in the country, either military or civil.

Despite all these considerations, the Peruvian army constituted a real force, which had to be respected by their enemies and with all its flaws, its potential was considerable.

Apart from the army, Peru possessed a relatively strong navy, which was all the more significant due to the inaccessibility of the Atacama Desert. The disputed provinces which were the main cause of the conflict could only be accessed by sea. It was obvious, that at least in the initial phase of the coming war, the navy would play a key role.

The core of the Peruvian naval forces was two ironclads: the relatively large broadside ironclad *Independencia* and much smaller ironclad turret ship (seagoing monitor) *Huascar*. Both these warships were ordered from British shipyards at the beginning of the conflict with Spain, which had broken out in 1864. They were delivered in 1866 during its final stages, and therefore did not take part in the fighting[21]. These were relatively old warships, but they were in good condition, since in February 1879 both were undergoing a thorough overhaul. Both ironclads were being reboilered and the *Independencia* was in dry dock, where her bottom was being scraped (the *Huascar* had her bottom cleaned earlier). As is apparent, both ships were temporarily out of commission, but upon completion of their overhaul, which took place shortly after the outbreak of the war, they were in perfect condition. Their main drawback was their relatively thin armour, since the armour plates protecting both vessels did not exceed 114 mm. It may have been enough to stop almost all projectiles fired by mid 19th century guns, but insufficient to protect them against modern heavy naval gun fire of the late 1870s. Additionally, the *Huascar*'s armoured turret which protected the ship's main armament, was still turned manually by its crew, therefore its full 360 degrees rotation took a quarter of an hour (!) and training the guns on the target took a considerable amount of time (which affected both the aim and the rate of fire).

Apart from both these ironclads, the ship with the most fighting potential was the corvette *Union*. This ship, along with three sister ships, had been built in France, ordered by the Confederate government. However, in early 1864, all four had been confiscated by the French government. The Peruvians, who were striving to strengthen their navy, seized the opportunity while a conflict with Spain was looming over the horizon. They purchased two of the ships, the aforementioned *Union* (ex. *Texas*) and the *America* (ex *Georgia*)[22]. Both corvettes reached the country before the end of the conflict with Spain and managed to take part in the battle of Abtao, fought on February 8, 1866. The *America* was later lost on August 8, 1868, when a tsunami wave created by an earthquake hit the harbour of Arica and washed her ashore. The *Union* survived until 1879 and was fully operational at the outbreak of hostilities. The corvette's combat potential was definitely lower than that of both the ironclads, but her advantage was speed – at 13.5 knots she was the fastest of all the warships that took part in the war. That, combined with her relatively strong armament, made her a valuable asset for the Peruvian navy.

The ironclads *Independencia* and *Huascar* were not the only armoured ships of the Peruvian navy. In 1868, the Peruvian government purchased, at a bargain price, two *Canonicus* class monitors, decommissioned after the end of the American Civil War, to serve as protection against another possible Spanish intervention (Peru and Spain were still formally at war). These were the *Atahualpa* (ex. *Catawba*) and the *Manco Capac* (ex *Oneota*)[23]. It took no less than 14 months (!) to tow the ships from the United States

The Peruvian monitor Atahualpa. In 1869, the Peruvians purchased two American monitors of the Canonicus class. By 1879 they had been obsolete, but could still be employed as the coastal defence units.

21 W. E. Warner, Warships of the Chincha Island Wars (1864–1866), Middletown 2105, pp. 185–187.

22 P. H. Silverstone, Warships of the Civil War Navies, Annapolis, Maryland 1989, p. 217; W. E. Warner, op.cit., pp. 122–124.
    The remaining two corvettes were purchased by the Prussians who named them the *Victoria* (ex. *Louisiana*) and the *Augusta* (ex. *Mississippi*).

23 P. H. Silverstone, op.cit., p. 10.

to Peru. This should come as no surprise, since these were coastal defence ships with low freeboard, extending only a foot above the water's surface and therefore had poor sea-keeping qualities. Finally, both monitors arrived at their destination where they were assigned for the protection of Callao against a possible enemy attack. They were armed with obsolete 450-pdr (15-inch) Dahlgren smoothbore muzzle-loaders of limited combat value. With poor sea-keeping qualities and speed not exceeding 5 to 6 knots, they could only be used for local defence (of selected harbours). Although their armament's striking power was significant, its range and accuracy was relatively low. Nevertheless, both monitors still had some fighting potential and could not be considered worthless.

Among the remaining warships of the Peruvian navy, the only ship which also had some fighting potential was the gunboat *Pilcomayo*, commissioned in 1875[24]. Apart from the gunboat, the Peruvian navy also had two armed side-wheelers, the *Limeña* and the *Oroya*, a small propeller steamer *Talisman* which served as an aviso, and an armed propeller transport *Chalaco*. In the coming conflict these would be used as transports and although they were armed, they were of little combat value. Shortly before the outbreak of the war, the Peruvians purchased three Herreshoff torpedo boats (*Republica*, *Alianza* and a third unnamed one) in the United States and the torpedo boat *Alay* in Great Britain. Also purchased were a few self-propelled Lay torpedoes (probably a total of 10). The first two ships reached Peru after the outbreak of hostilities, the third was never collected. The *Alay* was captured by the Chileans off the coast of Ecuador, while she was being transported to Peru. Initially, the torpedo boats were not to be armed with self-propelled torpedoes, but with spar torpedoes, which were also being fitted on some mobilised steam launches.

The Peruvian merchant navy was not large and in 1879, it had a total of 147 ships of 49,860 tons, including 8 steamers with a total tonnage of 1,768 tons, which were unfit for military service[25].

Peruvian naval personnel numbered less than 1,500 men. In January 1880, the so-called "naval brigade" was created. Some of its soldiers were Peruvian seamen and some were recruits enlisted in Callao. Soldiers of this unit (which numbered a few hundred men) would mostly man naval guns used in land fortifications, but also fight as regular infantry.

The Peruvian crews comprised both native inhabitants of the *costa*, as well as European mercenaries or immigrants who had came to Peru. There was a relatively large number of the latter in the navy, mostly holding positions which required technical knowledge and experience. Consequently, the seamanship of the Peruvian crews was satisfactory, but they lacked discipline and military training, which was especially apparent in the case of gunners (it was simply poor). Relieving from duty a large number of

---

24 What is interesting, is the fact that her initial name was to be the *Putamayo*, for the river flowing through Peruvian territory. However, due to an error, upon launching in Great Britain she was named the *Pilcomayo* for a river which does not even flow through Peruvian territory. Upon her arrival in Peru, her name was not altered.

25 *The Statesmen's Year-Book...*, vol. XVI (1879), op.cit., p. 567.

seamen of Chilean descent in April 1879 also had a disastrous effect on the level of training of Peruvian naval personnel, as they were replaced by fresh recruits.

There was a naval academy at Callao, but its curriculum put the emphasis on maritime, rather than naval training[26]. Nevertheless, the officer corps of the Peruvian navy was mostly competent, devoted to their duty and of high morale. The official Head and Commander in Chief of the Peruvian navy was Adm. Antonio de la Haza, who also held the position of Minister of War[27]. The direct command of the navy was in the hands of Commodore Miguel Grau, an experienced officer and a veteran of the war with Spain.

The main base of the Peruvian navy was the fortified harbour of Callao. Admittedly, its fortifications were old, as they dated back to the 1850s (and some even to the XVII century), nevertheless, it could provide all the warships of the navy with relative safety. Moreover, at Callao, the navy had a dry dock and a floating dry dock, which could accommodate any of its warships. It also had technical workshops which could make ongoing overhauls and repairs, even major ones. Callao was in fact the only harbour which could be considered a fortified naval base, as the remaining ones (with Iquique, Pisagua, Arica, Chimbote and Paita being the most important, yet these were mostly commercial harbours) lacked the necessary military infrastructure and the construction of fortifications in some of them only began after the outbreak of the war. Nevertheless, the facilities it provided allowed for the Peruvian warships to be well-maintained. Their bottoms were systematically cleaned and so were their boilers. All necessary repairs were carried out on a regular basis. At the outbreak of the war, in April 1879, both Peruvian ironclads were undergoing major overhauls with their boilers being replaced, which put them out of action. As soon as it had been completed, both the *Huascar* and the *Independencia* were able to put to sea and they were both in perfect condition.

Chile

At the end of the 1870s, Chile could probably be considered one of the most "European-like" of all the South American states. Its political situation was relatively stable, as opposed to that of Peru and Bolivia, which were constantly being shaken by rebellions and coups d'etat. There were regular elections at scheduled dates and the succession of authority was peaceful. That stability was positively reflected in the economic situation, therefore, it came as no surprise that Chile was considered one of the richest and best-developed South American countries.

On the eve of the war, following the 1875 incorporation of Bio Bio, Angol and Arauco territories and the treaty with Argentina concerning the division of Tierra del Fuego, the total area of the Chilean territory was about 510,000 km² (excluding Araucania inhabited by Indians). These territories were inhabited by a total of over 2.3 million people (not taking into account 70–80,000 Indians in the Araucanian territory). The majority of Chileans were white and mestizo. Indians constituted no more than a few percent of the population and Blacks were also few[28].

The territory of Chile covered a long strip of land between the Pacific Ocean and the Andes, from the Atacama Desert in the north to Tierra del Fuego in the south. It could be divided into the most populated central part with the best-developed economy, the northern part with the Atacama Desert and southern Patagonia, which was the subject of a border dispute between Chile and Argentina. It was divided from the central part by the Araucanian territory inhabited by Indians over which the central government had no complete control.

Anibal Pinto, the President of Chile.

The majority of Chileans lived by agriculture, however, besides individual farms there was also a relatively large number of plantations (mainly sugar cane). Apart from agriculture, the processing industry (mostly sugar) and mining also had an important role in the Chilean economy. The country's main export commodities were copper and sugar and to a lesser extent also silver, wheat and wool. Shortly before the outbreak of the war, the exploitation of saltpetre deposits would become more and more important. Chile possessed a relatively well-developed railroad system (it was the first South American

26 C. R. Markham, op.cit., p. 95.
27 T. B. M. Mason, op.cit, p. 18.
28 *The Statesmen's Year-Book...*, vol. XVI (1879), op.cit., pp. 524–525, vol. XX (1883), pp. 524–525.

Valparaiso, the largest Chilean harbour.

The harbour of Valparaiso, the ironclad Almirante Cochrane *can be seen in the centre.*

state to begin construction of railroads on a large scale), the total length of the tracks in 1878 was over 1,560 km, while another 330 km were under construction[29].

Chile's largest city was its capital Santiago, which in 1875 had a population of 130,000 people. The largest Chilean harbour of Valparaiso with its 100,000 inhabitants was not far behind as far as population was concerned. It must be noted that the number of residents of both these cities was growing steadily by a few percent per year[30].

The annual budgetary revenues of Chile in 1878 amounted to just under 20.5 million pesos, which equalled nearly 4.1 million pounds sterling, while the budgetary expenditures were approximately 21.4 million pesos, which was nearly 4.3 million pounds sterling[31]. On the eve of the war national debt equalled 64.4 million pesos (just under 12.7 million pounds sterling). Out of that sum nearly 46.5

---

29 Ibidem, p. 526.

30 Ibidem, p. 525.

31 The peso divided into 100 centavos was the currency of Chile. Similarly to the Peruvian sol, the Chilean peso was pegged to the French frank – one peso equalled 5 franks. The exchange rate of the peso was automatically given in British currency and was about 4 shillings (just like the Peruvian sol)., Ibidem, p. 527.

Warships of the Chilean navy: Almirante Cochrane *(1)*, Blanco Encalada *(2)*, Chacabuco *(3)*, O'Higgins *(4)*, Esmeralda *(5)*, Abtao *(6)*, Magallanes *(7)*, Covadonga *(8)*.

million pesos (9.3 million pounds) was attributed to foreign debt, incurred mainly in British banks[32]. It constituted a heavy burden on the Chilean budget (the interest themselves amounted to approximately 3 million pesos annually), however, it was regularly serviced until the outbreak of the war. Roughly half of the Chilean budgetary revenues came from direct and indirect taxes. The other half were the proceeds from the national railway and monopolies (by contrast to the income structure of Peru and Bolivia, where the majority of revenue came from duties and monopolies).

As far as the military was concerned Chile was only seemingly weaker than Peru. That illusion stemmed from the official size of the regular army, which in peacetime was limited. Due to its economic and population potential, Chile could actually mobilise a considerable force at short notice, which at least equalled in numbers those of the combined Peruvian-Bolivian ones and surpassed them in quality. Therefore, it was an equally strong opponent for the Peruvian and Bolivian forces.

The numerical strength of the Chilean army in peacetime was determined by the 1875 act of parliament at 3,573 soldiers (their actual number was no more than about 3,200)[33]. It was intended as an army with a large number of officers (about 400, including 5 generals), which could be easily expanded if necessary. These 3,500 troops were formed into 4 single battalion infantry regiments and an additional battalion which served on the Araucanian border, two cavalry regiments and an artillery regiment, not including a few engineering and medical units. In case of war recruits were to be drafted from the National Guard. Initially, it numbered as many as 30,000 men, however, since their armament and training were definitely insufficient, after 1873 its ranks were reduced to 18,000 men but more emphasis was put on their training (at least theoretically they drilled once a week). Moreover, a substantial number of weapons was purchased to uparm these units[34].

In the face of the coming conflict with Bolivia and Peru, in the spring of 1879 the Chilean Congress decided to expand the armed forces to 12,000 troops, and then to 40,000 (including the National Guards units designated to cooperate with the army), while the National Guard was expanded to 30,000 men (that number was increased later). Therefore, by the end of 1879, the Chilean armed forces numbered 22,000 troops[35]. The main source of new recruits for the expanded army was the National Guard, which after the outbreak of the war was divided into two formations: *Guardia Nacional Movilizada* of about 14,500 men, intended for operations with regular units and *Guardia Nacional Estático*, expanded in 1880 to 49,500 men, intended to serve in the rear units and as reserve for the front line units.

---

32 *The Statesmen's Year-Book…*, vol. XVII (1880), op.cit., pp. 522–523.

33 B. Vicuña Mackenna, op. Cit., …*Tarapaca*, vol. I, pp. 1340135. According to G. Esposito (op.cit., p. 19) on the eve of the war the Chilean army numbered approximately 3,000 troops, which is a probable estimate.

34 A. Curtis, op.cit., pp. 10–11; G. Esposito, op.cit., p. 23, B. W. Farcau, op.cit., pp. 47–48; *The Statesmen's Year-Book…*, vol. XVI (1879), op.cit., p. 523. On the eve of the outbreak of the war the size of the National Guard was even smaller and numbered less than 6,700 men (B. Vicuña Mackenna, op.cit., …*Tarapaca*, vol. I, p. 136).

35 *The Statesmen's Year-Book…*, vol. XVII (1880), p. 523; vol. XVIII (1881), p. 524; vol. XX (1883), p. 524.

The Chilean corvette Esmeralda.

That rapid and extensive expansion of the army was made possible by a considerable stockpile of weapons in the possession of the Chilean government. Back in the years 1873–1874, it had made extensive purchases of weapons abroad. Additional purchases were made shortly before the outbreak of the war and at its very beginning. Consequently, the Chilean army had approximately 12,000 Belgian Comblain M 1873 rifles (they were in the first place issued to regular units; later their numbers rose to 18,000 owing to additional purchases), 22,800 French Gras M 1874 rifles (modified Chassepot model), 10,000 Dutch Beaumont M 1871 (exclusively used by the *Guardia National Estático*), 2,000 Snider-Enfield M 1866 rifles, approximately 1,950 Korpatschek M 1878 rifles (for the navy), 4,800 Winchester cavalry carbines (various models) and a few thousand rifles of older patterns[36]. Thus, the Chilean army was in possession of a total of over 60,000 rifles, which was a sufficient number to arm the units that were going to be formed, both regular ones and those of the National Guard.

As far as artillery was concerned, the Chilean army initially possessed 16 modern Krupp rifled steel breech-loading guns (four 8 cm C/72 field and twelve 6 cm C/72 mountain guns), as well as 14 older French La Hitte rifled bronze muzzle-loaders (six 86 mm M 1859 field and eight M 1859 mountain guns of the same calibre). Shortly before the outbreak of the war and after its beginning more purchases were made (twelve 9 cm Krupp C/73, twenty-four similar C/80 guns, twenty-nine 7.5 cm Krupp C/79, thirty-eight C/79 mountain guns of the same calibre and six 63 mm Armstrong mountain guns), thus the number of both mountain and field guns in the Chilean army reached the number of about 150 pieces in the summer of 1880[37].

Apart from numerous field and mountain guns for the army, the Chileans also purchased 10 coastal artillery guns (two 254 mm Armstrong muzzle-loaders, four modern 21 cm Krupp breech-loaders and four 163 mm Armstrong guns), the majority of which was used to reinforce the defences of Valparaiso and Antofagasta.

The majority of the Chilean regular and National Guard troops were white and mestizo, while the officers were mostly white. Regular troops who served before the war were mostly well-trained and armed. They also had some combat experience gained in fighting the Araucanians (Mapuches). Rapid expansion of the armed forces made it somewhat difficult to sustain the quality of the newly formed units. However, since the new recruits came from the ranks of the National Guard, which was clearly superior to its Peruvian counterpart, those new units were relatively decent, quickly gaining experience on the battlefield. Also the *Guardia Nacional Movilizada*, well-armed and provided with an officer corps mostly made up of regular army officers, complemented the regular troops. In general, as far as ar-

---

36 G. Esposito, op.cit., p. 23, G. Esposito, A. Garcia Pinto, op.cit., pp. 117–118; *Historia ilustrada de la Guerra del Pacifico* (1879–1884), Santiago de Chile 1979, pp. 148–149.

37 G. Esposito, op.cit., p. 23; G. Esposito, A. Garcia Pinto, op.cit., p. 119; *Historia ilustrada*, op.cit., p 149, W. F. Sater, op.cit., p. 64. Out of the guns purchased abroad, mainly in Germany, 62 pieces were delivered by the end of 1879 (32 field and 30 mountain guns), the remainder arrived by the end of summer 1880., R. Gonzales Amaral, op.cit., pp. 15, 20.

mament and equipment was concerned, the Chilean troops should be evaluated as superior to their enemies. Their morale was also higher, as they were consciously fighting for their country and not out of loyalty to their military or political leaders (which was quite common in the Peruvian and Bolivian armies).

However, it would be an exaggeration to claim that the Chilean army was prepared for the coming war, as similarly to both the Peruvian and the Bolivian army, it was not. Admittedly, the better organization of the Chilean military machine allowed for more efficient mobilisation. However, the Chilean commanders had initially encountered the same problems while conducting operations as their enemies, while the soldiers similarly lacked in training and discipline. Although usually better equipped and supplied, initially the Chileans did not possess any significant qualitative advantage over their opponents. The outcome of the war was decided within the first few months, mostly by naval operations, as the Chilean navy bore the greatest responsibility in its initial phase.

The core of the Chilean navy was formed by two central battery ironclads *Blanco Encalada* and *Almirante Cochrane*. Both warships were built in Great Britain according to the design of the famous British ship designer Edward J. Reed. They had been ordered in 1872, in connection with the growing conflict with Argentina over the possession of the Tierra del Fuego territory. Following the initial settlement of the most contentious issues by means of the Fierro-Sarretea Treaty, both ironclads were theoretically made redundant and there had even been an idea to sell them. However, due to the turn of events in the north and the accelerated conflict with Bolivia and Peru, both finally remained under the Chilean flag.

The *Blanco Encalada* and her sister ship the *Almirante Cochrane* (the former was commissioned at the end of 1875, the latter in the following year), were relatively modern warships of considerable combat potential at the outbreak of the war. However, this was diminished by their poor state of repair. Ordering such large warships abroad, the Chilean authorities did not show any concern for a suitable local infrastructure that would service them. Consequently, the Chileans did not possess a dry dock (either floating or stationary), where they would be able to clean the bottoms of these ships (in 1879, the *Blanco Encalada* required scraping of her bottom more than the *Almirante Cochrane*, which was in a slightly better condition)[38]. In the coming war this was a serious problem which had an effect of the course of military operations[39].

Apart from the aforementioned ironclads the Chileans also had 4 corvettes. The oldest was the *Esmeralda*, built back in the 1850s. She had already been over 20 years old when the war with Peru and Bolivia broke out. She was a typical three-masted corvette with an open battery deck. In 1879, despite a few modernizations, both her wooden hull and her engine room were in really poor condition. Consequently, instead of the 8 knots she was able to reach when commissioned, she could barely steam at more than 6 knots. Therefore, her combat potential was seriously reduced and due to her age it was not feasible to make her undergo any extensive overhauls. For some time she had served as a training ship, but following the outbreak of the war, she was mobilised and recommissioned.

Another corvette, the *Abtao*, was also in a fairly deplorable state. Her construction had been ordered by the government of the Confederate States of America in 1863. However, after being seized by the British government she was purchased along with another corvette, the *Tornado*, by the Chileans, who were trying to reinforce their navy in the face of the war with Spain. While on her way to Chile, the *Tornado* was intercepted and captured off Madera by the Spanish frigate *Gerona* on August 22, 1866. However, the *Abtao*, under the temporary name of *Pampero*, managed to reach her destination at the beginning of 1867, although she did not take part in the conflict. After a decade of intensive service and lacking any major overhauls, she was in an awful condition (especially her machinery) and in 1878 she was sold to a shipping company to be converted into a sailing ship. However, following the outbreak of the war she was repurchased by the navy and despite her poor state (she was unable to reach more than 6 knots) she was recommissioned.

Chilean soldier.

---

38 A year before the outbreak of the war the *Almirante Cochrane* was dispatched to Great Britain for repairs and at the same time have her bottom scraped., T. B. M. Mason, op.cit., pp. 15–16.

39 The problem of marine growth on ships' bottoms was significant enough in Chilean and Peruvian waters, as it was more rapid in comparison to other, even tropical, areas.

Guns used by the Chilean army during the War of the Pacific (a postwar photograph).

Two corvettes, the *O'Higgins* and her sister ship, the *Chacabuco*, were in much better condition. Both warships were ordered in Great Britain after the outbreak of the war with Spain, but they were unable to leave that country before the official declaration of war in 1866. Therefore, they were interned by the British authorities and released after the armistice had been signed in 1868. When the war broke out they were not in the best condition (their hulls were in good shape, but their boilers were in need of repairs), but were of much greater value than the aforementioned two. They were not as fast as the Peruvian *Union*, but they were equal or even superior to her as far as armament was concerned. They were well-suited for the role of escort vessels or for providing artillery support for troops fighting on land.

Apart from the four corvettes, in 1879, the Chilean navy also had two gunboats. The first was the *Covadonga*, a former Spanish ship of the same name, captured off Papudo on November 26, 1865 by the corvette *Esmeralda*. She was commissioned in 1860, therefore she was no longer in her prime and despite modernizations her state left much to be desired. However, she was still in commission and had some combat potential.

The second gunboat (sometimes classified as a small corvette), was the *Magallanes*. She was ordered along with both ironclads in 1872 as a patrol and hydrographic service vessel to operate in the waters of the Tierra del Fuego. On the onset of the war, she was in good condition and had a considerable combat potential.

Chilean cavalry unit. Owing to careful selection of horses, the Chilean cavalry was clearly superior to the similar Peruvian or Bolivian units.

Right after the outbreak of hostilities, Chile ordered 13 steel-hulled torpedo boats of various sizes from the Yarrow shipyard in Great Britain. They were to serve as harbour defence vessels. Three of those (*Vedette*, *Colocolo* and *Tucapel*) were small vessels of 10–5 tons, confined to operate in coastal waters. The 30-ton *Janequeo* (the first warship of that name) was originally built for the Italian navy, but was acquired by the Chileans. The remaining 9 ships belonged to two classes: Glaura (6 ships) and Fresia (3 ships). Their displacement ranged from 35 (former) to 25 (latter) tons, which in favourable weather conditions made them even more useful. All these torpedo boats took part in military operations (the first were commissioned at the end of 1879) armed with spar torpedoes and mitrailleuses, since at that time the Chileans did not possess any self-propelled torpedoes.

Apart from strictly combat vessels, the Chilean navy also had a sidewheel aviso *Toltén*, ordered in 1872 along with both the ironclads. She could perform dispatch and transport duties and to some extent also limited combat missions. There were also a few auxiliary ships.

Unlike Peru, Chile had a relatively large merchant navy at its disposal. In 1877, it had altogether 87 ships of a total 22,434 GRT, including 22 steamers of a total 9,641 tons GRT[40]. The majority of these ships was unfit for military service, nevertheless this fleet constituted a significant support for the navy, mostly by providing troop transports (notably the ships of the Campañia Sudamericana de Vapores and the Campañia Esplotadora de Lota y Coronel). In return the shipowners could count on a system of state subsidies (on the basis of the act of May 5, 1874). Consequently, in 1879, the navy acquired several merchant ships for conversion into warships. The two smallest ones (*Lautaro* – ex. *Princessa Luisa* and *Toro*) were converted into patrol boats (sometimes classified as auxiliary gunboats), while the reminder served as transports, similarly to some previously chartered steamers. However, since the was still a shortage of mechanically propelled vessels for transportation of troops, it was also decided to employ sailing vessels for that purpose, thus several were chartered. When the main army force had already been redeployed north, 3 ships (*Loa*, *Amazonas* and *Angamos*) were armed and used as patrol boats or for shore bombardment.

On the eve of the war approximately 1,700 officers and sailors served in the Chilean navy, not taking into account the naval corps which comprised two coastal artillery battalions and the naval battalion, which at a later date operated on land together with the army[41]. Together with those units, navy per-

The Chilean National Guard units. After the outbreak of the war the Chilean government not only purchased a substantial number of weapons, but also equipment and uniforms in various countries. Consequently, a number of troops received German equipment and uniforms, including the characteristic pickelhaubes.

40 *The Statesmen's Year-Book...*, vol. XVI (1879), p. 526.
41 T. B. M. Mason, op.cit., p. 13.

sonnel numbered about 2,500 men, and it grew during the war with the acquisition of several ships purchased from private shipowners and those newly commissioned.

Similarly to those in the Peruvian navy, there were numerous naturalised foreigners who served in the Chilean navy. These sailors, recruited mostly from the area around Valparaiso and other coastal towns, were well-trained. A large group of officers (similarly to those in the Peruvian navy many of them were naturalised foreigners) gained their practical knowledge aboard Royal Navy ships. Included in that group was the Commander in Chief of the Chilean Navy, Juan Williams Rebolledo, the hero of Papudo, who fought in the war with Spain. The level of training of the Chilean seamen should be considered as at least good. Their seamanship was comparable to that of their Peruvian counterparts, but their military training was superior. The officer corps was trained at the naval academy in Valparaiso.

One of the Chilean navy's major disadvantages was the lack of sufficient shipyard facilities. The main naval base was the harbour of Valparaiso. Following the war with Spain the harbour was fortified, but it still lacked specialised shipyard facilities. The local arsenal was more like a military storage facility and its workshops had limited repair capacity. Fortunately, the warships of the Chilean navy could use the well-equipped workshops of the Pacific Steam Navigation Company. However, Valparaiso lacked a dry dock which could accommodate larger vessels (i.e. both ironclads), while the two existing floating dry docks could only accommodate vessels of no more than 1,000 tons.

Apart from Valparaiso, Chilean warships could use other harbours, primarily Coquimbo and Caldera. However, these could only be considered auxiliary. Following the capture of Antofagasta, the town was hurriedly fortified and became a temporary base for Chilean warships. However, it was mainly used as a staging point for the redeployment of land troops north.

The President was the supreme commander of all Chilean armed forces, both the army and the navy. Since April 18, 1879, direct leadership was in the hands of Gen. Basilio Urrutia, the Minister of War in the Chilean government. Following his resignation, he was replaced by Col. Cornelio Saavedra Rodriguez. At the beginning of 1879, command over the land forces was given to the relatively old (he was 74) Gen. Justo Artegua Cuevas, veteran of the War of Independence. He was an experienced combat soldier, but with virtually no proficiency in commanding larger units. He owed his appointment mainly to his political connections (he was a conservative party deputy of the congress). However, it must be noted, that at that time Chile had no officers capable of conducting operations on such a large scale as those they were to face in the coming conflict. Therefore, their choice should be considered optimal. The command of the navy was given to Rear Adm. Juan Williams Rebolledo, veteran of the war with Spain in the years 1864–1866, where he distinguished himself as the commander of the corvette *Esmeralda* by capturing the Spanish gunboat *Covadonga* (that action granted him the status of a national hero). He was a good and experienced officer, but had a tendency to be extremely overcautious (he obsessively feared defeat), which did not correlate well with the offensive strategic plans of the Chilean high command and could be considered a serious weakness.

Table no. 1. Comparison of the Chilean and Peruvian naval forces at the onset of the war.

Type	Chile		Peru	
	Numbers	Displacement (t)	Numbers	Displacement (t)
Broadside or central battery ironclads	2	6,740	1	3,500
Turret ironclads	-	-	1	1,745
Monitors	-	-	2	4,200
Corvettes	4	approx. 6,000	1	1,827
Gunboats	2	1,400	1	600
Total	8	14,140	6	11,872

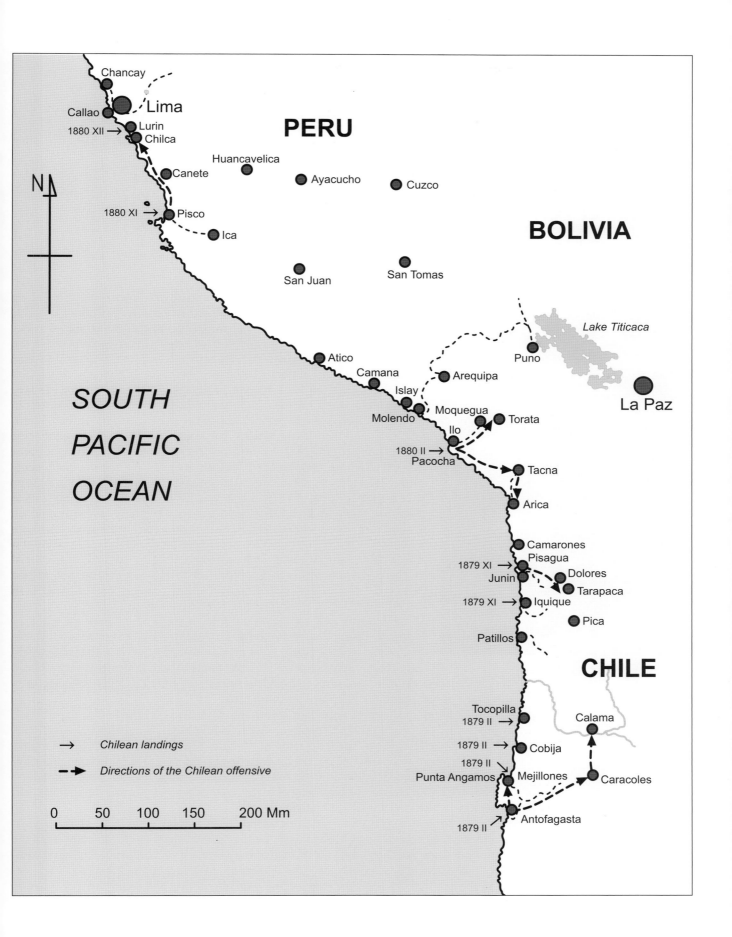

Chancay

Callao ● ● Lima

PERU

1880 XII → Lurin
Chilca

N

Canete

Huancavelica ●

● Ayacucho

● Cuzco

BOLIVIA

1880 XI → Pisco

● Ica

San Juan ●

● San Tomas

SOUTH

PACIFIC

OCEAN

● Atico

Camana ●

Islay ●

● Arequipa

Lake Titicaca

● Puno

Molendo

Moquegua ● ● Torata

● La Paz

Ilo

1880 II → Pacocha

● Tacna

● Arica

● Camarones
Pisagua

1879 XI →

Junin

● Dolores

● Tarapaca

1879 XI → Iquique

● Pica

Patillos

CHILE

Tocopilla
1879 II →

Calama ●

1879 II → Cobija

1879 II
Punta Angamos

Mejillones

● Caracoles

1879 II ↗ Antofagasta

→   *Chilean landings*

➤   *Directions of the Chilean offensive*

0   50   100   150   200 Mm

Theatre of operations of the Chilean/Bolivian-Peruvian War.

3. Invasion of the Bolivian costa and the outbreak of the war

Rear Admiral Juan Williams Rebolledo, the Commander in Chief of the Chilean navy.

The operation of taking the Bolivian coast by Chilean troops began on February 14, 1879, when, at about 06.00 in the morning, the Chilean ironclads *Almirante Cochrane* and *Blanco Encalada* and the corvette *O'Higgins* under overall command of Rear Admiral Williams Rebolledo dropped anchor in the Antofagasta roadstead. Aboard these ships there were over 500 Chilean soldiers commanded by Colonel Emilio Sotomayor. Immediately after anchoring, Col. Sotomayor headed for land, straight to the Bolivian Prefect Severino Zapata, who was responsible for the administrative management of the town. He informed him that, due to the termination of the 1874 agreement by the Bolivian authorities and their taking actions that would undermine Chilean interests, he was taking control of the entire Bolivian coast. Shortly thereafter, at about 08.00, the Chilean troops landed. They effortlessly took over the town, being warmly greeted by its inhabitants. Out of 6,000 residents who lived in Antofagasta at the beginning of 1879, as many as 5,000 were Chilean citizens, while fewer than 600 were Bolivians[1]. Prefect Zapata could only protest against the fact and then, along with his family, he took refuge in the Peruvian Consulate building. Thirty-five Bolivian policemen under his command scattered as soon as they noticed the incoming Chilean troops.

The Chileans immediately installed there their own administration and on the next day, the ironclad *Blanco Encalada* departed to capture the harbours of Tocopilla and Cobija, while the corvette *O'Higgins* headed towards Mejillones. All these towns were taken without firing a shot[2]. Simultaneously, a unit of troops was dispatched from Antofagasta towards the largest mining settlement of Caracoles and the nearby Solar del Carmen, which were both taken on February 16. As approximately 95% inhabitants of both settlements were Chilean citizens (mainly miners working in local silver and saltpetre mines), the entering Chileans soldiers were greeted with cheers as had previously happened in Antofagasta.

Following the capture of the most important towns and settlements on the Bolivian coast, Col. Sotomayor put further operations on hold, trying to organize administration and national guard units in the previously captured territories. To fill the ranks of the latter he enlisted the local Chilean miners (their arms and equipment were delivered aboard the corvette *O'Higgins*). At the same time, in the following days, the Chileans landed further troops in Antofagasta, therefore, by the end of the month their numbers rose to over 2,000. Thus, at the beginning of March, in the captured province the Chileans had nearly 4,000 troops, which constituted a substantial force[3].

Initially, Sotomayor had no plans for conducting operations farther inland as he was busy organizing local administration and enlisting Chilean miners for the national guard units. Moreover, all of the major coastal settlements and those close nearby had already been captured. Outside Chilean control was only one strategically important location – the settlement of Calama on the River Loa. It was important due to the fact that it was on the road leading deep into Bolivia and could have been used as a foothold for a potential Bolivian counter-offensive. At that time, an offensive was unlikely to happen. Therefore, Sotomayor decided that there were more pressing matters to attend to than taking it over. However, on March 7, he received an explicit order to capture it. So on March 21, a unit of approximate-

---

1   A. Curtis, op.cit., vol. I, p.43.

2   *Boletin...*, op.cit., pp.8-9; B. Vicuña Mackenna, op.cit., ...*Tarapaca*, vol. I, p. 19.

3   B. Vicuña Mackenna, op.cit., ...*Tarapaca*, vol. I, p. 173.

ly 550 Chilean soldiers (4 infantry companies, a cavalry company and two guns with a small supply train of carts) under command of Col. Eleuterio Ramirez were dispatched towards Calama.

Ramirez's troops arrived at their destination on March 23. On their way, the Chileans managed to capture a few Bolivian scouts, so while they were closing on Calama, Ramirez had already been aware that it was being defended by an improvised unit of 135 soldiers and civilians under command of the local Prefect Ladislas Carera Vargas. Since the defenders had burned the bridges leading to the town, Ramirez decided to immediately cross the River Loa at two locations where fords were located, as he assumed the defenders would make their stand in the nearby buildings of the town. Meanwhile, the Bolivians took positions near the fords and surprised the crossing Chilean troops, inflicting some casualties and forcing them to retreat in the initial stages of the engagement. Unwisely, some of the Bolivians rushed to chase the escaping enemy and were soon encircled by overwhelming Chilean forces. Seeing the demise of their friends, the remaining defenders of Calama retreated following a short fight with Ramirez's troops, who captured the town.

In the entire engagement the Bolivians lost a total of 20 killed and 34 taken prisoners (including the previously captured scouts). The Chileans had 7 killed, 6 seriously wounded and some with slight

Antofagasta.

29

Emilio Sotomayor, the commander of the unit which captured Antofagasta in February 1879.

wounds[4]. These were not serious losses and the entire engagement at Calama should be considered a skirmish rather than a battle. However, it was the first engagement of the war where blood was drawn and both sides suffered losses. Following the capture of Calama, the entire area of the province of Antofagasta was under the control of Chilean troops.

The Chilean capture of the Bolivian coast was considered an act of open aggression in La Paz and on March 1, 1879, President Daza officially declared that Bolivia was at war with Chile. In a burst of patriotic effusion, volunteers were being recruited for the army to strengthen its numbers and launch a counter-offensive. Among the volunteers were members of the Creole aristocracy and middle classes, as well as farmers and miners. Within 5 to 6 weeks the newly created units incorporated over 6,000 men, but there were not enough arms and equipment for all of them. Moreover, they needed time for training. It was clear that in that situation, the recapture of the *costa* by the Bolivians would depend on Peruvian intervention, since both countries had been allies since the treaty of 1873.

Meanwhile, the Peruvians were initially reluctant to enter the conflict. Their society was generally in favour of the Bolivian cause, but everyone was perfectly aware that in the case of war, Peru would not gain anything and in its interest was maintaining the existing status quo. Diplomatic solutions could also be used to that end.

Consequently, the Peruvian government undertook a mediation effort. President Prado's Envoy, José Antonio Lavalle, went to Santiago to stop the escalation of the conflict. Following his arrival, the Peruvian diplomat offered the Chileans a proposal in which they would withdraw their forces from the captured Bolivian territory, which would fall under neutral administration. Collected taxes (mainly mining concessions and duties) would be split equally between Bolivia and Chile. Acceptance of these terms would make further talks concerning achieving a compromise satisfying all sides possible[5].

Lavalle's proposal was not accepted by the Chilean side, which demanded the Peruvian government break off the alliance treaty with Bolivia signed in 1873 and declare neutrality. Obviously, Lavalle could not accept these terms, therefore, under the pretence of consultation, he headed back to Lima at the end of the month. Although the departure of the Peruvian diplomat did not mean the end of talks, the Chileans had already made up their minds and were ready for war. The reasons for that decision were numerous. On one hand, the authorities in Santiago thought that they would be able to alleviate the effects of the growing crisis by gains in Bolivia and Peru. These were also the thoughts of ordinary Chileans, who assumed that the war would bring them rich acquisitions and well-paid jobs for many

Water distillation plant at Antofagasta. Due to the desert location of the town, it was an essential installation, as the existence of its inhabitants depended on its functionality.

4   A. Curtis, op.cit., vol. I, p. 47, There are various figures concerning the losses suffered by both sides at Calama.
5   C. R. Markham, op.cit., p. 91.

in the saltpetre industry. Therefore, the society supported the war and the government could not really oppose these tendencies, since after the concessions to Argentina concerning Tierra del Fuego (which had not been received well) it had to show more determination. Especially since voters could have forgiven concessions concerning unimportant territories in the south, but would not be as willing to be as understanding in the case of forfeiting at the last moment the rich regions of the Atacama which had just been taken over.

Consequently, on April 2, the Chilean Congress agreed to launch military operations against Peru and on the 5th day of the month the Chilean-Peruvian war was officially declared.

Entering the conflict, the Chileans set keeping control of the captured Bolivian coast as their main objective. After the declaration of war it was expanded to include taking control over the rich deposits of saltpetre in the Peruvian province of Tarapaca. Quite soon, the Chilean military leaders recognized the fact that taking over Tarapaca would only be possible after the capture of the Peruvian provinces of Tacna and Arica, located north of the said province. These two were to serve as a sort of buffer zone,

Mining settlement of Placida de Caracoles (as seen in 1873).

where a concentration of Chilean troops would be stationed. They would be able to repulse a Peruvian counter-offensive and later serve as a bargaining card during peace negotiations.

By contrast, both Bolivians and Peruvians wanted to remove the Chileans from Antofagasta to reclaim the territories captured by them and restore the status quo. The plans of both countries were essentially limited to that objective. However, due to the fact that the Atacama Desert was inaccessible and Calama with basically the only road leading from Altiplano to the coast had been captured by the Chileans, the Bolivian army had to march to Tacna. There, it would join the Peruvian troops and only then launch an offensive against Antofagasta. Therefore, on April 15, a Peruvian-Bolivian agreement was signed in Lima, which defined the objectives of the war and determined that the Bolivian side would provide 12,000 troops, while the Peruvians would provide 8,000 and their navy[6].

The latter would play a special role in the coming war. The theatre of operations included mostly the region of the Atacama Desert, which divided the belligerents. Therefore, both the Chileans, who wanted to move operations to Tarapaca and later farther north to Tacna and Arica, and the Peruvians and Bolivians, who wanted to stop the Chilean offensive against Tarapaca and then recapture Antofagasta, had to control the sea first. Transporting such large armies through the desert was improbable. There were neither railroads, nor even roads or trackways (all roads in the desert led from the harbours on the coast to mines or mining settlements located farther inland) which would facilitate such undertaking. In those conditions the troops and their supplies could only be transported by sea. Land routes could only be used by Peruvian or Bolivian troops and they were limited to Tacna and Arica. Farther south there were no such routes. Still the relocation of troops that way was more difficult and took more time. Consequently, in the first phase of the conflict it was the navy which played the major role.

Officers of the 4.Line Regiment, who constituted the majority of the landing party which had taken Antofagasta in February 1879.

6 Farcau B. W., op.cit., p.57. It turned out fairly soon that the Bolivians were unable to meet these obligations and provide as large a contingent (in mid April, Daza marched out from La Paz towards Tarapaca with only 4,500 poorly armed and equipped troops. To dispatch them the Bolivians used up the entire supply of arms and equipment they had).

4. Blockade of the southern coast of Peru and the battle of Chipana

The first problem for the belligerents was the concentration of a sufficient number of troops in the deployment areas for conducting further military operations. For the Peruvians and Bolivians these were the areas of the province of Tarapaca with its crucial harbour of Iquique, as well as Pisaqua, Tacna and Arica. For the Chileans it was the recently captured Antofagasta.

Apart from the need to concentrate troops in the designated areas, which would allow for the launching of active military operations, there was still the case of the Chilean citizens living in Peru and Bolivia. Their total number was estimated at 30–40,000, with the majority of them being permanent residents of the Bolivian *costa* and the borderland Peruvian provinces. However, there was also a large group living in Lima and Callao. Already on March 1, the Bolivian government issued an order to Chilean citizens living within the borders of Bolivia to leave the country within 8 days under threat of internment and confiscation of property. This warrant caused no serious perturbations, since the huge majority of the Chilean citizens living in Bolivia inhabited the coastal province of Antofagasta which had already been captured by the Chileans. Larger problems arose when on April 15, a similar order was issued by President Prado. There was a total of approximately 20,000 Chilean citizens living in Peru (they constituted half the population of Iquique – over 3,800, in Tarapaca it was one-fourth of the population). Evacuation of such a large number of people posed a serious logistic problem. During the entire operation the Peruvian authorities often exhibited ruthlessness, turning a blind eye to abuse by officials or soldiers. Consequently, large groups of Chileans were camping out in extreme conditions for days, being exposed to all kinds of privations. Some of them managed to get out of Peru on their

Evacuation of the Chilean citizens from Iquique after Peru had entered the war.

Iquique. own aboard neutral ships, some were evacuated from the coast before the declaration of war by Chilean ships (some 8,600). Others were evacuated by warships following the commencement of hostilities. Over a thousand failed to leave Peruvian territory and they were interned in Lima[1].

The side effect of such treatment of Chilean citizens living in Peru (Peruvians and Bolivians living in Chile were not forced to leave the country, however there was less than a thousand of them), was the enlistment of about 7,000 Chilean refugees into the army, which later had an impact on the behaviour of the Chilean troops following their intrusion into Peruvian territory. Former miners and railroad workers expelled from Peru (these were in the majority) burned to give as good as they had got, which led to an escalation of violence on both sides of the conflict, but mainly by the Chilean side.

In preparations concerning the concentration of troops before larger scale military operation, the Chileans had it easier. Since April 5, they could easily move along the coast to Antofagasta, where they began the concentration of their troops. At the outbreak of war, they had already had over 4,500 soldiers there – 2,500 regular troops transported from their country and almost the same number of national guard formed from local miners of Chilean origin. Moreover, also after the official declaration of war the Chilean sea lines of communication were still relatively safe since both Peruvian ironclads, the only warships capable of taking control of the sea, were being overhauled and incapable of putting to sea. The Peruvians would not risk any operations against the Chilean shipping without them. That was a well-known fact for the Chileans[2].

The Peruvians faced a much more difficult task as far as this process was concerned, all the more so as their army was deployed mostly in order to ensure internal order. Therefore, a large number of troops were stationed deep inland and their concentration required time[3]. Already on March 7, the transport *Limeña* left Callao heading for Iquique, carrying over 750 troops, 4 field guns and a significant number of arms for the units that were to be formed on the spot (approximately a thousand troops were enlisted there on the basis of these resources, including 300 Bolivians who worked locally and formed a separate battalion). Simultaneously, over a thousand troops were dispatched to Arica by land from the largest garrisons located inland at Cuzco and Ayacucho. On April 2, the transport *Chalaco* left Callao with over a thousand troops and 4 heavy coastal artillery guns. Some of these (one battalion) was landed in Arica, the rest was delivered to Pisagua. Following that assignment, *Chalaco* immediately headed to Mollendo, were she embarked a unit of over a thousand troops recruited from local gandarmes and Guardia Civil. This unit was transported to Pisagua and on April 8, the ship returned to Callao. Overall command of the forces at Tarapaca was taken over by Gen. Juan Buendia, who arrived from Iquique in the beginning of April.

1   G. Blunes G., *Guerra del Pacífico. De Antofagasta a Tarapaca*, Valparaiso 1911, p. 188; B. Vicuña Mackenna, op.cit., ...*Tarapaca*, vol. I, pp. 482–483.

2   Information provided by Chilean intelligence was confirmed by the Chilean ambassador, who had left Lima at the beginning of April and arrived to Santiago before the official declaration of war., B. W. Farcau, op.cit., p. 55.

3   The main regular troops garrisons were in Cusco, Ayacucho, Lima, Callao and Chorillos, Ibidem, p. 55.

Chilean blockade of Iquique.

The command over the garrisons at Arica was given to Rear Adm. Lizardo Montero, who at approximately the same time had arrived with additional reinforcements to the harbour of Mollendo[4].

Meanwhile, with the official declaration of war, the Chilean navy began its operations, arriving off Iquique in the morning of April 5, with the ironclads *Blanco Encalada* and *Almirante Cochrane*, corvettes *O'Higgins*, *Chacabuco* and *Esmeralda*, along with the transport *Lamar*, under personal command of Rear Adm. Williams. The Chilean admiral immediately declared that from April 15, he would begin the blockade of the harbour (and the entire southern coast of Peru). Civilians and neutrals were given 10 days to leave the area.

However, the action undertaken by Williams did not satisfy President Pinto, who expected much greater activity and so did the commander of the land forces. It was assumed that, taking advantage of the temporary immobilisation of both Peruvian ironclads, the Chilean admiral would attack the enemy fleet at Callao and destroy it, thus taking control of the sea at the very onset of the war, which would instantly give the Chilean side an enormous advantage and allow them to maintain the initiative. Rear Adm. Williams was perfectly aware of the fact that the navy would be of crucial importance in further military operations and it made him extremely cautious. Naval defeat would have been fatal. The Chilean commander was mindful of the fact that the harbour of Callao was well fortified and even assuming that both Peruvian ironclads were immobilised, an attack would pose a serious risk and any losses may have had serious implications. Therefore, instead of attacking the enemy in his main base, he decided to blockade the southern Peruvian harbours which would prevent them from exporting guano or saltpetre and thus causing substantial material losses. In his calculations Williams expected that this move would eventually force the Peruvian navy to leave harbour and attempt to break the blockade. This would lead to a decisive battle in open waters on his terms. In the case of such a scenario, the Peruvian warships could not have counted on the support of coastal batteries, giving the Chileans not a decisive, but still a slight advantage.

While the main force of the Chilean navy was anchored in the Iquique roadstead, the transport *Copiapó* left Valparaiso, heading north. She carried a unit of troops with supplies and was to join Rear Adm. Williams' force and later reinforce the forces concentrated at Antofagasta. By means of an undersea telegraphic cable connecting Valparaiso and Callao, the Chilean authorities in Santiago had freedom of communication with Antofagasta, but had no direct contact with the squadron at Iquique. Therefore, the gunboat *Magallanes* would be dispatched first to inform about the arrival of the transport. Additionally, she would also carry further orders and instructions to Rear Adm. Williams (the Chilean vessel left Antofagasta in the evening of April 11).

The aforementioned cable may have been facilitating the Chilean command's contact with individual units stationed on the coast, mainly those in Antofagasta, but it also allowed the Peruvians to listen to the exchange of telegrams. Consequently, quite early, Peruvian intelligence learned about the departure of the *Copiapó* and the fact that the transport was sailing without any escort (the Chilean command,

---

4   A. Curtis, op.cit., pp.49–50, B. Vicuña Mackenna, op.cit., ...*Tarapaca*, vol. I, pp. 492–494.

The Chilean gunboat
Magallanes.

The Chilean gunboat
Magallanes.

being aware of the fact that both Peruvian ironclads were still immobilised at Callao, clearly ignored the danger). President Prado immediately ordered the still operational warships, the corvette *Union* and the gunboat *Pilcomayo*, to put to sea with orders to intercept the Chilean transport[5].

Captain Aurelio Garcia y Garcia, who was in command of the Peruvian force, decided to ambush the Chilean transport in vicinity of Punta Chipana, where the River Loa flows into the Pacific Ocean, half way between the harbours of Tocopilla and Iquique. The Peruvian commander's plan was logical, however Captain Garcia y Garcia was unaware of the fact that the gunboat *Magallanes* had been dispatched ahead of the transport. Thus, when on April 12, he spotted the smoke of an unknown vessel on the horizon, he was convinced that it was the *Copiapó*.

At the moment the Chilean ship was spotted (at about 10.00), the *Union* (Captain Garcia y Garcia and Captain N. Portal) and the *Pilcomayo* (Commander A. Guerra) were sailing near the coast, between the mouth of the river Loa and Punta Arena. Both Peruvian warships had the backdrop of the land and they were more difficult to spot than the gunboat *Magallanes* (Lt. J. J. Latorre) steaming in open water. Therefore, it was not surprising that the crew of the latter only spotted the enemy after a while, which allowed the Peruvian ships to cut her way of escape south. Left with no choice, the commander of the Chilean gunboat, Lt. Juan Jose Latorre, ordered his ship to accelerate to full speed and turned the vessel straight towards the north to reach Iquique as soon as possible. The Chileans aboard the gunboat were fully aware of gravity of the situation – the enemy had an enormous advantage and moreover, the corvette *Union* was also much faster. Some among the crew of the *Magallanes* had reportedly considered possible capitulation or scuttling their ship, but Latorre cut all the speculations short and decided to run away. If the plan failed, he decided to fight to the end. He must have reckoned with the possibility of defeat, since at the onset of the engagement he burned the orders and instructions which he was to hand over to Rear Adm. Williams upon his arrival[6].

Captain Garcia y Garcia made a mistake at the beginning of the chase by not taking advantage of the *Union*'s superior speed and cutting off the Chilean warship's escape route to Iquique. Consequently, this bought the *Magallanes* some time and having the window of opportunity to escape north open, she took the chance and accelerated to full speed. Even that oversight by the Peruvian commander would not have mattered, as the *Union* had a considerably superior speed and initially everything indicated that the Chilean gunboat would be caught before she reached the safe haven of Iquique.

At approximately 10.30, the moment when the chase began, the distance between the *Magallanes* and the Peruvian warships was 4.3 km and at 11.50, it had dropped to 3.5 km. *Pilcomayo* then passed behind the Chilean warship's stern and took a seaward position. The *Union* kept position closer to the shore, gradually accelerating, she was inexorably gaining on the *Magallanes*. Due to the considerable distance at which they were firing, most of the shells missed, but after 12.00, the *Union*'s fire began to straddle the Chilean warships and finally the Peruvians managed to score a hit. A 162 mm round bounced off the water and demolished a lifeboat aboard the *Magallanes*, but inflicted no significant damage or human casualties. The Chileans did not pay any attention to the *Pilcomayo*, which was far behind, only replying to the *Union*'s fire. When at about 12.55, the distance between the *Magallanes*

---

5   A. Curtis, op.cit., p. 51, B. W. Farcau, op.cit., p. 68.

6   B. W. Farcau, op.cit., p. 68; J. Lopes, *Historia de la Guerra del Guano y el Salitre*, Lima 1980, p. 123.

and the *Union* dropped to 2.3 km, two hits on the enemy ship were observed at short intervals from the deck of the Chilean warships. Following those, the Peruvian ship immediately slowed down and a cloud of smoke and steam could be seen billowing out above her deck[7].

That event caused the Peruvian ship to cease the pursuit, while the *Magallanes* safely arrived off Iquique on the same day to join the forces under Williams' command. The damage sustained by the *Union* must have been quite serious because following her return to Callao, she was dry docked and only returned to service after about three weeks.

After the battle off the mouth of the River Loa (also known as the battle of Chipana or Punta Chipana), which could hardly be considered more than a skirmish, both sides claimed victory. It must be objectively stated that the Chileans were the successful side, as the *Magallanes* managed not only to escape the stronger enemy, but also inflict damage to one of his ships, which put her out of action for some time. In the entire engagement the Chileans expended a total of 42 rounds (four 178 mm, nineteen 160 mm and the same number of 95 mm rounds), the Peruvians fired less than 200 (the *Union* some 150, while the *Pilcomayo* fired 42 rounds)[8]. The Peruvians managed to score only one hit on the Chilean gunboat, which caused no serious damage, while the Chileans probably scored one or two hits on the *Union*. As the result of the damage sustained by the Peruvian ship, she had 36 crewmen dead or wounded (however, it is unclear if these were caused by the Chilean hits)[9].

Although the battle of the mouth of the Loa River was only a minor skirmish, it had serious consequences, both military and political. First of all, the Chileans got the message that the enemy should not be underestimated and as long at the Peruvian navy existed, any maritime transport should be under escort of warships. It turned out that the Peruvian warships could operate quite freely under the nose of the passive main force of the Chilean navy. That particular fact irritated President Pinto and

7   *Boletin...*, op.cit., p. 42 (Lt. Latorre's report). In his report, Captain Garcia y Garcia did not mention the hits received by his ship, the damage sustained was later ascribed to a malfunction (A. Curtis, op.cit, p. 52; *Voina mezhdu yuzhno-amerikanskimi republikami Peru, Chili I Bolivya. Morskaya khronika*, part. 2, "Morskoi Sbornik" No. 7/1879, p. 28). However, Peruvian accounts are so unclear that it is impossible to rule out the possibility of the *Union* in fact being hit or the fact that a Chilean shell or shells may have caused the serious damage to her power plant.

8   *Boletin...*, op.cit., p. 42 (Lt. Latorre's report); G. Blunes, op.cit., *De Antofagasta...*, p. 211; A. Curtis, op.cit., p. 52; F. A. Machuca, op.cit., vol. I, pp. 74–75.

9   *Voina mezhdu...*, part. 2, "Morskoi Sbornik", No. 7/1879, p. 27.

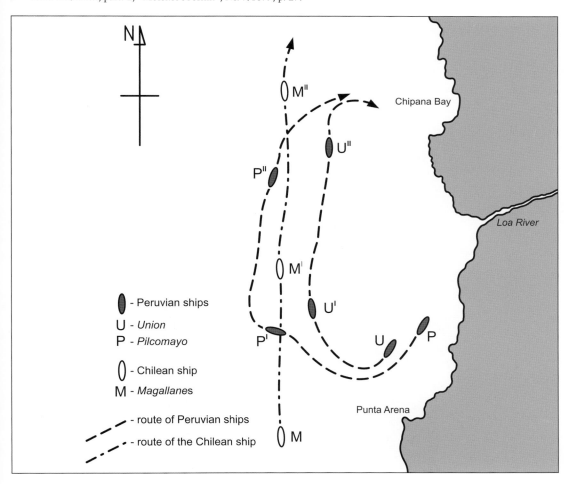

Battle of Chipana.

Commander Juan Jose Latorre, the commanding officer of the gunboat Magallanes *during the battle off the mouth of the Loa River.*

in effect led to the resignation of the current cabinet with a new government being set up on April 18 around the new Secretary of Internal Affairs, Antonio Varas (he replaced Belisario Prat). In the new government, Gen. Basilio Urrutia was appointed the new Secretary of War[10].

The skirmish at the mouth of the Loa River naturally caused a wave of criticism aimed at Rear Adm. Williams, who was accused of idleness. In the wake of that criticism the Chilean admiral decided to undertake more energetic actions. On April 15, after leaving the corvette *Esmeralda* and the gunboat *Covadonga* (which had previously arrived there) at Iquique, he sailed south with the ironclad *Blanco Encalada* and corvettes *Chacabuco* and *O'Higgins*, simultaneously dispatching the ironclad *Almirante Cochrane* and the gunboat *Magallanes* north. Officially, the Chilean admiral was thus going to force the Peruvian navy to leave Callao and engage in a decisive battle. In practice, he wanted to do anything that would make him look less passive.

On the same day, the force led by Williams himself arrived at the harbour of Pabellon de Pica (Chanabaya), where they took possession of a small Peruvian sailing ship and destroyed 21 lighters used for transporting guano. Then he headed to Huanillos (Guanillos), which was bombarded, causing some damage to the harbour and the lighters concentrated near the shore. Three days later, a force under command of Captain Simpson (commander of the ironclad *Cochrane*) arrived at Mollendo. In retaliation for firing at the boat sent to reconnoitre, the Chilean warships bombarded the railroad station and the custom house building. The firing did not cause any serious damage ashore, but some rounds which had missed their target exploded in the vicinity of the town, killing one person and wounding five others. On April 18, a similar incident took place at Pisagua, where Williams' force arrived. Also there, in retaliation for firing at the boat sent to reconnoitre (2 Chilean sailors from the corvette *Chacabuco* were killed and 6 were wounded[11]), the ironclad *Blanco Encalada* and the corvette *Chacabuco* fired on the town. The Chilean bombardment ignited fires in civilian buildings and caused considerable damage (2 people were killed). What was worse, the British Consulate building was destroyed and numerous foreigners living in the town suffered heavy material losses, which resulted in later claims for compensation[12].

By April 21, the Chilean force had again gathered in the Iquique roadstead. The actions undertaken proved futile and their effects were negligible. In no way did they affect the course of military oper-

---

10 G. Blunes, op.cit., *De Antofagasta…*, p. 237, A. Curtis, op.cit., p. 53; B. W. Farcau, op.cit, pp. 68–69. In Chile the government was de facto an auxiliary body serving the president, in whose hands was the ultimate legislative power (the government was not elected by the parliament), although the secretary of internal affairs played a most important role.

11 According to some sources the Chileans tried to put a landing party ashore, but they quickly abandoned the idea.

12 A. Curtis, op.cit., pp. 52–53; T. B. M. Mason, op.cit., p. 28; *Voina mezhdu…*, part. 2, "Morskoi Sbornik" No. 7/1879, pp. 29030.

Deck view of the Chilean gunboat Magallanes.

ations. Consequently, the criticism of Rear Adm. Williams grew stronger. Eventually, he suddenly decided to attack Callao. It was a decision which had been expected of him for a month by both the president and the high command of the army.

On April 16, one by one the Chilean warships began to leave the Iquique roadstead. The Peruvian garrison in the town was constantly in telegraphic contact with Arica and Callao, so the Chilean admiral tried not to do anything suspicious to alert the enemy about the planned operation. By nightfall, only the corvette *Esmeralda* and the gunboat *Covadonga*, which were to maintain the blockade of the harbour, remained at the location. The remaining warships (the ironclads *Blanco Encalada* and *Almirante Cochrane*, the corvettes *O'Higgins*, *Chacabuco* and *Abtao*, the gunboat *Magallanes* and the steamer *Matias Cousiño*, which served as a collier) put to open waters, until they could no longer be observed from the shore and then the entire force headed north. Rear Adm. Williams was going to use the old corvette *Abtao*, which was part of the force, as a fireship. After loading her with explosives she was to be steamed into the harbour to explode in the vicinity of the Peruvian ironclads. The skeleton crew of the corvette-fireship was then to be picked up by the gunboat *Magallanes*. She was to be accompanied by steam launches from both ironclads, armed with spar torpedoes, which were to enter the harbour immediately after the *Abtao*'s charge

Captain Aurelio Garcia y Garcia, the commanding officer of the corvette Union *during the battle off the mouth of the Loa River.*

and attack the surviving Peruvian warships. The entire operation was to be concluded by the bombardment of the harbour. The corvettes *O'Higgins* and *Chacabuco* were to target the coastal fortifications, while both ironclads were in the first place to destroy the remaining Peruvian warships[13].

On the night of April 21/22, the Chilean squadron arrived at Callao. It was plagued by strokes of bad luck and therefore, for technical reasons, the preparations of the *Abtao* for the planned attack were well behind schedule and so were the preparations of the steam launches that were to accompany her. Consequently, the preparations had not been completed before the break of dawn. When the sun had risen (at 04.30 hours), the Chileans observed from the deck of their ships that the Peruvian ironclads were not in the harbour. Thus, the attack at Callao no longer had any purpose. The Chilean squadron only paraded at the entrance of the harbour, beyond the reach of the Peruvian guns and after 11.00, sailed south.

The fact that the *Huascar* and *Independencia* were not present at Callao seriously troubled Rear Adm. Williams, who was rightly worried about the possibility of a Peruvian attack against one of the harbours under Chilean control. Therefore, he was going to return to Iquique as soon as possible. The situation was complicated by the fact that at night, before the arrival at Callao, the steamer *Matias Cousiño*, which served as a collier, got separated from the squadron in the darkness. Meanwhile, the Chilean warships were short on fuel. To reach Iquique as soon as possible, Williams decided to transfer coal from the corvettes *O'Higgins* and *Chacabuco* to the remaining vessels, which steamed south faster. The corvettes followed them under sail.

Meanwhile, on May 14, the Peruvian government met at Lima, with Bolivian President Daza also being present. It was decided that the main allied forces should be concentrated in the area of Tacna-Arica. Accordingly, the Peruvians decided to transport an additional 4,000 troops to Arica by sea, while a Bo-

---

13 A. Curtis, op.cit., p. 54.

The Peruvian corvette Union, *the main opponent of the* Magallanes *in the battle off the mouth of the Loa River.*

The bombardment of Pisagua by the Chilean squadron under command of Rear Adm. Williams on April 18, 1879. The attempt to reconnoitre the enemy positions cost the Chileans one boat sent to the bottom and human losses.

livian corps of at least the same strength would march to Tacna by land. President Prado himself was going to travel to Arica along with the Peruvian troops, leaving Vice President La Puerta in office in Lima. The Peruvian troops were to be carried aboard the transports *Oroya*, *Chalaco* and *Limeña*, escorted by both Peruvian ironclads, which had just completed their overhaul. It was initially planned to also dispatch to Arica the monitor *Manco Capac*, in order to reinforce the harbour's defences. However, technical difficulties forced Prado to leave that ship in Callao. Consequently, at the same time when Williams' warships were leaving the Iquique roadstead, 3 Peruvian transports carrying troops and supplies under the escort of the *Huascar* and *Independencia* left Callao. Due to a mechanical breakdown aboard the transport *Chalaco*, the Peruvian convoy had to make a stop in vicinity of the Chincha Islands. The malfunction was soon repaired and the remainder of the journey went smoothly. On May 18, the Peruvian ships called at Mollendo to refuel and finally arrived at Arica on May 20. The Peruvians were lucky, as at night following their departure from Mollendo they passed by the Williams' squadron. The Peruvian ships were steaming close to the shore, their enemy on the other hand was moving far from the shore so as not to be spotted. The attack on Callao was to be a surprise and premature detection of the Chilean warships by the Peruvians would have thwarted the plans.

Immediately upon arrival at their destination, the Peruvians began disembarking their troops and unloading supplies. The transport *Oroya* headed for Pisagua at once, with 500 troops and supplies. Upon going on shore, President Prado learned about the absence of the main Chilean naval force at Iquique (a telegram with the information had already been sent from Iquique on the day after Williams' force left, heading north). In those circumstances, suspecting an easy victory and destruction of the vessels blockading Iquique, Prado ordered the *Huascar* and the *Independencia* to leave Arica and attack the Chilean vessels stationed there. Both ironclads put to sea in the evening hours, calling at night at Pisagua to refuel and make sure the main Chilean forces are not at Iquique. Upon confirmation of the said information, the *Huascar* and the *Independencia* immediately put to sea and headed straight for Iquique.

5. Battle of Iquique

On May 21, the blockade of Iquique was maintained by the corvette *Esmeralda* (Commander A. Prat) and the gunboat *Covandonga* (Lt. C. Condell) with the transport *Lamar*, which had arrived after May 17. The command of that small force anchored in the roadstead was in the hands of Commander Arturo Prat, commander of the Chilean corvette. The Chileans had already been aware of the arrival of considerable Peruvian naval and army forces which had reached Arica, therefore, they were anxiously on the lookout for a superior enemy naval force. Both *Esmeralda* and *Covandonga* were old, slow warships and their escape from the enemy vessels was out of question. Despite the weakness of his forces, Prat was determined to fight to the end, no matter what enemy they would face.

The approaching Peruvian ships were first spotted at 06.05 by a lookout on the *Covadonga*. Both Chilean warships immediately beat to quarters and then anchored in the southern section of the bay, as close to the shore as possible (no more than 200 metres), with the town behind them. Prat thought that, on the one hand the position would discourage the Peruvian ironclads which had much larger drafts than the Chilean warships, and on the other, it would make it difficult for them to fire, as the rounds that overshot the Chileans would possibly hit the town. However, staying so close inshore, the Chileans were exposed to harassing fire from the shore. They decided it would be a lesser evil (they assumed the Peruvians had no artillery in the town). The transport *Lamar* weighed anchor immediately after confirmation that the approaching ships were Peruvian and hoisting the American ensign, fled south at full speed, leaving the area of the upcoming battle.

Iquique (a view from the western side).

The Chilean corvette Esmeralda.

Battery deck of the corvette Esmeralda. *In 1879, the ship was armed with 120 mm (40-pdr) Armstrong muzzle loaders, which were unable to penetrate the armour of the Peruvian ironclad* Huascar, *the adversary the Chileans had to face.*

The Iquique roadstead along with the Chilean warships stationed there were spotted from the decks of the Peruvian ironclads at about 07.00. The *Huascar* (Captain M. Grau) was then approximately 2 NM in front of the *Independencia* (Captain J. G. Moore), the distance to the harbour was still some 5 NM[1]. Shortly thereafter, the port captain arrived from Iquique aboard the flagship ironclad with information (incorrect, but delivered in good faith), that the Chilean anchorage was probably protected by mines[2]. Therefore, Grau decided not to engage the enemy at very short range and ordered the commander of the *Independencia* to attack the *Covadonga*, while he himself would target the *Esmeralda*. At about 08.20, when the distance between the *Huascar* and the *Esmeralda* dropped below 2,000 metres, Grau ordered the gunners to open fire and the Peruvians fired the first shot of the battle[3]. Shortly thereafter, the Chileans also opened fire, while the *Independencia*, steaming behind the flagship, joined the battle at about 08.30, targeting the *Covadonga*.

For the next hour the Chilean and Peruvian warships were firing at each other at a distance of approximately 800–900 metres, but the Peruvian fire was extremely inaccurate[4], while the Chileans could not penetrate the armour of the enemy ships, although they scored at least a few hits. At about 09.00, the *Independencia*, which in the meantime had closed the distance to the enemy to about 600 metres, eventually managed to hit the *Covadonga*. The round hit the stern of the Chilean warship, but went through the hull without exploding. Therefore, the Chilean gunboat suffered no significant damage, but her commander, Captain Condell, decided to slip anchor and head south, running away from the battle, concluding that he would not be so lucky next time. He was immediately followed by the *Independencia*, while the *Huascar* remained in the Bay of Iquique, still fighting the *Esmerlada*.

Commander Arturo Prat, the commanding officer of the corvette Esmeralda.

Due to the inaccurate fire of the Peruvian ironclad, the *Esmerlada* was still operational (although at the outset of the battle there was a boiler malfunction, which reduced her already slow speed to a mere 3 knots). At about 10.00, her situation dramatically changed. Although four heavy coastal guns had been delivered to Iquique to be used as coastal artillery, they had not been deployed. The troops stationed in the town had a battery of 4 field guns (the Chileans were unaware of that fact), which had been deployed ashore, some 450 metres from the corvette's anchorage. Shortly before 10.00, they opened fire. As long as the *Esmerlada* was under fire from small arms, as annoying as it had been, it could be ignored since it constituted no serious threat. With the artillery fire, the situation became serious, so Prat ordered the ship to weigh anchor and slowly steamed deeper into the bay to escape beyond the range of the Peruvian guns.

The leaving of the previous anchorage by the *Esmeralda* urged Grau, who had already been clearly frustrated by his gunners' incompetence, to decide the battle by ramming the enemy ship. He had been worried to do this so far, being convinced that the *Esmeralda* was protected by a minefield. He ordered his ironclad towards the Chilean warship and approaching her, she fired two shots from her 10-inch guns. One of the Peruvian rounds hit the midships of the Chilean corvette, slightly above the waterline and exploded in the engine room, demolishing it and killing all the occupants[5]. The Chilean corvette was immobilised and moreover, a fire broke out on her deck. Shortly thereafter (at 10.30), the *Huascar* rammed the side of the *Esmeralda*. The impact, however, was at too oblique an angle and the speed of the ironclad was only 8 knots, therefore, her ram glanced off the hull of the corvette, causing no real damage. While the two ships were touching for a moment, Prat took advantage of that, leaping on the deck of the ironclad to board her. The commander's desperate move surprised even his subordinates, consequently, only one petty officer managed to follow him to the deck of the *Huascar*. Soon, the crew of the ironclad opened small arms fire, killing Prat on the spot and severely wounding Sgt. Aldea, who later died in captivity[6].

Immediately after the first ramming attempt, Grau ordered a repeat of the attack. It was an easy task, as at that time the Chilean warship was practically helpless and unable to make any moves. The second

1   *Voina mezhdu...*, part. 3, "Morskoi Sbornik" No. 8/1879, p. 35 (M. Grau's report), p. 39 (J. G. Moore's report).

2   G. Blunes, op.cit., *De Antofagasta...*, p. 292; A. Curtis, op.cit., p.56; B. W. Farcau, op.cit., p. 72.

3   *Voina mezhdu...*, part. 3, "Morskoi Sbornik" No. 8/1879, p. 36 (M. Grau's report). It is often stated that the Peruvian ironclad fired the first shots at about 08.00 (A. Curits, op.cit., p. 55, C. r. Markham, op.cit., p. 109; T. B. M. Mason, op.cit., p. 31).

4   In the entire engagement the *Huascar* fired forty-seven 254 mm rounds, scoring only one hit. Correspondencia Jeneral de la Comandancia Jeneral de la 1. Division Naval bajo el mando del contra-almirante don Miguel Grau, comendante del "Huascar", Santiago 1880, p. 19; W. L. Clowes, Four Modern Naval Campaigns, London 1902, p. 81; T. B. M. Mason, op.cit., p. 32.

5   C. R. Markham, op.cit, p. 110. From 20 to 30 Chileans were killed then.

6   It is sometimes stated (probably erroneously), that at that moment three Chileans boarded the *Huascar*: Prat, Sgt. Juan de Dios Aldea and one unnamed sailor, whose further fate remains unknown., A. Curtis, op.cit., p. 57.

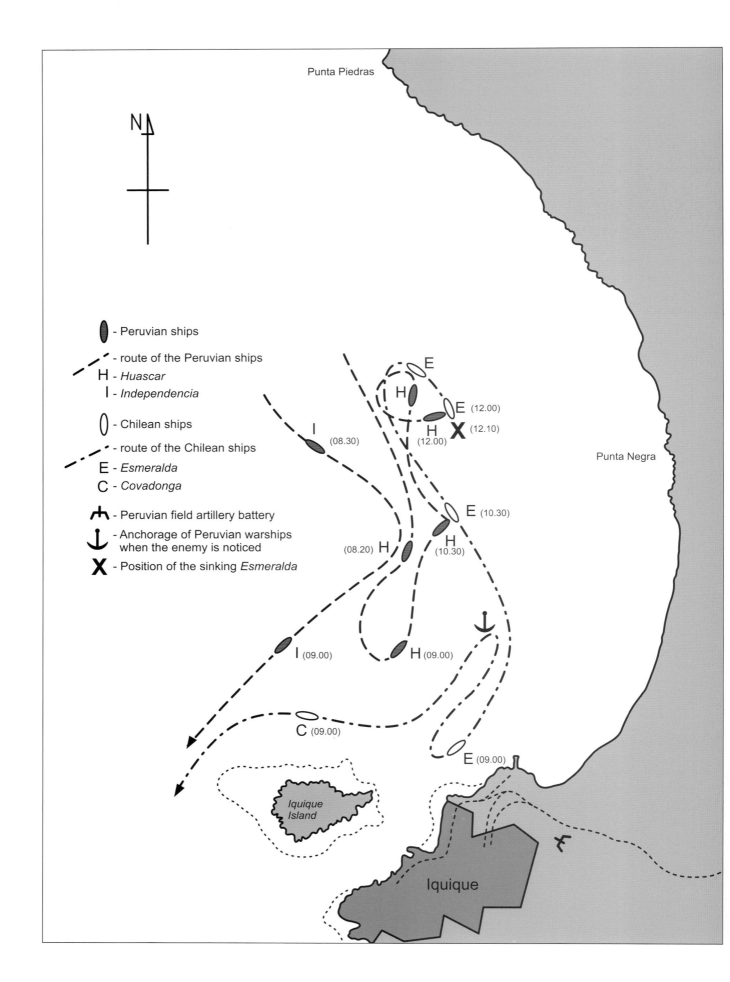

Punta Piedras

N

Punta Negra

Legend:

◖ - Peruvian ships

- - route of the Peruvian ships

H - *Huascar*

I - *Independencia*

◯ - Chilean ships

- route of the Chilean ships

E - *Esmeralda*

C - *Covadonga*

⚓ - Peruvian field artillery battery

⚓ - Anchorage of Peruvian warships when the enemy is noticed

X - Position of the sinking *Esmeralda*

E

H

E (12.00)

H (12.00)

X (12.10)

I (08.30)

E (10.30)

H (10.30)

H (08.20)

I (09.00)

H (09.00)

C (09.00)

E (09.00)

Iquique Island

Iquique

Battle of Iquique (engagement between the Huascar *and the* Esmeralda).

44

A model of the Chilean gunboat Covadonga.

attack came from the *Esmeralda*'s stern. The Peruvian ironclad hit her side at a 45° angle. Even that did not send the Chilean warship to the bottom, as the *Huascar* stopped her engines too early and therefore the impact was too weak. Although the *Esmeralda* sprung a leak shortly after the collision, she was still afloat. The moment the two ships were together, Lt. Ignacio Serrano, following his commander's example, leaped onto the deck of the Peruvian monitor along with 12 sailors. Trying to reach the enemy ship's conning tower, Serrano encountered Lt. Jorge Velarde and shot him with his revolver (two Peruvian sailors accompanying him were wounded). Shortly thereafter, he himself succumbed to small arms fire of the *Huascar*'s crewmen. The sailors who followed him were mostly killed with their commander and only two or three managed to jump overboard and swim back to the *Esmeralda*[7].

The Chilean corvette was then truly in dire straits. The ship was completely immobilised and was slowly taking on water. Half of the crew was dead or wounded and the ship's guns were silent. Despite that, Lt. Louis Uribe, who took command of the ship after Prat's death, had no thoughts of surrender. However, the heroic stand of the Chilean warship's crew could not affect the course of the battle in any way. The *Huascar*'s third attack would end in the sinking of the *Esmeralda* and so it happened. At about noon, the ironclad, steaming at over 10 knots (the engines were stopped only 20 metres from the target), hit the side of the Chilean corvette at nearly a right angle. She went down at about 12.10[8]. Immediately after sinking the Chilean corvette, the Peruvians began rescue operations, taking aboard the ironclad 63 survivors, including Lt. Uribe[9]. It took no more than half an hour, and then the *Huascar* immediately headed south, where the *Independencia* was fighting the *Covadonga*.

Lieutenant Carlos Condell, the commanding officer of the gunboat Covadonga *during the battle of Iquique.*

Shortly after abandoning the *Esmeralda*, the commander of the *Covadonga*, Lt. Condell, ordered his ship to head south trying to keep her well inshore to make it difficult for the much larger ironclad *Independencia* to pursue her. The Chilean commander was aware of the fact that the enemy warship had the advantage in speed, but also that her draft was much deeper (by about 3.5 metre) than that of the *Covadonga*. In view of these, the escape along the shoreline, close to the shoals, although also dangerous for the *Covadonga*, gave her some hope of survival. Even more so, as the Chileans had already found out that the Peruvian gunners were poorly trained. Escape to open waters would have probably resulted in the interception of the gunboat by the ironclad sooner or later, ending in the destruction of the former.

Lt. Condell's plan proved sound, as it quickly turned out that although the *Independencia* closed the distance to the chased gunboat to a mere hundred metres (at times it dropped to 200 metres), it could not have intercepted, sunk or forced her to surrender. Initially, the Peruvian ship, passing the shoals around Iquique on the western side, overtook the Chilean gunboat and tried to stop her with a broadside, but with no effect. Condell swiftly manoeuvred around the ironclad, escaping to a nearby bay. Repeating a similar manoeuvre would have been difficult

---

7   Prat is sometimes credited with shooting Lt. Velarde dead (e.g. see C. R. Markham, op.cit., p. 110), but in reality, the Peruvian officer died during the second attempt to ram the *Esmeralda*., A. Curtis, op.cit., p. 57.

8   *Voina mezhdu…*, part. 3, "Morskoi Sbornik" No. 8/1879, p. 37 (Grau's report).

9   Ibidem, p. 37; *Boletin…*, op.cit., pp. 186–187.

The Peruvian ironclad Huascar, *the opponent of the* Esmeralda *during the battle of Iquique.*

and dangerous, therefore, Captain Moore of the *Independencia* decided to keep his ship behind the stern of the gunboat and kept on firing at her with the bow 9-inch (250-pounder) chaser, waiting for the right moment to ram her.

Heavy fire from the gunboat soon put the ironclad's heavy bow chaser out of action[10] and two consecutive attempts to ram the *Covadonga* failed (the first took place approximately 2 NM south of Iquique, and the second abreast of Molle), as every time she managed to avoid the ironclad's bow. Moore did not want to risk running aground. Consequently, with every attempt, the *Independencia* had to turn towards open water, which slowed down the pursuit and gave the Chilean gunboat some more time to escape. Moore made the third attempt to ram the *Covadonga* after a two-and-a-half-hour pursuit, when both vessels reached Punta Gruesa, roughly 10 NM south of Iquique. At 11.45, avoiding the ironclad's ram, the *Covadonga* turned towards the shore, with her hull scraping an uncharted rock[11].

10   There are two accounts of the event in which the bow 9-inch Vavasseur chaser was put out of action. According to the first one, it was taken out by the direct hit of a 163 mm round fired by the gunboat (see e.g. B. W. Farcau, op.cit., p. 74). In the second one, it was silenced by intense small arms fire from the deck of the *Covadonga* (e.g. A. Curtis, op.cit, p. 58). Captain Moore's report (*Voina mezhdu…*, part. 3, "Morskoi Sbornik" No. 8/1879, p. 40) is inconclusive, the Peruvian commander emphasised the intense small arms fire directed at his ship, even attributing it to a machine gun, although none was mounted aboard the *Covadonga*. It is then highly probable that the Peruvians were unable to operate the bow chaser due to the intense small arms fire from the *Covadonga*.

11   B. W. Farcau, op.cit., p. 74.

The Peruvian ironclad Independencia.

Miraculously, her hull was not damaged, but the ironclad, closely following her (in his report Captain Moore emphasized the fact that the *Independencia*'s ram nearly scraped the side of the Chilean gunboat, so both ships had to be really close[12]), ran hard aground and stuck fast[13].

The impact in the proximity of the engine room was so great that it tore the hull of the Peruvian ironclad open. She soon began taking on water, simultaneously listing to port, which prevented the gunners from firing the guns, all the more so because the battery deck was quickly being flooded. Condell immediately took advantage of the situation, turned the *Covadonga* around, placed her behind the stern of the grounded ironclad and began to shell her.

Soon, the Chilean rounds set the ironclad on fire and with no chance to continue the fight, Moore ordered his crew to abandon ship. Since some of the lifeboats were destroyed during the battle, and there was not enough room for all of the crewmen, the Peruvian commander ordered taking the first batch ashore and returning to the ironclad to collect the remainder. This proved impossible, as all the lifeboats were wrecked. Therefore, the commander of the *Independencia* remained aboard his ship along with 20–30 officers and sailors until 13.30, when the *Huascar* appeared on the horizon, steaming from Iquique. Upon spotting the incoming ironclad, the *Covadonga* immediately ceased fire and headed south towards Antofagasta[14]. Upon arrival at the wreck site, the *Huascar* rescued the reminder of the crew and then gave chase of the Chilean gunboat. This lasted until nightfall. With no chance to catch her, the ironclad returned to Iquique. The remaining survivors from the *Independencia* also reached the town after some time.

The battle of Iquique ended in a Peruvian victory, but it was truly a Pyrrhic one, which even the victors, had they known the outcome, would have wanted to avoid. The Chileans lost an old corvette with 135 officers and sailors, 63 (including numerous wounded ones) were captured. The *Covadonga*

Captain Juan Guillermo Moore, the commanding officer of the ironclad Independencia *during the battle of Iquique.*

---

12 *Voina Mezhdu...*, part. 3, "Morskoi Sbornik" No. 8/1879, p. 40 (J. G. Moore's report).

13 It is sometimes stated that at the critical moment the *Covadonga*'s small arms fire killed the ironclad's helmsman (his position was on the main deck), which purportedly caused the *Independencia* to run aground (W. L. Clowes, op.cit., p. 83; Hancock A. U., *A History of Chile*, Chicago, 1893, p. 281; T. B. M. Mason, op.cit., p.33). However, Captain Moore does not mention it in his report, emphasizing that the depth of water around the rock on which the ironclad had run was 11 to 12 metres, which meant that his ship ran aground on an uncharted rock far from the shore. Both Chileans and Peruvians were unaware of its existence, therefore both ships could not have tried to avoid it.

14 *Boletin...*, op.cit., pp. 168–169, 187–188, 716–717. During the entire engagement, the *Covadonga* expended a total of sixty-five 163 mm rounds (27 shells and 38 armour-piercing solid shots) and sixty-eight 76 mm rounds., *La Guerra maritime entre le Péru et la Chili*, "Revue Maritime et Coloniale", part 1, vol. 65 (1880), p. 84 (Condell's report).

Battle of Iquique – the initial phase of the engagement.

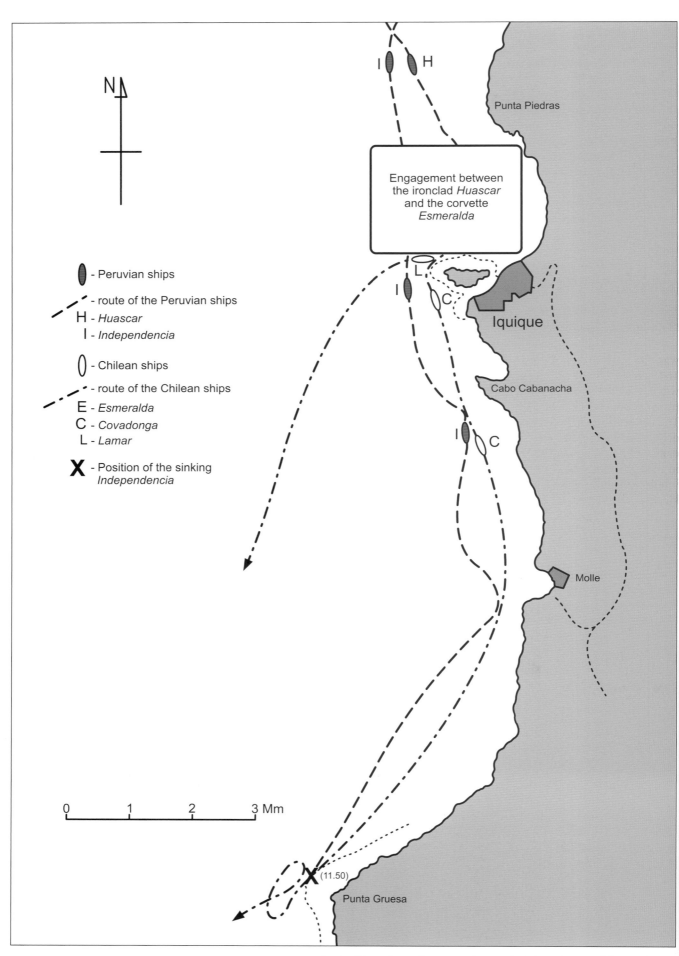

- Peruvian ships
- route of the Peruvian ships
- H - *Huascar*
- I - *Independencia*

- Chilean ships
- route of the Chilean ships
- E - *Esmeralda*
- C - *Covadonga*
- L - *Lamar*

X - Position of the sinking
Independencia

Engagement between
the ironclad *Huascar*
and the corvette
Esmeralda

Punta Piedras

Iquique

Cabo Cabanacha

Molle

(11.50)

Punta Gruesa

N

0   1   2   3 Mm

Battle of Punta Gruesa (engagement between the Independencia *and the* Covadonga*).*

was damaged, losing 3 killed and 6 wounded (her hull was hit by a total of two 203 mm and one 163 mm shell, two others damaged the rigging[15]). The Peruvians lost the ironclad *Independencia*, which was considered a total loss and was burned by her crew (earlier they had managed to salvage two guns from the upper deck). She had 18 officers and sailors killed or wounded (mainly due to small arms fire). The *Huascar* suffered some damage but remained operational. She damaged her bow (a minor leak was detected) in ramming of the *Esmeralda*. The tripod foremast was also seriously damaged and was in danger of toppling over (it was removed upon arrival at Callao). The most serious of all the hits received in the battle with the *Esmeralda* was the one in the turret gun port – a 120 mm shell had entered the interior of the turret, but failed to explode. Only a single officer (Velarde) of the *Huascar*'s crew was killed and 7 sailors were wounded[16].

Battle of Iquique – the moment of the sinking of the Esmeralda.

---

15 F. A. Machuca, op.cit, vol. I, p. 132.

16 Losses according to: *Boletin…*, op.cit., p. 141; B. W. Farcau, op.cit., p. 72; *Voina mezhdu…*, part. 3, "Morskoi Sbornik" No. 8/1879, pp. 43 (Condell's report), 45. There are various figures concerning the losses suffered by the *Esmerlada*, depending on the number of survivors rescued by the *Huascar* (some sources mention 50 and 47 – the author decided to accept Grau's report, which tells about rescuing 63 Chileans). It is sometimes stated that *Huascar* had only 3 sailors wounded. This could be possible not taking into account those who suffered minor wounds and were not put out of action.

The ironclad Independencia *after running aground on an uncharted rock. (Thomas Somerscales)*

However, the most important fact was that the Peruvians lost the ironclad *Independencia*. It drastically reduced the strength of the Peruvian navy. This called into question Prado's plans of taking back Antofagasta by a naval assault and landing. In the new reality, in the situation where the Chilean navy was clearly stronger, this would be an incredibly risky task. Therefore, immediately after receiving the news concerning the loss of the *Independencia*, the Peruvian president decided to give up the plans of the offensive and concentrate on the defence of Arica and Tacna[17]. The weakening of the Peruvian navy had a tremendous impact on further military operations in general. It may have even decided its entire outcome.

Political repercussions of the battle of Iquique were another issue. The heroic commander of the *Esmeralda*, Arturo Prat, was elevated to the status of a national hero overnight, while Chileans were swept by a wave of true "Pratomania", which could not be underestimated, as it strengthened national support for the war. Consequently, even those who had been sceptical about it were beginning to change their minds. Incidentally, Prat's death gave the conservatives an opportunity to attack the ruling liberals (although, quite ironically, Prat himself was known for his rather liberal views!) for leaving the warships blocking Iquique alone. In all that commotion, the commander of the *Covadonga*, Lt. Condell, who had turned defeat into victory, was somehow forgotten. If he was mentioned, it was in the context of the one who had deserted his superior at a critical moment. The wrecking of the *Independencia*, being a key moment of the battle and one of the crucial moments of the entire conflict, was considered more of an unlucky event than Lt. Condell's intentional action. There was some truth in that, but also a fair amount of injustice, since owing to the Chilean gunboat commander's wise tactics, the events took the right turn. However, the Chilean high command could appreciate Condell's merits, although he did not gain the corresponding fame.

Immediately after the battle of Iquique Arturo Prat's body was buried on May 22, at the Iquique cemetery. However, in 1888 it was exhumed and interred with honours in a mausoleum at Valparaiso. The date of May 21 (the day of the battle of Iquique) is celebrated as the Chilean Navy Day. The photo shows Prat's second burial ceremony in 1888.

17 Lopez J., *Historia de la Guerra del Guano y la Salitre*, Lima 1980, p. 188.

6. Naval operations in the period between the battle of Iquique and the battle of Angamos (May-October 1879)

The battle of Iquique completely altered the balance of naval power, with the advantage in Chilean hands. In those circumstances Grau came to the conclusion that the said advantage could only be overcome by activity. By holding the initiative and attacking Chilean commerce and harbours, he could paralyse the enemy's operations and thus prevent the Chilean army's invasion of Peruvian territory. In the current situation, it was difficult for the Peruvian-Bolivian side to consider any offensive actions. Defending Tarapaca became the priority, and the key to success of that undertaking was preventing the Chileans from transporting the army invasion force, which was being concentrated in Antofagasta, by sea to Peruvian territory.

In the morning of May 24, after the transport *Chalaco*, which had meanwhile arrived with supplies at Iquique, was dispatched to Arica, the *Huascar* left the harbour heading south. The next day at dawn, an unidentified steamer was spotted on the horizon by the Peruvian ironclad's lookouts. She turned out to be the Chilean transport *Itata*[1]. A four-hour-long chase failed (following the ramming of the *Esmeralda*, the *Huascar*'s bow was damaged and she was incapable of reaching her top speed) and the Peruvians were only able to intercept the small sailing ship *Recuperado* which was accompanying the transport. It turned out that she was a former Peruvian vessel previously captured by the *Itata*. With a shortage of crewmen to man the prize, Grau ordered her torched and then headed for Mejillones, where he arrived on the same day. He encountered no resistance there and proceeded to destroy a few lighters used for transporting guano (which could have been useful for the Chileans as troop landing vessels) and the schooner *Clorinda*[2].

Rear Admiral Miguel Grau Seminario.

In the evening, the *Huascar* put to sea again, heading for Antofagasta. At dawn, approaching her destination, he spotted the transport *Rimac* leaving the harbour. The ironclad gave an ineffective chase, but being unable to catch the enemy, Grau returned to patrol off Antofagasta. Thus, he gave the Chileans time to finish unloading the transport *Itata* (the very same that had escaped him earlier), which was in the harbour. Consequently, when the *Huascar* appeared off Antofagasta again, the *Itata* had managed to leave the harbour and was running away at top speed towards open waters. The Chilean steamer yet again managed to slip away from the *Huascar* (the chase lasted for about two hours). The Peruvian ironclad returned to Antofagasta.

---

1   Also on May 15, the transports *Rimac* and *Itata* had been dispatched from Vaparaiso to Antofagasta, carrying a large amount of supplies and 2,500 troops. The Chileans, oblivious to their previous experiences, rather blithely dispatched both ships with no escort, not assuming that they might encounter enemy warships. The faster *Rimac* reached Antofagasta on May 24. G. Blunes, op.cit., *De Antofagasta...*, p. 322, A. Curits, op.cit., vol. I, p. 60.

2   *Voina mezhdu...*, part 4, "Morskoi Sbornik" No. 9/1879, pp. 26–27 (M. Grau's report).

The ironclad Huascar. *Brilliantly commanded by Rear Admiral Miguel Grau she was able to impede Chilean ooperations, thus preventing the invasion of Peruvian.*

In the harbour, apart from a number of neutral ships, was the gunboat *Covadonga*. The harbour itself was protected by three 254–178 mm guns and two field artillery batteries. At 15.15, following a short reconnaissance of the enemy positions, the *Huascar* opened fire, targeting the water distillation plant (the Peruvians clearly tried not to hit the town, as they later justified, for fear of hurting numerous foreigners living in Antofagasta). The Chilean coastal batteries and the *Covadonga* immediately responded, beginning an artillery exchange which lasted for approximately two hours. The *Huascar* fired a total of sixteen 254 mm and 8 smaller calibre rounds, while the Chileans expended a total of about 80 rounds of various calibres. They managed to score one heavy calibre hit on the ironclad, which hit close to the waterline and pierced the armour, but failed to penetrate the hull (therefore, the damage was minor)[3].

Undeterred by that failure, on May 27 the *Huascar* returned off Antofagasta and cut the submarine cable connecting the town with Valparaiso. In the evening she steamed north, arriving off Cobija in the morning of the following day. There, she destroyed 6 small sailing vessels and then left. Shortly thereafter, the Peruvian ironclad intercepted the schooner *Coqueta*, which was manned by a prize crew and sent to Callao. Then, she captured the large barque *Emilia*, which followed suit. On May 29, the *Huascar* returned to Iquique, where Grau received orders to steam to Ilo to recoal[4]. On her way to the said harbour, on May 30 at about 17.00, the Peruvian ironclad encountered the Chilean transport *Matias Cousiño*, cruising off Arica. She had previously been "lost" by Williams' squadron during its raid against Callao. Following a two-hour-long chase, Grau finally gave up and steamed north, arriving off Ilo in the morning of May 31. After recoaling, the ironclad steamed to Arica, and then, on June 2, to Pisagua. There she received orders to search for the Chilean corvettes *O'Higgins* and *Chacabuco*, which, following an unsuccessful raid against Callao, were returning under sail and according to the intelligence gathered by the Peruvians were still at sea.

On June 3, the *Huascar* put to sea again and in the evening of the same day, while steaming approximately off Huanillos, spotted two unidentified vessels on the horizon. Initially, the Peruvians had assumed that these were the two corvettes they were searching for, which, sailing with no coal aboard, would have been an easy prey for the ironclad. Grau ordered his ship to head in their direction, but in the morning he found out that they were not *O'Higgins* and *Chacabuco*, but the ironclad *Blanco Encalada* and the accompanying gunboat *Magallanes*. Immediately after realizing the mistake, the *Huascar* turned north, however, the Chilean warships gave chase.

The moment it began, at about 07.00, the distance between the Peruvian ironclad and the enemy was approximately 8 km, but it was gradually and inexorably decreasing. Following the battle of

3   Ibidem, p. 28; *Boletin…*, op.cit, pp. 169–170; T. B. M. Mason, op.cit., pp. 34–35. Grau's report does not mention any hit scored by the Chilean coastal batteries.

4   On May 28, shortly before dawn, *Huascar* passed Williams' squadron in the vicinity of Punta Mejillones. The Chilean warships had been spotted by the Peruvian ironclad, while she remained unnoticed., *Voina mezhdu…*, part. 4, "Morskoi Sbornik" No. 9/1879, p. 29 (Grau's report).

The Chilean transport Itata.

Iquique, the *Huascar* still had her bow damaged, which prevented her from reaching top speed and moreover, the coal she loaded at Ilo was of inferior quality. Consequently, she was unable to reach a speed of more than 9 knots. Therefore, the Chileans were gradually reducing the distance by about 700 m an hour. At about 11.30, when the distance between the opponents dropped to 4.7 km, Captain Riveros, the commanding officer of the Chilean ironclad, ordered his ship to take a turn to be able to fire a broadside at the *Huascar*. This manoeuvre turned out to be a mistake, since the range was still too great to score a hit and the time lost allowed the Peruvian warship to increase the distance. At the same time, the Peruvians came up with the idea of using a mixture of paraffin and turpentine to improve the effectiveness of the coal, so they maintained their distance until nightfall, when they managed to break away from the enemy after an eighteen-hour-long pursuit[5].

Finally, on June 7, the *Huascar* called at Callao, being enthusiastically welcomed by its residents. In recognition for his conduct, the ironclad's commanding officer, Miguel Grau, was soon promoted to the rank of rear admiral (but he still retained command of the ship). The ironclad itself was repaired. Her tripod foremast, damaged during the battle of Iquique, was removed and the maintop was fitted with an iron screen for a Gatling gun (Grau insisted on it, bearing in mind the effectiveness of the Chilean small arms fire during the battle of Iquique).

The repairs to the Peruvian ironclad lasted less than a month, until the beginning of July. In the meantime the Chileans enjoyed a relative freedom in naval operations, although the blockade of Iquique

---

5 G. Blunes, op.cit., *De Antofagasta…*, pp. 336–339; A. Curtis, op.cit., vol. I, pp. 61–62; T. B. M. Mason, op.cit. p. 35.

The bombardment of Iquique by the Chilean warships on July 16, 1879.

53

Copiapó.

was still maintained by the ironclad *Almirante Cochrane*, the corvette *Abtao*, the gunboat *Magallanes* and the transport *Matias Cousiño*. Antofagasta was defended by the ironclad *Blanco Encalada* and the corvette *Chacabuco*. At the beginning of June, the army concentrated at Antofagasta which was to invade Peruvian territory, had already reached the number of 8,700 troops (these also included a 640 men strong naval battalion). Apart from these forces, there were about 1,860 additional troops in the Araucanian area, while 6,500 were in reserve or undergoing training (troops were constantly being recruited)[6].

Meanwhile, at the beginning of July, the *Huascar*'s repairs were completed and on the 6th the ship put to sea again along with the transport *Chalaco*. Both ships headed south and arrived at Arica on July 9. There, Rear Adm. Grau met with President Prado, who ordered him to attack the Chilean warships blockading Iquique. The Chilean warships spent every night out at sea in fear of night-time torpedo attacks[7], leaving only the corvette *Abtao* in the roadstead. She was to be the target of the *Huascar*'s nocturnal attack. Grau was dubious about Prado's plan, as he considered it extremely risky. However, he accepted the order and on the same day left Arica, heading farther south. The Peruvian ironclad arrived off Iquique at about 01.00 at night. No more than two hours later, the lookouts aboard the ship spotted the transport *Matias Cousiño*, which stopped its engines and struck its colours immediately after the ironclad had fired a warning shot. Before the Peruvians were able to take possession of the prize, the Chilean gunboat *Magallanes* arrived from the south, alerted by the gunfire. The Peruvians had initially mistaken the gunboat for the ironclad *Almirante Cochrane*. The *Huascar* left its prize, whose crew took advantage of the situation and quickly escaped the area, avoiding capture. Shortly thereafter, the ironclad opened fire at the *Magallanes* at a distance of less than 300 metres. The gunboat replied when the distance dropped to mere 160 metres.

Aware of the poor training of his gunners, Grau ordered ramming the Chilean gunboat (the ironclad's crew quickly figured out who the enemy was), but this proved an extremely difficult task in the darkness, therefore both attempts failed. However, both ships passed at a distance of only a few dozen metres, firing at each other. They ceased fire only when the ironclad *Almirante Cochrane* arrived at the scene from the south. Bearing in mind Prado's directives, which prevented him from engaging enemy ironclads, the Peruvian ironclad's commanding officer ordered his ship to retreat. The *Cochrane* tried to

---

6   A. Curtis, op.cit., pp. 63–64.

7   Chilean intelligence received information concerning the Peruvian purchase of a few Lay self-propelled torpedoes, and the arrival of mercenaries who were trained in operating them. Therefore, they correctly assumed, that these torpedoes could be delivered to Iquique in order to attack the Chilean squadron.

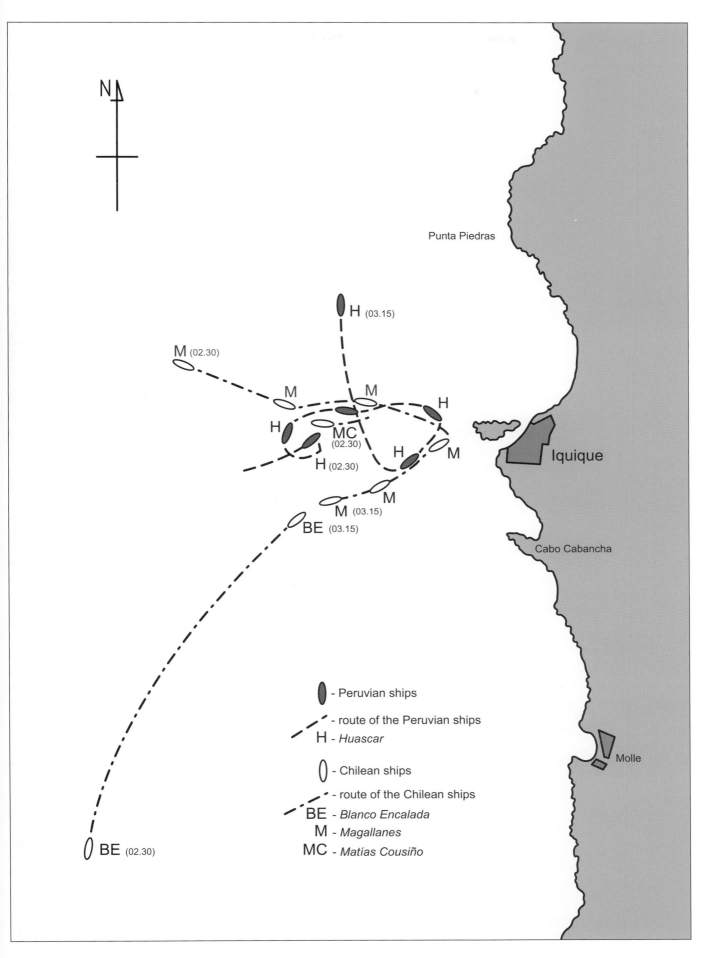

The second battle of Iquique

pursue the enemy, but after 30 miles gave up and turned back. The undisturbed *Huascar* set course to the north and arrived at Arica in the morning hours of July 10[8].

Thus, the second engagement off Iquique was inconclusive as both sides suffered no losses. During the battle the *Huascar* fired a total of six 254 mm shells, scoring no hits. The *Magallanes* fired only one round each from her 178 mm and 160 mm guns and seven 95 mm ones, scoring two hits on the Peruvian ironclad which caused no damage[9]. Following that engagement, the Chilean warships would no longer leave the Iquique roadstead for the night.

On the same day that the *Huascar* left Callao, the Peruvian gunboat *Pilcomayo* arrived off Tocopilla harbour after escorting the transport *Oroya*, carrying supplies for the Bolivian troops, from Arica to Pisagua. There, she destroyed 13 lighters and the barque *Matilda* flying the Nicaraguan flag (upon inspection of her papers, it turned out that she was a Chilean vessel)[10]. Soon, however, the ironclad *Blanco Encalada* and the corvette *Chacabuco* appeared on the horizon, steaming from Antofagasta and the *Pilcomayo* immediately headed north. The Chilean warships tried to chase her, but after a few hours gave up and on the next day returned to Antofagasta, where they spent the following week[11]. At that time Rear Adm. Williams decided to steam to Iquique and take command of the forces blockading the harbour, dispatching the *Almirante Cochrane* off Antofagasta (Iquique was then blockaded by the *Blanco Encalada*, the *Abtao*, the *Magallanes* and the *Limari*). On the very same day, suspecting the Peruvians of planning (or even already launching!) a torpedo attack against the Chilean warships anchored in the roadstead, Williams ordered the bombardment of the town without prior notice[12]. This lasted from 19.00 until 22.00 hours and caused relatively serious damage (one Bolivian soldier was killed, two Peruvian ones were wounded and in addition, three children were killed and 8 civilians were wounded). That rather unsettling and unprovoked action (the Peruvians had not been preparing any attack and took no action which could have caused such suspicions) resulted in strong protests from neutral consuls residing in Iquique[13].

The bombardment of Iquique infuriated Prado, who ordered Rear Adm. Grau to shell Antofagasta and destroy the water distillation plant located in the town. Consequently, the *Huascar* left Arica, accompanied by the corvette *Union*[14] and headed south. Due to the fact that Chilean warships were at Antofagasta, Grau decided not to bombard the town and headed farther south to attack the Chilean coast. Therefore, between July 18 and 22, the Peruvian ironclad appeared in succession off Chanaral, Carrizal, Bajo, Pan de Azucar, Huasco and Caldera, destroying lighters used for transporting goods to

8   *Boletin...*, op.cit., p. 718; A. Curtis, op.cit., vol. I; T. B. M. Mason, op.cit., pp. 36–37.

9   The Chileans, in fear of torpedo attacks, had loaded their guns with grape shot, much more effective against small steam torpedo launches than regular shells. Surprised by the *Huascar*, they had been unable to reload their guns, therefore the Peruvian ship was peppered with a hail of grape shot, which could not have inflicted any damage.

10 G. Blunes, op.cit., *De Antofagasta...*, pp. 341–342; Vicuña Mackenna B., op.cit., *...Tarapaca*, vol. II, p. 62.

11 *Voina mezhdu...*, part. 5, "Morskoi Sbornik" No. 10/1879, p. 15.

12 The Chilean commander communicated his reasons for the bombardment of Iquique in a note dated July 17, Ibidem, p. 18.

13 Reports of the defenders and foreigners staying at Iquique mentioned 30 to 40 shells being fired at the town by the Chilean warships (*Voina mezhdu...*, part. 5, "Morskoi Sbornik" No. 10/1879, p. 16). According to official reports the Chilean warships fired 42 shells at the town (Vicuña Mackenna B., op.cit., *...Tarapaca*, vol. II, p. 103).

14 The *Union* left Callao on July 13, loaded with arms and supplies for the troops at Arica, and delivered them two days later., *Voina mezhdu...*, part. 5, "Morskoi Sbornik" No. 10/1879, p. 15).

Capture of the Chilean transport Rimac *by the corvette* Union *and the ironclad* Huascar.

Lay torpedo.

ships. In the meantime she also captured three ships (two loaded with copper and one with coal), which were sent to Callao with prize crews. The raid ended at Copiapó, where the infantry troops stationed there, armed with a battery of field guns, put up a resistance, discouraging the Peruvian commander from a serious involvement with the harbour and town. Besides, Grau already had other plans, since he had learned from the captain of one of the neutral ships at Caldera about the departure north of two Chilean transports loaded with reinforcements and supplies for Antofagasta.

The transports *Rimac* and *Paquete de Maule* had indeed departed Valparaiso on July 20, carrying both troops, arms and supplies for the invasion army in Antofagasta. Despite the fact that the Chileans were perfectly aware of the *Huascar*'s presence in the naval war zone, they decided to dispatch the ships without escort[15]. Only an order was sent to Captain Simpson to take the ironclad *Almirante Cochrane* and immediately steam south to provide escort to the transports. Unfortunately, the Chilean ironclad could not have departed in the designated manner, since she had to recoal first and that took her a couple of hours. Meanwhile, the transports had not encountered the *Almirante Cochrane* at the rendezvous and therefore they decided to split up and proceed to Antofagasta separately. The *Paquete de Maule* hugged the coast, while the *Rimac* kept some 20 to 36 nautical miles out to sea. The commanders of

---

15 Both transports were to put to sea on July 18, but since Chilean intelligence was informed about the *Huascar*'s appearance in vicinity of Mejillones, their departure was postponed by two days. G. Blumes, op.cit., *De Antofagasta...*, p. 384.

The capture of the Rimac *by the* Huascar *and the* Union.

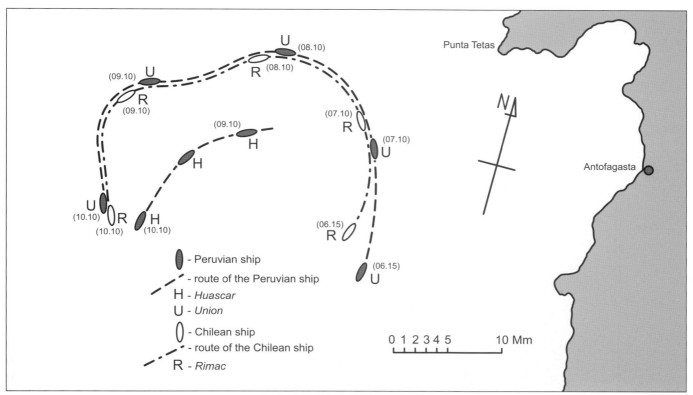

57

The Chilean corvette Abtao. *She was the target of the* Huascar's *attack on August 27/28, 1879.*

the Chilean vessels feared an encounter with the Peruvian warships, however, they thought such a possibility was slim. They had no idea that Grau had already known about their journey and had set a trap.

Meanwhile, the Peruvian commander, assuming that both transports were heading for Antofagasta, decided to wait for them in the vicinity of that harbour, slightly to the south of its location. The ironclad *Huascar* took position closer to the shore, while the corvette *Union* was farther out to the sea. In the morning of July 23, it was the latter who first spotted the *Rimac*, some 18 NM south-west of Antofagasta. The interception task turned out to be easier, since the Chilean vessel mistook the *Union* for the previously expected ironclad *Almirante Cochrane*. However, the Chileans quickly realised who they were dealing with (although they initially identified the *Union* as the *Pilcomayo*) and the *Rimac* fled (the pursuit began after

A 7-inch (178 mm) Armstrong gun aboard the corvette Abtao.

06.15), but the fast *Union* was gradually gaining on her. Catching up with the Chilean transport from her starboard side, the *Union* was slowly forcing her to turn to the port. After a four-hour chase the *Rimac* had already been steaming south. The Peruvian corvette managed to reduce the distance to a mere 600 metres. The last chance of escape was gone when the *Huascar*, arriving from the north-eastern direction, cut her off. Left with no other alternative, at 10.10, the *Rimac* struck her colours and surrendered to the Peruvian warships. She arrived at Arica on July 25, along with her captors[16].

The prize turned out to be extremely valuable! Aside from the fact that the *Rimac* itself was a fast steamer, useful for various military purposes, she carried 240 cavalrymen and 215 horses of the "Carabineros de Yungay" Regiment, a considerable amount of arms, ammunition and equipment, animal feed and 400 tons of good quality coal[17]. The capture of the *Rimac* had undoubtedly been Rear Adm. Grau's most spectacular success to date. What was also important, there were some valuable documents on board, which provided the Peruvians with information concerning the routes of the Chilean transports carrying weapons and war material purchased in Europe.

Problems with transportation of armaments purchased abroad were significant for both sides of the conflict. Due to the fact that the war had broken out quite unexpectedly, all of the belligerents were caught unprepared. Consequently, following the outbreak of hostilities, Peru, Bolivia and Chile began frantic purchases abroad to supplement their insufficient supplies of armament and equipment.

The Peruvians purchased most of their arms and war material in the United Stated and Europe[18]. They transported them aboard ships flying the American flag to Colon on the Caribbean coast and then by railroad coming thorough the Isthmus of Panama to Panama. They were collected from there by government steamers. Since both the isthmus and both aforementioned harbours were at that time within the borders of Columbia, whose government sympathized with Peru and Bolivia, these operations encountered no difficulties, despite Chilean protests[19]. By September 1879, the Peruvian transports had sailed at least five times on the route from Panama to Callao. The first, in late May, was the steamer *Talisman*. In early June, the *Chalaco* made a second journey and then the *Talisman* made another run at the end of the month. In July, the transport *Limeña* headed for Panama to bring back another batch of arms, ammunition and other war material, while the *Oroya* travelled on the same route in August (the latter, among other things, brought to Callao two small torpedo boats purchased in the United States). All these voyages went smoothly, since at that time the Chilean navy was unable to conduct operations so far north as to prevent them.

By contrast, the Chileans acquired most of the arms and supplies necessary for military operations in Europe. These were transported mostly by British or German ships sailing around Cape Horn.

One of the first vessels which brought a large amount of weapons and ammunition to Valparaiso following the outbreak of the war was the German steamer *Luxor*. During her second voyage, the ship called at Callao and was detained there. A prize court, however, finally decided there were no grounds to seize the ship and she was later released. A considerable amount of arms and supplies was delivered to Chile in June by the German steamer *Zena*. In the beginning of July, another one, the *Veloz*, arrived (carrying a couple of torpedo boats which had been built for Chile in Great Britain). In August, the arrival of two more ships transporting arms, ammunition and other war material, the *Glenelg* and the *Genovese*, was being expected at Valparaiso. The Peruvians learned about the voyage of the *Glenelg* from the documents they had taken aboard the captured steamer *Rimac*. In that situation, President Prado ordered the corvette *Union* to head for the area in the vicinity of Punta Arenas, which the aforementioned transport had to sail through, to intercept her[20]. The Peruvian warship left Arica on July 31, however, to avoid any encounters with enemy warships she did not hug the coast, but initially sailed west and after travelling for over a hundred miles, she turned south. The *Union* reached Punta Arenas on August 18. The Chilean

---

16 G. Blunes, op.cit., *De Antofagasta…*, pp. 392–395; *Boletin…*, op.cit., pp. 282, 313–315; A. Curits, op.cit., vol. I, p. 66, Vicuña Mackenna B., op.cit., *…Tarapaca*, vol. II, pp. 157–159.

17 Vicuña Mackenna B., op.cit., *…Tarapaca*, vol. II, p. 141.

18 The Bolivians used Peruvian help in transporting the purchased war material and armament. Alternatively, some smaller amounts were delivered via Argentina

19 Following the outbreak of the Chilean-Bolivian war the government in Bogota declared its neutrality. Simultaneously, on June 2, it declared free movement of goods through its territory to Peru. However, soon thereafter, there was a change of local government (Panama had enjoyed autonomy within Columbia since 1855), which backed out from earlier declarations, announcing prohibition on transportation of any war material for the belligerents (it affected mostly Peru and Bolivia; some said that the decision had been influenced by generous bribes handed over by the Chilean consul residing in Panama). However, the new restrictions were never implemented and transportation of arms and supplies for Peru and Bolivia could freely flow through the Isthmus of Panama., B. W. Farcau, op.cit., p. 79.

20 The *Glenelg* was carrying in her hold 16 modern Krupp guns, 4,000 Gras rifles and a considerable amount of ammunition (G. Blunes, op.cit., *De Antofagasta…*, p. 401), while the *Genovese* had on board 3 mitrailleuses, 3,000 rifles, 10 million rounds of rifle ammunition and a large number of uniforms (F. A. Machuca, op.cit., vol. I, p. 162).

A 9-inch (299 mm) gun of the coastal battery Bellavista at Antofagasta.

governor was unable to prevent the Peruvians from resupplying at local warehouses. He also informed them that the steamer *Glenelg*, which they expected, had already passed around Cape Horn and sailed on to Valparaiso (she arrived there on September 8). The commanding officer of the corvette, Captain Garcia y Garcia, had suspected that another ship carrying war material bought for the Chilean army in Europe was on the way, but without exact information he decided not to wait and soon set off for Arica, arriving there on September 14 (any potential search attempts for the ship carrying contraband was thwarted by bad weather). Six days later (on September 20) the *Union* arrived at Callao. Shortly afterwards, the latter of the aforementioned transports, the *Genovese*, passed Punta Arenas. However, at that time the Chilean high command had already had information concerning the *Union*'s sortie and dispatched the corvette *O'Higgins* along with the armed transport *Amazonas* to escort the *Genovese*. They accompanied the transport to Valparaiso, where she arrived safely on September 17[21].

Rear Adm. Grau was perfectly aware of the fact that the operations he had been conducting so far, albeit successful, were at best able to postpone the invasion of Peruvian territory by Chilean troops. The only chance to decide the outcome of the war in favour of the anti-Chilean coalition would be to eliminate the Chilean naval superiority gained after the battle of Iquique. That required the destruction of at least one of the Chilean ironclads. At the end of August, Peruvian intelligence acquired information that the ironclad *Almirante Cochrane* had broken down and was incapable of moving on her own (the Peruvians thought that this was the reason why she had not been able to escort the *Rimac*), therefore she was towed to Caldera for repairs by the steamer *Itata*. When this report reached Arica, Grau did not hesitate and on August 1 left harbour, heading south to destroy the Chilean warship. Off Calder he found only the steamer *Lamar*, but did not attack her. Instead, he decided to look for the purportedly damaged *Cochrane* at Coquimbo. However, while at sea, the *Huascar* was caught in a fierce storm and forced to turn back. On August 6, she returned to Caldera with the intention to destroy the *Lamar*. Upon spotting the oncoming ironclad, the Chilean transport beached herself behind the mole in an area inaccessible to the Peruvian warship. Discouraged, Grau then steamed to Tantal and off the harbour he was spotted by the *Blanco Encalada* and *Itata* steaming north. Trying to avoid an engagement with the ironclad, Grau immediately ordered his ship to turn back north and following a short chase he disengaged from the enemy. On the way back, the Peruvian ironclad called at Cobija, Tocapillo and Iquique (On August 3, the Chileans lifted the blockade of the harbour), to finally drop anchor back at Arica on August 10.

Undeterred by the failure of his latest sortie, Grau, in agreement with President Prado who still resided at Arica, decided to make one more attempt to destroy the Chilean ironclad. On this occasion he wanted to use the Lay torpedoes which were in Peruvian possession[22]. Assuming that the easiest way

---

21 *Voina mezhdu...*, part. 6, "Morskoi Sbornik" No. 11/1879, p. 6. Later two more ships carrying arms and supplies for the Chilean army arrived at Vaparaiso, sailing around Cape Horn. These were the *Maranhese*, *Hylton Castle* (November 1879), *Kielder Castle* (April 1880), *Bernard Castle* (August 1880) and *Almvick Castle* (February 1881), A. Curtis, op.cit., vol. I, pp. 67–68; F. A. Machuca, op.cit., vol. I, pp. 161–162; R. Gonzales Amaral, op.cit., p. 18.

22 At least three Lay torpedoes and a trained operator were delivered to Peru in the end of June aboard the transport *Talisman*. On July 6, they were delivered to Iquique aboard the transport *Chalaco*. The Lay torpedoes were relatively large devices with a

Damaged mast of the corvette Abtao *after her engagement with the* Huascar *on August 28, 1879, at Antofagasta.*

to encounter one of the Chilean ironclads would be to head for Antofagasta, the *Huascar* put to sea again on August 26. On her way there, she called at Iquique and embarked two Lay torpedoes and their operator. The ironclad entered the Antofagasta roadstead during the night of August 27/28.

It is difficult to ascertain if Grau, making his decision to strike, had been aware that there were not any Chilean ironclads at Antofagasta at that time. Admittedly, the *Blanco Encalada* had been stationed there in the beginning of the month, but she put to sea along with the transport *Itata* upon receiving news of the reported presence of Peruvian warships off Paposo (it later turned out that this false alarm was triggered by the appearance of the Chilean steamer *Toro*) before the *Huascar*'s arrival. Anyway, on the night of August 27/28, the only ships present in the harbour were the corvette *Abtao*, the gunboat *Magallanes* and the transports *Limari* and *Paquete de Maule*.

Slipping into the harbour, Grau tried to maintain a low profile so as not to be detected by the Chileans. He succeeded and managed to approach to a distance of less than 200 metres from the *Abtao*. One of the torpedoes was then launched, but after travelling for a dozen metres or so, it turned 180 degrees and headed straight back at the ironclad! This unexpected situation was probably caused by the fact that the torpedo's steering cables became entangled with the ironclad's propeller. That caused it to change its direction and also prevented any adjustments that would correct that error. Lt. Fermin Diez Canseco saved the day, diving into the water and turning the incoming torpedo away from the ironclad (the torpedo was moving on the surface)[23]!

That unfortunate turn of events discouraged Rear Adm. Grau from using torpedo armament again, as he completely lost confidence in it (which should not be surprising). The *Huascar* returned to Iquique were she landed the second torpedo and on the next day, the Peruvian rear admiral returned off Antofagasta again to repeat his attack. However, at that time he wanted to engage in an artillery duel in broad daylight.

It could not have been a surprise attack. The approaching *Huascar* was spotted from Antofagasta as early as 11.00. Two and a quarter hours later she was fired upon, first by the corvette *Abtao* and then (at 13.09) by the gunboat *Magallanes*. Soon, the southern coastal battery also joined the fight (13.20)[24].

---

weight of over 1.2 tons and a diameter of 60 cm. They were powered by a reciprocating engine fuelled by compressed carbon dioxide gas. The operator controlled them by means of electrical signals sent through two cables. Their maximum speed was about 8 knots (it was not constant as it decreased with the depletion of the compressed gas) and the maximum theoretical range was about 2 km. F. A. Acuña, *Las Fuerzas Sutiles y la defensa de costa durante la Guerra del Pacifico*, Lima 2001, pp. 111–115, 123.

23 Ibidem, pp. 85–91; A. Curtis, op.cit., p. 69; T. B. M. Mason, op.cit., p. 39.

24 Antofagasta was defended by a total of three coastal batteries: the northern one (also known as Bellavista) armed with one 229 mm ML and one 178 mm ML gun and the central and southern ones (el Sur), each armed with one 178 mm ML gun. Additional protection was provided by a field battery of four 8 cm Krupp guns, but its involvement in that battle was limited.

The Chilean squadron at anchor.

Meanwhile, the *Huascar* closed the distance to the shore to slightly less than 3 km and from that distance she also opened fire at 13.50.

Initially, her main target was the corvette *Abtao*. At that time the Peruvian ironclad's gunners were more accurate than usual and after about an hour they scored their first hit on the Chilean corvette, which inflicted serious damage to her engine. At about 14.30, they scored a second hit, which also caused severe damage. The *Abtao* was basically put out of action with 18 killed and at least 12 wounded. Then, after 15.00, the *Huascar* changed her position (which resulted in a 40-minute interlude in the engagement) and then reopened fire, concentrating it on the Chilean coastal batteries (mostly the Bellavista battery), silencing them by 16.30 (the 229 mm gun had already been damaged after its first discharge, the recoil force damaged its carriage and prevented it from taking further part in the battle) and finally also fired at the water distillation plant damaging one of its units (the *Limari* also received a random, harmless hit on the stern)[25]. Firing her final round at 16.51, the Peruvian ironclad sailed away at about 17.00. During the entire engagement the *Huascar* fired a total of twenty-six 254 mm and two 120 mm rounds. The Chileans (both ships and coastal batteries) fired a total of 113 rounds (the *Abtao* – 44, the *Magallanes* – 23 and the coastal batteries – 39, additionally 7 rounds were fired by the field guns)[26]. The *Huascar* was hit only once, a 178 mm fired by the *Abtao* (or the central battery, which only fired a single shot during the entire engagement) hit the funnel, killing one crewman and wounding another one. The damage was not serious. The Chileans had several dozen killed and wounded including 30 aboard the *Abtao*[27].

Following the attack on Antofagasta, the *Huascar* also visited the harbours of Taltal, Tocopilla and Mejillones, destroying boats and lighters. She made a short call at Iquique on August 30 and on the next day returned to Arica. On the same day the ironclad put to sea again to escort the transport *Chalaco* to Iquique, where both ships arrived on September 2. She put to sea the next day heading back to Arica, where she arrived after two days steaming.

25 The water distillation plant at Antofagasta had an output of 128,000 litres of fresh water per day, which was a sufficient amount to cover the needs of the town's residents. However, it was not enough to fully satisfy the needs of the troops stationed there., B. Vicuña Mackenna, op.cit., ...*Tarapaca*, vol. II, p. 25.

26 *Boletin...*, op.cit., pp. 329–335; F. A. Machuca, op.cit., vol. I, p. 156.

27 A. Curtis, op.cit., vol. I, pp. 69–70; *Voina mezhdu...*, part. 6, "Morskoi Sbornik" No. 11/1879, pp. 6–7; Ibidem, part. 7, "Morskoi Sbornik" No. 12/1879, pp. 10–14.

7. Battle of Angamos

The Peruvian capture of the transport *Rimac* caused serious uproar in Chile. Protesters took to the streets demanding decisive action concerning naval operations and the launch of an invasion against Peruvian territory. Their anger was mainly focused on the government of Antonio Varas (there was even an incident in which a mob threw stones at the Minister of War and the Navy, Gen. Urrutia, while he was entering the entrance to the Senate building), which finally resigned at the beginning of August. The new government was formed under Domingo Santa Maria, the Minister of Internal Affairs[1]. Rafael Sotomayor was appointed the new Minster of War and the Navy. In that situation, it was impossible for Williams to remain in command of the navy.

Aware of the widespread sentiment, Rear Adm. Williams lifted the blockade of Iquique on August 3 and headed to Valparaiso, leaving the main naval force to protect Antofagasta. In anticipation of his dismissal, on August 10 the Chilean admiral handed in his resignation, officially for health reasons. Naturally, Williams' resignation was accepted and he was replaced by Captain Galvarino Riveros, the former commanding officer of the ironclad *Blanco Encalada*. His former position was given to Commander Guillermo Pena. Also the commanding officer of the ironclad *Almirante Cochrane*, Captain Enrique Simpson was replaced by Commander Juan José Latorre (former commander of the gunboat *Magallanes*).

Captain Galvarino Riveros, the new Commander in Chief of the Chilean Navy, who replaced Rear Admiral Williams in August 1879. The victory at Angamos granted him promotion to rear admiral.

Both President Pinto, as well as the new head of state and the Minister of War and the Navy, expected the new commander of the navy to seize control of the sea and make it possible to redeploy the invasion army onto Peruvian territory. In that situation, Riveros concluded that his top priority was putting the ironclad *Huascar* out action. Since the *Huascar* had the advantage of speed over the Chilean warships, in mid August Riveros decided to send the ironclad *Almirante Cochrane*, which was in poor condition, for an overhaul at Valparaiso. Apart from minor repairs, arming the ship with mitrailleuses, installing modern searchlights and the necessary reboiling, Riveros especially ordered her bottom to be cleaned. Since there was no dry dock capable of accommodating the ironclad at Valparaiso, it had to be laboriously scraped by divers. Therefore, all these procedures took a long time and concluded at the beginning of the second half of September. Consequently, following the overhaul, the *Almirante Cochrane* was capable of making over 12 knots, almost as much as the *Huascar*. The *Blanco Encalada* underwent similar procedures at Mejillones, although they were not as complex. Additionally, the corvettes *Chacabuco* and *O'Higgins* were also reboilered and underwent the necessary repairs[2].

Consequently, the Chilean navy was rather passive throughout the whole of September, being focused on protection of Antofagasta and transportation of approximately 3,000 troops and provisions for those already stationed there in a convoy from Valparaiso to the former location. The said convoy comprised 8 transports (*Amazonas, Loa, Limari, Matias Cousiño, Huanay, Paquete de Maule, Santa Lucia* and *Tolten*), escorted by the *Almirante Cochrane* and *O'Higgins* (which had both just finished their overhaul). It left Valparaiso on September 21, arriving at its destination four days later. Then, the main forces of the Chilean navy were again concentrated at Antofagasta. On September 28, command over those was taken by Captain Riveros, who hoisted his flag on the ironclad *Blanco Encalada*.

On the same day, Chilean intelligence provided the information that the *Huascar* was at Arica, while the *Union* was at Callao. Upon receiving this, Riveros called for a council of war aboard his flagship. Apart from the commanders of the warships present at Antofagasta, it was also attended by the

---

1   Ironically, it was Santa Maria, who as a minister in the Vargas' government was responsible for sending the unescorted *Rimac* and the *Paquete de Maule* to Antofagasta.

2   A. Curtis, op.cit., vol. I, pp. 68–69.

Minister of War and the Navy, Rafael Sotomayor, who was with the army, and the representative of the President, Eusebio Lillo Robles[3]. At the meeting it was unanimously decided to take advantage of the *Huascar*'s stay at Arica and attack the harbour. However, since the Peruvians had already managed to fortify the harbour, it was decided that a surprise nocturnal attack with the use of steam launches armed with spar torpedoes would have a better chance of success. As a result of these arrangements, on October 2, the Chilean squadron, including the ironclads *Blanco Encalada* and *Almirante Cochrane*, the corvette *O'Higgins*, the gunboat *Covadonga* and the transports *Loa* and *Matias Cousiño*, departed the harbour of Antofagasta and steamed north towards Arica.

The information concerning the whereabouts of the Peruvian warships received by Riveros turned out to be already outdated. In the meantime, the *Union* had already joined the *Huascar* at Arica and in the evening of September 30, both ships put to sea again escorting the *Rimac*, which was carrying reinforcements and supplies to Pisagua. Upon completion of that assignment, Grau decided to steam farther south along with the corvette, as he still assumed that the *Cochrane* was incapacitated and therefore, he would be able to destroy her if he managed to find her to slightly equalize the balance of naval power. On the night of October 2, in darkness, the *Huascar* and the *Union* missed Riveros' squadron steaming towards Arica at distance of some 40 to 50 NM (neither side was aware of the presence of the other). In the morning of the next day, both ships sailed by the harbour of Mejillones and in the evening of October 4, they captured the Chilean barque *Coquimbo* (which was sent with a prize crew to Callao). After midnight, both ships arrived at Coquimbo. After inspecting the bay in the hope of encountering the Chilean warships, the *Huascar* left shortly before dawn and along with the *Union* headed for Los Vilos. In the morning of the following day, the Peruvian warships called at the Tongoy harbour roadstead. There, due to the worsening weather conditions, Rear Adm. Grau decided to turn back north. On the night of

There were also changes at other positions. Commander Juan Jose Lattore, who distinguished himself as the commander of the gunboat Magallanes, *was given the command of the ironclad* Almirante Cochrane. *During the battle of Angamos his contribution was instrumental in the defeat of the* Huascar.

October 7/8, at about 01.30, both Peruvian warships were again off Antofagasta. The *Union* was in the open sea off Punta Tetas, while the *Huascar* entered the harbour's roadstead, but since there were no targets worth engaging, she soon left. At about 03.00, the ironclad joined the corvette and both ships headed north[4].

---

3   There was a specific division visible between Lillo and Sotomayor – the former was mainly responsible for the navy, with the latter for army matters.

4   *La Guerra maritime…*, "Revue Maritime et Coloniale", part 1, vol. 65 (1880), p. 92; *Voina mezhdu…*, part. 6, "Morskoi Sbornik" No. 1/1880, p. 19 (Garcia y Garcia's report).

Riveros' flagship, the Chilean ironclad Blanco Encalada.

Meanwhile, on the night of October 3, the Chilean squadron arrived off Arica. While the steam launches, which were to launch the attack, were being unloaded, one was damaged. Consequently, Captain Riveros decided to postpone the entire operation by 24 hours. At 03.00 on October 4, the two steam launches were again launched, but the *Matias Cousiño*, which was towing them, dropped them too early. They had to cover too long a distance on their own and arrived off Arica at dawn. In that situation, an attack was out of question, but the Chileans had the chance to notice that the *Huascar* was not in the harbour. Riveros captured several local fishermen, who informed him that both the *Huascar* and the *Union* had left Arica some time ago and headed south. The Chilean commander immediately realised what kind of an opportunity he had. Since both Peruvian warships departed Arica quite a long time ago heading south, they should be coming back shortly. Meanwhile, the Chilean squadron was cutting them off from their base. The only thing that had to be done was to set a trap, await the inevitable return of the *Huascar* and the *Union*, and then intercept and destroy them in battle[5].

In order to achieve that goal, it was decide to split the forces. Riveros with the division of slower warships (*Blanco Enclada*, *Covadonga* and *Matias Cousiño*) would patrol the waters closer inshore, while Latorre, in command of the faster division (*Almirante Cochrane*, *O'Higgins* and *Loa*) would take position some 30 to 40 NM out to sea, simultaneously steaming slightly farther to the north in relation to the first division. It was assumed that the Peruvian warships steaming north would have to run into one of them and even if they manage to run away from Riveros' ships, they would be caught by Lattore's division[6].

The Chileans decided to set a trap for Grau's ships in the waters between Mejillones and Antofagasta. Therefore, the Chilean squadron immediately headed south, arriving at Mejillones before noon of October 7. There, the ships recoaled and Riveros received a dispatch which informed him that the *Huascar* and the *Union* had been spotted off Tongoy and at that time both ships were steaming north. That meant they could be expected to arrive at any moment[7]. In this case, at about 22.00 on the same day, Riveros' division put to sea, followed

Rear Admiral Miguel Grau.

---

5   Shortly before the departure of the Chilean squadron off Arica on October 5, at about 09.30, the gunboat *Pilcomayo*, which had been staying in the harbour, put to sea to reconnoitre. Twenty minutes later, the Chilean corvette *O'Higgins* and the gunboat *Covadonga* headed for the Peruvian warships. The former engaged her at about 10.30. The battle took place at a distance of approximately 6 NM from Arica and lasted for an hour. The *O'Higgins* fired a total of 16 rounds, while the *Pilcomayo* fired 21. Neither sides scored any hits (the battle was fought at a long distance). After 11.30, the *Pilcomayo* turned back to Arica, while the Chilean warships followed Riveros' main force (B. Vicuña Mackenna, op.cit., ...*Tarapaca*, vol. II, pp. 256, 262–264).

6   G. Riveros, *Angamos*, Santiago 1882, p. 10, A. Curtis, op.cit., vol. I, p. 71.

7   G. Riveros, *Angamos*, op.cit., pp. 21, 28–29.

The Chilean corvette O'Higgins. She accompanied the ironclad Almirante Cochrane during the battle of Angamos. She unsuccessfully chased after the Peruvian corvette Union, *and therefore, she did not take part in the battle.*

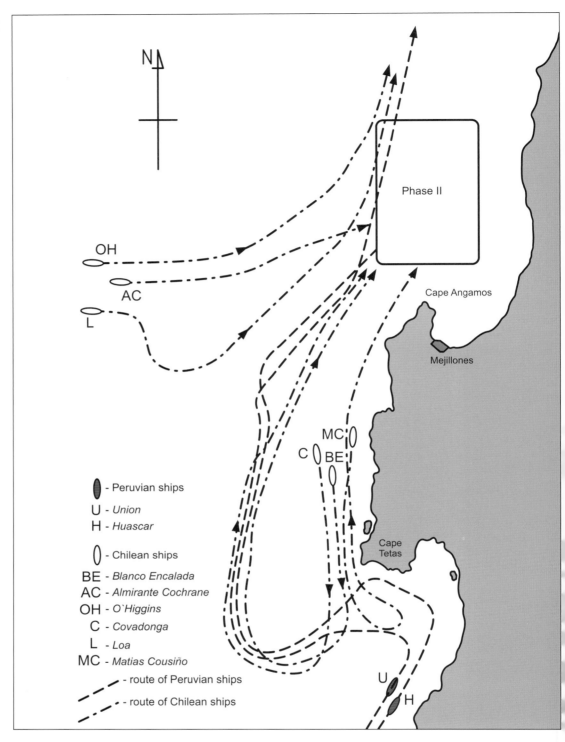

by Lattore's three hours later. However, in the meantime, the Chilean plans were slightly modified under the influence of orders given by Minister Sotomayor. The ships under Riveros' command were to head farther south and patrol the waters off Punta Tetas in the vicinity of the coast, while Lattore's division was to steam about 20 NM out from the shore in the vicinity of Mejillones[8].

Shortly before 03.30, in the moonlight, the lookouts aboard the *Blanco Enclada* (Captain G. Riveros, Commander G. Pena) and the *Covadonga* (Lt. Cdr. M. J. Orella) almost simultaneously spotted the smoke of two unidentified vessels in the distance. The Chileans were still not certain if these were the Peruvian warships they were looking for, but everything pointed to the fact that this was the case. And that was true, they were the *Huascar* (Rear Adm. M. Grau, Commander M. M. Carvajal and Lt. Cdr. E. Aguirre) and the *Union* (Captain A. Garcia y Garcia), which met up just after the ironclad's "visit" to the Anotfagasta roadstead. The Peruvians spotted the Chilean warships almost at the same time, but they were also unsure as to who they were dealing with. Rear Adm. Grau had believed that even if these

8   Ibidem, p. 24.

Battle of Angamos – the initial phase of the engagement, when the Huascar *was only engaged by the ironclad* Almirante Cochrane.

were the Chileans, he would be able to run away from them to Arica, taking advantage of his ships' superior speed.

The situation resolved itself by sunrise. Both sides were able to see who they were dealing with, as the ships could be easily identified. Therefore, both Grau and Riveros were certain who their opponents were. The Peruvian admiral did not seem to be concerned with the encounter. He ordered to alter course to south-west and to increase speed to 10¾ knots, which, as he had thought, should suffice to disengage from the enemy. Indeed the distance to Riveros' warships was gradually increasing (they were steaming at no more than 8 knots). In that situation, the Peruvian commander concluded that he was far enough away to pass them on the western side, so at 05.40 he ordered his ships to set their previous northern course and even slightly reduced speed in order not to overload the engines. An hour and a half later, at 07.15, the Peruvian lookouts spotted other warships coming from the north-western direction. After a quarter of an hour, the Peruvians identified one of them as the ironclad *Almirante Cochrane* (Lt. Cdr. J. J. Latorre). Grau immediately realised the gravity of the situation – he had just found himself between two enemy divisions, one of which was cutting off his escape route north. The Peruvian commander decided that the only option to save his ships was to escape, he had not lost hope as he still believed in his superior speed. However, he came to the conclusion that an artillery duel with the Chilean ironclad was a possibility, therefore, he immediately ordered the commanding officer of the *Union* to leave the ironclad and push through to Arica on his own. It should not, however, be considered as some sort

Later phase of the battle of Angamos – the Huascar *is desperately fighting, encircled by both Chilean ironclads.*

Battle of Angamos – Phase II.

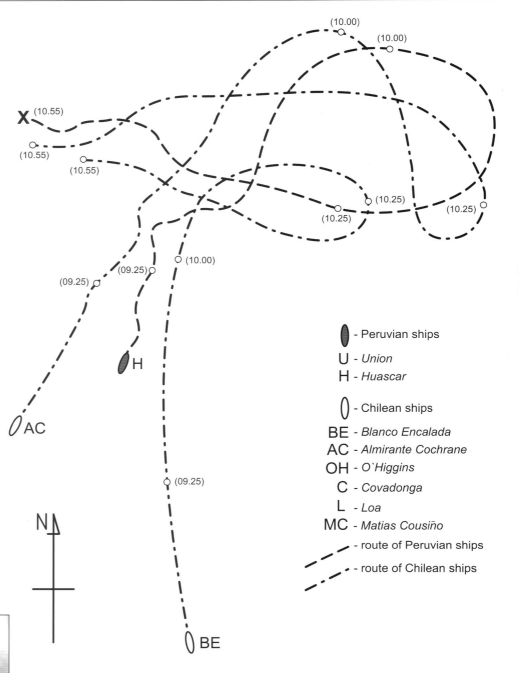

Commander Manuel Melitón Carvajal, Rear Admiral Grau's Chief of Staff. Wounded during the battle of Angamos he was taken prisoner along with the ship.

of desperate decision in which Grau would sacrifice the ironclad to at least save the corvette. The Peruvian admiral had simply concluded that was the optimal solution. Staying with the *Huascar*, the *Union* would not have been able to help her in any way, simultaneously being exposed to damage or destruction. Therefore, an attempt to escape on her own provided her with a better chance of success[9].

Captain Garcia y Garcia, the corvette's commanding officer, ordered the ship to increase speed to 13 knots and after 07.45, he overtook the ironclad and crossing the bows of the Chilean warships approaching from the west, he almost effortlessly opened his route of escape north. The *Union* was almost immediately being chased by the corvette *O'Higgins* (Lt. Cdr. J. Montt) and the armed transport *Loa* (Lt. F. J. Molina), but the Peruvians managed to maintain a safe distance. After some time, the *Loa* managed to close to a firing distance from the escaping corvette (she fired a total of 5 rounds at her), but she was never a serious threat. Since the *O'Higgins* was a couple of miles behind, Garcia ya Garcia at one time considered the possibility of turning back and destroying the poorly-armed transport in a surprise attack. Following a council of war with his officers, he abandoned the idea since his priority was to keep his ship intact and such an action

9   *Boletin…*, op.cit., p.369; A. Curtis, op.cit., vol. I, pp. 72–73; T. B. M. Mason, op.cit., p. 41.

68

Final moments of the battle of Angamos.

The place of Rear Admiral Grau's death – the Huascar's conning tower smashed by a well-aimed Chilean short.

Lieutenant-Commander Elias Aguirre Romero, second in command of the Huascar. *He died in the battle.*

would have been too risky. Consequently, the chase lasted until nightfall and only when the ships were off the mouth of the River Loa, the Chileans turned south accepting their failure. The undisturbed *Union* called at Arica on the next day and then, on October 12, she arrived at Callao[10].

The moment the *Huascar* and the *Union* split, the Chilean ironclad *Almirante Cochrane* was about 4 NM WNW from the *Huascar*, while the *Blanco Encalada* was about 6 NM to the south of her. If Lattore's ship had not had her bottom cleaned and could have only achieved a similar speed to that of the *Blanco Encalada*, the Peruvian ironclad would probably have managed to get out of the trap, risking only a long distance duel. However, the *Almirante Cochrane* was then capable of making 12 knots, roughly as much as the *Huascar* and therefore she was quickly closing the distance, so that at 09.01 it was only 2 NM. About 10 minutes later, when the distance between the ships dropped to 1.5 NM (2.7 km), the *Huascar* was the first to open fire, beginning the battle[11].

Already the second shot fired by the Peruvians skipped off the surface of the ocean and hit the stern of the Chilean ironclad, causing minor damage as it failed to explode. The *Almirante Cochrane* only replied 5 minutes later, when the distance between both ships dropped to one mile (1.8 km). The Chileans were also accurate, hitting the *Huascar* twice with the first salvo. The first shot hit the forecastle and the second struck the port side, slightly above the waterline, in front of the turret, exploding inside the hull and killing or wounding 12 crewmen. A moment later, the Peruvians managed to hit the Chilean ironclad for the second time. A shot fired from a distance of 550 m struck the 6-inch armour of the central battery at a 30 degrees angle and disintegrated without causing any significant damage. It was probably at that moment when Grau concluded that he would not succeed in an artillery duel, so he decided to resolve the battle by ramming the Chilean warship. Therefore, at 09.40, the *Huascar* turned to port trying to get close to the enemy, but the *Cochrane* performed an evasive manoeuvre and continued on a course parallel to the Peruvian ship. Shortly thereafter, at about 09.45, a heavy Chilean shot struck the conning tower of the *Huascar* and easily pierced its 3-inch thick armour, exploding inside and literally blowing all those present inside, including Rear Adm. Grau, into pieces[12]. Simultaneously, the force of the explosion damaged the steering wheel in the compartment below, so the ironclad turned to port. However, the damage was quickly repaired and the ship was back on her previous course, but in the meantime he had received a few more hits. One of the shots penetrated the turret, piercing the armour and exploding inside, killing or wounding its entire crew (Commander Carvajal, Rear Adm. Grau's Chief of Staff, was seriously wounded then), which put the *Huascar*'s main battery temporarily out of action. The guns remained intact and were soon manned by a new crew. However, these were ordinary seamen, therefore it was not surprising that the accuracy of the Peruvian ironclad's fire dropped from then on. Anyway, soon the starboard 254 mm gun was damaged and the *Huascar*'s firepower was reduced by half.

At that moment, the outcome of the battle was practically decided, but the heavily damaged Peruvian ironclad kept on fighting. Trying to finally decide the battle, Lattore made an attempt to ram the enemy ship, but the *Huascar* managed to avoid the attack with the *Almirante Cochrane* passing a mere 5 metres behind her stern, firing a broadside in her direction. One of the shots damaged the steering gear of the monitor and one from the next salvo exploded in the nearby engine room, showering it with debris (however, the engine remained operational). Despite all of this, the *Huascar* continued the fight, so Latorre made a second attempt to ram, which again failed. Then the *Blanco Encalada* arrived at the scene of the battle.

Riveros' flagship crossed the *Huascar*'s path, almost two miles in front of her bow and then turned to starboard, heading east. A few minutes later, steaming on a reverse course to the Peruvian ship, she opened fire at her at about 10.10. To avoid collision, the *Almirante Cochrane* had to turn to port (her

10 *Boletin...*, op.cit., p. 422; *Voina mezhdu...*, part. 6, "Morskoi Sbornik" No. 1/1880, pp. 20–23 (Garcia y Garcia's report).

11 There are significant discrepancies in the reports of individual Chilean commanders as to the time and place of different events. e.g. Lattore states that the *Huascar* opened fire at 09.20, while according to Riveros the time was 09.15. Riveros claims that the *Blanco Encalada* joined the battle at 10.10, while according to Lattore the time was about 10.25 and Molina states that it was at 10.15 (G. Riveros, op.cit. pp. 48–49; A. Curtis, op.cit., vol. I, p. 73). The differences may have arisen from a silent rivalry between Latorre and Riveros as to which one of them contributed more to the capture of the Peruvian ironclad. The author decided to accept the accounts which, according to him, were the most probable.

12 The Peruvian admiral did not stay inside the conning tower during the battle, but directed his ship with his head and shoulders showing above the hatch atop it. The explosion of the Chilean projectile must have ripped his body apart, throwing it into the sea. Only a piece of his foot was found after the battle., T. B. M. Mason, op.cit., p. 43.

Arrival of the heavily damaged Huascar, *captured at Angamos, to Valparaiso.*

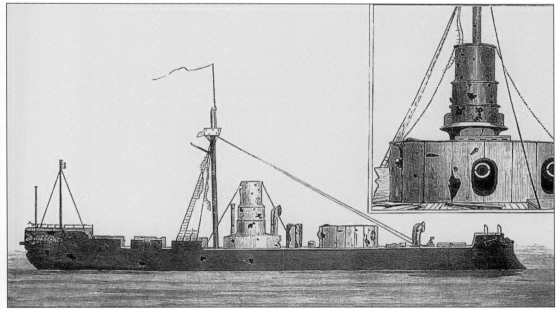

Damage sustained by the Huascar *at the battle of Angamos.*

stern was then struck by enemy shot for the third time), momentarily disengaging from the *Huascar*, but then the *Blanco Encalada* commenced firing at the Peruvian ironclad. At about 10.25 there was a short ceasefire, as one of the rounds shot the *Huascar*'s ensign away, and the Chileans presumed she had struck her colours. Lt. Enrique Palacios immediately hoisted another one (for which he paid with his life) and the *Blanco Encalada* resumed firing at the Peruvian warship. Then a heavy shot once again pierced the armour of the Huascar's turret, killing or wounding its entire crew, including Lt. Cdr. E. Aguirre, who was directing the ship from there. The port side 254 mm gun was still operational and after being manned fired two or three more shots at the *Blanco Encalada*, but the *Huascar* had already become virtually helpless and being surrounded by the Chilean ironclads, she was doomed.

At that time, the situation aboard the Peruvian ironclad was tragic. At least a quarter of her crew had already been either killed or wounded, the rest was in shock caused by the tragedy they witnessed unfolding around them and demoralized by the death of their commanders. The steering gear was damaged and steam was escaping from fractured pipes (also the pressure in one of the boilers dropped). There was no chance of escape (in the meantime, the gunboat *Covadonga* had also arrived at the scene and joined in the firing), therefore, Lt. Pedro Garezon (the seventh officer on the seniority list!) who was

Huascar's turret after the battle (damage sustained during the battle is clearly visible).

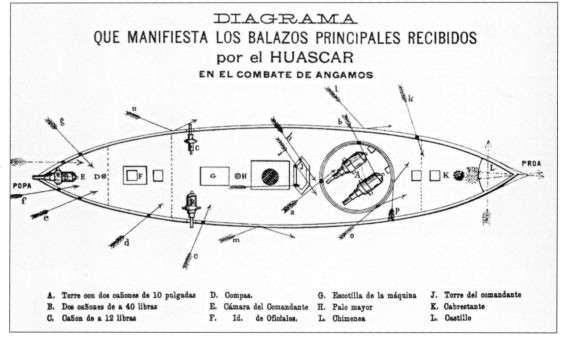

Diagram showing the damage sustained by the ironclad Huascar *during the battle of Angamos.*

in command of the *Huascar* at that time, following a brief council of war, decided to scuttle the ship by opening the Kingston valves[13].

At about 10.55, the *Huascar* stopped its engines and the crew began to abandon the ship. However, the scuttling of the Peruvian vessel was prevented at the last moment by a Chilean boarding crew dispatched from the *Blanco Encalada* (the first Chilean sailors boarded the *Huascar* at about 11.10). Their commander threatened the chief engineer of the *Huascar*, with a revolver pressed against his temple, to close the valves. Despite a considerable amount of water which had entered the ironclad's hull, she remained afloat and with the help of calm seas and still operational pumps, could be taken to Mejillones.

---

13 Contrary to an often presented account, the *Huascar* neither struck her colours, nor surrendered at the end of the battle.

Two days after the battle, with the most serious damage being temporarily patched up, she was sent to Valparaiso for repairs, arriving there on October 20[14].

During the battle the *Almirante Cochrane* fired a total of forty-five 229 mm, twelve 95 mm and sixteen 76 mm rounds, while the *Blanco Encalada* expended thirty-one 229 mm, six 95 mm and the same number of 76 mm rounds. Both ships scored together twenty 229 mm hits (12 shots hit the *Huascar*'s hull, 9 of them pierced the armour, out of the 3 that hit the turret 2 penetrated the armour, 1 destroyed the conning tower and 4 only damaged the forecastle, bulwarks and superstructure without affecting the ship's structure)[15]. The *Huascar* fired a total of forty 254 mm rounds, scoring three hits on the *Almirante Cochrane*, which had 10 crewmen wounded (later one of them died of the wounds he had sustained). The Peruvians had 34 killed and 162 officers and sailors, including 26 wounded, were taken prisoner[16].

The battle of Punta Angamos finally gave the Chileans command of the sea. From then on they could easily supply their troops by sea and invade Peru at any area they chose, which would ensure their advantage. Simultaneously, the Peruvians lost the possibility of seizing the strategic initiative and systematically supplying their troops at Iquique, Pisagua and Arica by sea. It was decisive for the further conduct of military operations.

Admiral Grau's statue at Callao (in a park of his name).

---

14 *Boletin...*, op.cit., pp. 369–376, 443–444. After a complete overhaul, during which the damaged armour plates were replaced, the shell holes were patched up, the engine room damage was temporarily repaired and a new foremast was erected, the *Huascar* was ready to be commissioned again on December 8, 1879., W. L. Clowes, op.cit., p. 104.

15 *Boletin...*, op.cit., pp. 403–404, 468–469; G. Riveros, op.cit., p. 78; *Voina mezhdu...*, part. 7, "Morskoi Sbornik" No. 2/1880, p. 12. An analysis of the damage sustained by the *Huascar* can also be found in: *The Capture of the "Huascar"*, *"Engineering"* 5.03.1880; *Madan, Incidents of the War between Chili and Peru, 1879–80.*, JRUSI vol. XXV (1881), p. 699; A. Curtis, op.cit., vol. I, pp. 76–76.

16 *Boletin...*, op.cit., pp. 370–372; A. Curtis, op.cit., vol. I, p. 75. T. B. M. Mason (op.cit., p. 46) states that the *Huascar* had 32 officers and sailors killed, while the number of wounded was 48, while according to F. A. Machuca, the Peruvian losses were 52 killed and 144 taken prisoner, including many wounded (op.cit., vol. I, p. 199)

8. Landing at Pisagua and the Chilean capture of the province of Tarapaca

Initially, President Prado assumed that the Peruvian navy would be able to seize control of the sea to at least such a degree that would allow them to recapture Antofagasta. After the battle of Iquique he realised that in view of the apparent Chilean naval superiority any offensive action was doomed from the beginning, therefore he decided to switch his strategy to defensive. This meant that he would have to provide protection to the entire coast exposed to Chilean invasion, at least over a distance from Iquique as far as Arica, or even farther to Ilo. To garrison the individual harbours, he had to divide his forces, which in the case of an invasion would give the Chileans an opportunity to achieve local superiority with ease.

By mid October the Chileans had already mustered over 18,000 troops, 10,000 of which were stationed at Antofagasta[1]. Since the very beginning, the Chilean high command considered various options for further action. President Pinto was a proponent of an immediate attack against the capital of Peru. That course of events called for landing troops in the vicinity of Callao, capture of that harbour and then an offensive against Lima. That plan would bring a chance of a swift conclusion to the war, however, it was also extremely risky. Therefore, the military officials suggested that it would be more advisable to attack one of the harbours in the Peruvian "saltpetre" provinces to acquire a suitable base for further operations. However, that could neither be Iquique, where the Peruvian main force was based, nor Arica, whose defences were considered too strong. An attack against one of the harbours in the province of Moquegue (Ilo was one of the options) was being considered. Its capture would have cut off the Peruvian-Bolivian forces concentrated at Tarapaca, Arica and Tacna from the centre of the country. The next move was to be a strike against Tacna, but then a problem of a political nature arose. The Chilean authorities counted on the Bolivians to pull out of the war, as the chances of their regaining

---

1   Apart from in Antofagasta, there were approximately 6,700 troops stationed in the area of Valparaiso and Santiago and less than 1,900 at the Araucanian borderlands., G. Blunes, op.cit., *De Antofagasta...*, pp. 343–345.

The Chilean transport anchored in the Antofagasta roadstead.

74

Antofagasta had already vanished and the country had not the motivation to continue any further military operations. The main forces of President Daza were stationed at Tacna and in the case of heavy fighting, the losses suffered by his army may have hindered peace negotiations with Bolivia. Therefore, it was finally decided to attack Pisaqua, a small harbour in the northern part of the province of Tarapaca.

As long as the *Huascar* was on the loose, the Chileans were not willing to dispatch their troop transports by sea. However, since maintaining such a large number of troops at Antofagasta, which had poor access to fresh water supplies (it was basically dependent on the output of the local distillation plant and deliveries by sea), had already by June come to pose serious problems for the Chileans, they even considered attacking the enemy by land. Iquique was to be the destination of the troops stationed in Antofagasta and the soldiers were to march for two weeks through the desert, along the coast, being supplied where possible by sea. On the optimistic assumption that a single soldier's 1.5 litre daily supply of water was sufficient, that option was theoretically viable. However, it soon turned out that each soldier would have to receive at least twice as much water rations and anyway, substantial losses on the march route should still be expected[2]. In that situation all ideas of invading the area by land turned out to be completely unrealistic.

At the beginning of October the desperation of the Chilean high command was reaching its peak. Consequently, it was considered to invade even if the *Huascar* was at large, posing a serious threat to the Chilean lines of communication. It was, among other things, the reason for the mid-July change at the post of the commander of the expeditionary army. The cautious Gen. Arteaga (who otherwise distinguished himself as a good organizer) was replaced by a man more bold and open to the government's suggestions, Gen. Erasmo Escala. However, the capture of the *Huascar* dispelled any Chilean doubts and on October 28, at Antofagasta, they finished embarking fewer than 10,000 troops (including a 640 strong naval battalion), 1,100 horses and mules and 32 guns aboard 15 transports (*Itata, Amazonas, Abtao*[3], *Lamar, Limari, Matias Cousiño, Santa Lucia*[4], *Tolten, Angamos, Copiapó, Huanay, Paquete de Maule, Toro* and *Elvira Alvarez*[5])[6]. The escort

General Erasmo Escala, commander of the Chilean army which captured Pisagua.

---

2   B. W. Farcau, op.cit., pp. 90–91.

3   After sustaining heavy damage in the engagement with the *Huascar* at Antofagasta on August 28, the corvette *Abtao* was not considered fit to serve as a warship and therefore it was decided to use her as a transport.

4   That ship had a water distillation plant installed on board. Its daily output was over 14,500 litres of fresh water.

5   A sailing vessel which carried mainly cavalry horses and beasts of burden. She was being towed by the transport *Copiapó*.

6   *Boletin…*, op.cit., p.408; A. Curtis, op.cit., vol. I, p. 81.

The harbour of Pisagua.

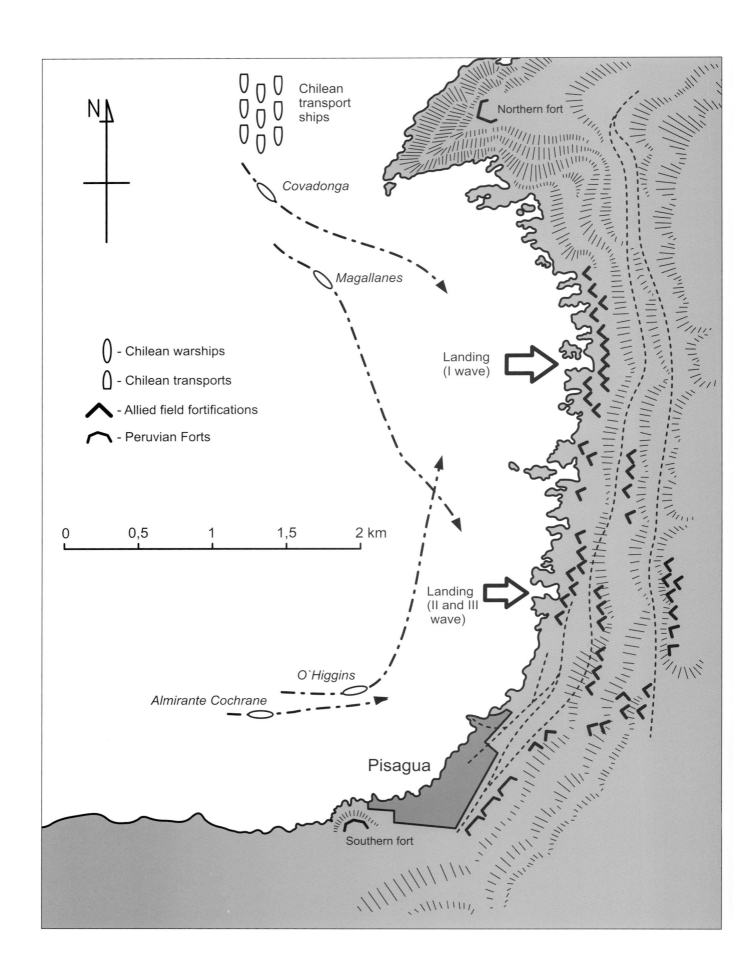

N

Chilean
transport
ships

Covadonga

Magallanes

○ - Chilean warships
◑ - Chilean transports
⌃ - Allied field fortifications
⌐ - Peruvian Forts

0   0,5   1   1,5   2 km

Northern fort

Landing
(I wave)

Landing
(II and III
wave)

O`Higgins

Almirante Cochrane

Pisagua

Southern fort

The Chilean landing at Pisagua.

Pisagua in 1879.

comprised the ironclad *Almirante Cochrane*, the corvette *O'Higgins* and the gunboats *Magallanes* and *Covadonga*. The escorting warships were under command of Captain Lattore (Rear Adm. Riveros was at that time in Valparaiso, where his flagship, the ironclad *Blanco Encalada*, was undergoing an overhaul). Gen. Escala, accompanied by the Minister of War and the Navy, Rafael Sotomayor, was in command of the land forces.

At the moment the Chilean convoy was leaving Antofagasta, the Allies had a slightly stronger force available to them in the southern Peruvian provinces. However, they were dispersed over a large area. The combined Allied forces in the province of Tarapaca were under command of the Peruvian Gen. Juan Buendia, whose headquarters were located at Iquique. The bulk of the Peruvian forces was also concentrated around that town. There were over 2,000 troops in the town itself and another 1,900 at Molle, located a half a day's march south. Additionally, there were over 2,000 troops and 50 cavalrymen stationed at La Noria, approximately 30 km inland, south-east of Iquique, with up to 200 infantrymen as a defence unit in the area of Monte Soledad. There were also over 4,500 Bolivian troops under Buendia's command. Four battalions (with a total of 2,000 troops) were garrisoned at Patillos, Pabelon de

Pisagua, a present day photograph (southern direction – towards the city).

Pica, Huanillos and Chichumata. Over a thousand were stationed in the vicinity of Agua Santa in the northern part of the province, while 900 were part of the Pisagua garrison[7]. Therefore, Buedina had a total of approximately 6,300 Peruvian and roughly 4,500 Bolivian troops at his disposal in Tarapaca[8]. However, it has to be kept in mind that the main Bolivian forces under command of President Daza were stationed relatively close, at the nearby Tacna. Their numbers were estimated at about 2,500–3,000 troops. At Arica, where President Prado's headquarters were located, there were at least an additional 2,000 Peruvian troops.

Making a decision to attack Pisagua, the Chileans were going to surprise its defenders. Part of the force (slightly over 2,100 troops under Col. Urriola) was to land at Junin, some 10 km south of Pisagua, and attack the rear of the town defenders' positions as soon as the landing commenced. However, it was assumed that the first wave would reach the shore at dawn, so that the embarkation itself would take place under cover of darkness, unseen by the enemy on land. As so often happens, in reality things did not go according to plan. Firstly, the convoy got lost and the time was not calculated correctly, therefore, the troop transports arrived at Pisagua too late and the planned element of surprise was gone. Consequently, the landing of the detached force at Junin was also delayed (it only began at 11.00, on November 2) and these troops arrived at the scene of the battle when it had already been concluded. Finally, the Chilean high command had made a sort of embarrassing mistake calculating the capacity of the landing boats at their disposal – it had not been taken into account (!) that roughly half of the available space would be taken by the rowers. Thus, only half of the planned 900 troops could be landed at once.

Pisagua was a relatively small town located in the southern part of an approximately 5 km long bay, which served as a comparatively good anchorage for all sorts of watercraft. The beach was partially sandy, which facilitated the landing, but almost at the very shore, steep cliffs several dozen metres tall rose up, which would have been a serious obstacle for the attackers. In the northern and southern parts of the bay, south-west of the town, there were two improvised forts armed with a single 163 mm Parrott gun each. The El Hospicio railroad station, located a few hundred metres north-east of the town, constituted a separate defensive position. The garrison of Pisagua had the two, aforementioned battalions of Bolivian infantry with a total of approximately 900 men and a local battalion of the Peruvian National Guard with a total of roughly 250 men. The number of Pisagua defenders, including the gun crews of the aforementioned coastal guns, was about 1,200 men. They were under command of the Peruvian Col. Isaac Racavárren, but quite accidentally, on the day of the Chilean landing, Gen. Buendia had arrived at Pisagua to inspect the troops, and therefore he took command over all the Allied forces the moment the battle commenced[9].

7   A. Curtis, op.cit., vol. I, pp. 78–80.

8   G. Blunes, op.cit., *De Antofagasta...*, p. 535.

9   Ibidem, pp. 78–80, C. R. Markham, op.cit., pp. 136–137.

Immediately after spotting the enemy (in the early morning of November 2), the defenders manned their positions – the Bolivians on the cliffs and at its foot, with the Peruvians at both forts, around the town and at El Hospicio station. At about 07.00, the Chilean warships steamed into the bay. The *Blanco Encalada* and the *O'Higgins* targetted the southern fort and the town, while the *Magallanes* and the *Covadonga* began shelling the northern fort. The Chilean ironclad quickly silenced the southern fort, putting its gun out of action. The defenders of the northern fort had been shelling the Chilean warships for over an hour before they too were forced to flee their positions. After silencing both forts the Chilean warships steamed slightly further into the bay and began firing at the Bolivian positions on the cliff face (the *Almirante Cochrane* was also bombarding the town). At about 09.30, the first wave of landing boats (about 450 men) headed towards the beach. They approached the northern part of the bay in the vicinity of the Blanca beach, some 2.5 to 3 km from the town. The landing Chileans troops met with heavy resistance and were pinned down by the fire of the Bolivian infantrymen positioned on the cliff face. Consequently, the next wave landed an hour later, slightly more to the south, where it could count on the artillery support provided by the ironclad *Cochrane* and where the resistance was somewhat weaker. Nevertheless, even there the Chilean troops met stiff resistance and only after the arrival of the third wave of the landing at about noon, were they gradually pushing the enemy from his positions.

Finally, Gen. Buendia ordered a retreat when, at 13.00, he received information about the landing of Chilean troops at Junin. Both the Peruvians and the Bolivians began falling back towards San Roberto. At about 14.00, the Chileans took the El Hospicio station and after 15.00, when the first soldiers of the detachment that had landed at Junin began to arrive, the battle was already over[10].

Lieutenant Isaac Recavarren, the commander of the Peruvian garrison at Pisagua.

It ended with a Chilean victory and the capture of Pisagua, which provided them with a foothold on Peruvian territory which could be used for further operations. That success cost them 72 killed and 170 wounded (including 8 killed and 19 wounded sailors), which could be considered a bargain price. The defenders' losses were comparable and they could be estimated at slightly over 200 killed and wound-

---

10 *Boletin...*, op.cit., pp. 424–430, 433–435, 452–453.

Southern fort at Pisagua (the photograph was taken after the town was taken by the Chileans).

The landing of the Chilean troops at Pisagua.

The Chilean warships (the Blanco Encalada and the O'Higgins can be seen in the foreground) bombarding the Peruvian positions during the landing at Pisagua.

ed, as well as 65 taken prisoner (mostly wounded)[11]. The naval artillery bombardment inflicted heavy damage to the town and at least several dozen civilians were killed.

The news of the fall of Pisagua reached Arica and Tacna on the very same day. Immediately upon receiving it the Bolivian President Daza travelled to Arica to consult the situation with Prado. It was

---

11 Ibidem, pp. 431–432; A. Curtis, op.cit., vol. I, p. 83, B. Vicuña Mackenna (op.cit., ...*Tarapaca*, vol. II, p. 526) states that 66 Chileans were killed and 169 were wounded, while G. Blunes (op.cit., *De Antofagasta*..., p. 559) and F. A. Machuca (op. cit., vol. I, p. 266) estimate the Chilean losses at 58 killed and 173 wounded (including 10 killed and 17 wounded sailors). The defenders suffered most from the fire of the Chilean warships, which had expended a total of 610 rounds of large and medium calibres. During the bombardment of the Peruvian and Bolivian positions, the *Cochrane* fired 58 heavy rounds and thirty-nine 95 mm ones, the *O'Higgins* – 180 rounds, the *Covadonga* – 110, the *Magallanes* – 55 and the transport *Loa* – 3 rounds (*Boletin*..., op.cit., pp. 430–431). B. Vicuña Mackenna (op.cit., ...*Tarapaca*, vol. II, p. 530) presents slightly different figures: the *Cochrane* – 128 rounds (including 58 heavy ones), the *O'Higgins* – 180, the *Magallanes* – 112 and the *Covadonga* – 180.

The Chilean landing at Pisagua.

decided that the Bolivian troops stationed around Tacna would head south as soon as possible to reinforce the Allied army in Tarapaca. On November 8, Daza commenced the redeployment of the available troops (approximately 2,400 soldiers[12]) by railroad to Arica. On November 11, the Bolivian troops reinforced by a few Peruvian units (mostly cavalry) headed south, reaching the town of Chaca on the next day and on November 14 they arrived at Camarones. However, a swift decision concerning the launch of the offensive, which had not provided enough time for its proper preparation, as well as the exhausting march through the desert caused the Bolivian troops arriving at Camarones to be in terrible condition. The Bolivians spent the next two days resting. Without the possibility of providing his troops with a sufficient amount of supplies and bearing in mind that any further march would be just as difficult, on November 16 President Daza ordered a retreat and on the 20th, he and his troops were back at Arica[13]. The failed attempt to relieve Gen. Buendia's army had a disastrous effect on the morale of the Bolivians and seriously undermined Daza's authority, which resulted in later political repercussions in Bolivia.

Meanwhile, Gen. Buendia, following his retreat from Pisagua, decided to gather all the forces he had at his disposal at Agua Santa (80 km south-east from Pisagua) to be able to launch an offensive. The order also concerned the main body of troops stationed around Iquique, therefore, after leaving a unit of over a thousand troops under command of Col. Rios in the town, the remaining troops were transported by railroad to Pozo Almonte, where on November 8 they joined other units gathered

---

12 Some of those were still not fully armed. Luckily, the arrival of the Bolivian troops at Arica coincided with that of the gunboat *Pilcomayo* with a cargo of 1,500 rifles and 6 guns, which solved the problem. (B. W. Farcau, op.cit., p. 99).

13 Barros Arana D., *Historia de la Guerra del Pacífico (1879–1880)*, vol. I, Santiago 1880, pp. 186–187.

Pisagua following the Chilean naval bombardment.

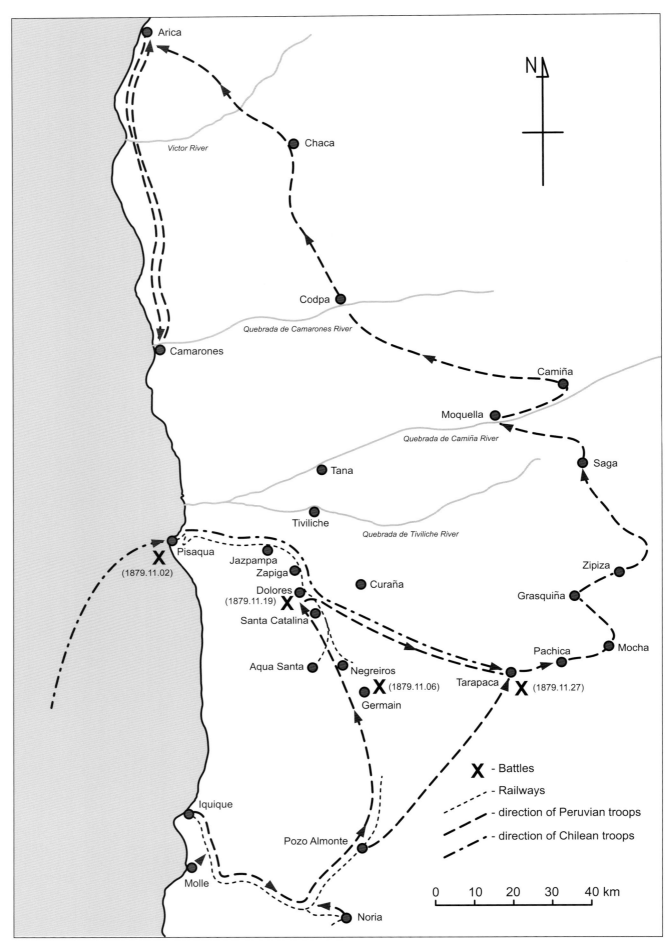

Arica

Victor River

Chaca

Codpa

Quebrada de Camarones River

Camiña

Camarones

Moquella

Quebrada de Camiña River

Saga

Tana

Tiviliche

Quebrada de Tiviliche River

Zipiza

Pisaqua
X
(1879.11.02)

Jazpampa

Zapiga

Curaña

Grasquiña

Dolores
(1879.11.19)
X

Mocha

Santa Catalina

Pachica

Aqua Santa

Negreiros

Tarapaca **X** (1879.11.27)

X (1879.11.06)

Germain

X - Battles

- Railways

- direction of Peruvian troops

- direction of Chilean troops

Iquique

Pozo Almonte

Molle

0   10   20   30   40 km

Noria

Tarapaca Campaign.

from other regions. Following a short rest, on November 18 they reached Agua Santa. At that moment Gen. Buendia theoretically had about 9,000 troops under his command (approximately 5,500 Peruvians and 3,500 Bolivians). However, in reality his forces were much weaker as numerous soldiers were sick and desertion was rampant, especially among the Bolivian troops.

The situation of the Allied army was even worse, as in the meantime, after landing at Pisagua, the Chileans troops started moving inland along the railroad. After defeating a Peruvian-Bolivian cavalry force[14] near the mining station of Germain on November 6, they arrived at Dolores (where there were wells which could provide them with a substantial supply of water). Thus, they crossed the shortest overland route (about 10 days march) between Iquique and Arica. There, they took strong defensive positions in the hills of San Francisco, located south of Dolores. These were manned by slightly more than 6,000 troops (over 3,500 remained at Pisagua and guarded lines of communication) awaiting the enemy. In that situation Gen. Buendia had no other choice but to try to seize the initiative and attack the enemy. The failed attempt to push him back towards Pisagua made on November 19 is known as the battle of San Francisco or the battle of Dolores. The Allies lost a total of 220 killed and 228 wounded, while the Chilean losses amounted to 61 killed and 178 wounded[15]. What was important was the fact that the defenders held their positions and Gen. Buendia had to retreat towards Tarapaca.

The lost battle of San Francisco was not a serious defeat as the Allied losses were not significant, however, its consequences were severe. Most of all, the morale of Buendia's army declined, which seriously affected their discipline. It was especially apparent among the Bolivian troops. The Bolivians had already accepted the loss of the *costa* (as they were never really attached to it) and ironically, they considered the ongoing war as a Peruvian matter (although Peru had gone to war to defend Bolivia!). The defeat at San Franciso resulted in the disintegration of the Bolivian troops, who fled back to their country, leaving the Peruvians to themselves. The situation of the latter was also far from being perfect, as there was a shortage of almost everything. Finally, on November 22, the Peruvian troops reached Tarapaca, where they stopped to rest and regroup.

The Allied defeat at San Francisco also caused Col. Rios' troops, which had been left at Iquique, to leave the town on November 20. They joined the main force at Tarapaca after six days of marching. Thus, the main harbour of the province remained defenceless and it was captured without fighting on November 23, by a small landing party from the ironclad *Almirante Cochrane*[16].

Meanwhile, in the north, the Chileans were initially not pursuing the enemy. Soon, however, their intelligence provided information concerning the Bolivian retreat and the deplorable state of the Peruvi-

---

14 The victory was won by a 180 man strong Chilean cavalry unit and the battle itself had serious repercussions, as the victorious Chileans committed mass killings of the wounded, taking only 4 prisoners (including one officer; the Allied losses were about 70 killed, while the Chileans had 3 killed and 6 wounded). The news of this event spread quickly which resulted in the escalation of atrocities.

15 A. Curtis, op.cit., vol. I, p. 90. According to B. Vicuña Mackenna (op.cit., ...*Tarapaca*, vol. II, pp. 659–660) the Chilean lost 60 killed and 148 wounded.

16 49 crewmen of the *Esmeralda*, who had been imprisoned at Iquique, were liberated then. Soon thereafter, the town was garrisoned by troops of the 7. Regiment, transported aboard the corvette *Abtao*, the gunboat *Covadonga* and the transport *Itata.*, *Boletin...*, op.cit., pp. 477, 592.

General Juan Buendia Noriega, the victorious Peruvian commander at the battle of Tarapaca.

an troops at Tarapaca. In that situation, a 2,500 strong force under command of Col. Arteaga was hastily formed. On November 26, it reached the settlement of Dubija and on the next day it attacked the Peruvian positions on the outskirts of Tarapaca. The Chileans clearly underestimated their opponents, whose forces were much stronger than they had expected (apart from about 3,600 troops in Tarapaca, there were an additional 1,200 soldiers at Pachica) and managed to repulse the attack and then launch a counter-attack, forcing Arteaga's troops to retreat. The battle of Tarapaca ended in a clear Peruvian victory. They managed to stop the enemy and inflict serious losses on his troops. The Chileans lost 518 killed, 189 wounded and 66 taken prisoner, while the Peruvians lost 238 killed and 294 wounded[17].

That victory did not improve the desperate situation of Buendia's Peruvian troops. Apparently, Peruvian morale was noticeably boosted, but deprived of ammunition and provisions, the soldiers were unable to continue. Therefore, the Peruvian general decided to retreat the long way, over the mountains, towards Arica. On November 28, his troops left Tarapaca and following an exhausting march through Pachica, Mocha, Grasquiña, Saga, Moquella, Camiña and Chaca, on December 18 he arrived at Arica with about 4,000 men. Thus, the Peruvians lost the province of Tarapaca.

The Bolivian attempt to retake the *costa* by means of an inland offensive launched from the Bolivian territory of Altiplano was a separate episode. This task was to be undertaken by Gen. Narcisso Campero, who commanded approximately 2,500 troops concentrated south of Oruro. In October Campero's troops began marching over the mountains, but extremely bad weather and difficult terrain conditions slowed them down considerably, therefore they only arrived at Salina de Garcia-Mendoza at the end of November. The difficulties encountered made Campero realise that he would not be able to launch the planned offensive, so he began to consider leading his troops to Tarapaca to join Buendia's army. However, at Garcia-Mendoza he received the news concerning the fall of Pisagua and the battle of San Francisco. Consequently, he decided that the march to Tarapaca was pointless and took his troops back to Oruro.

---

17 A. Curtis, op.cit, vol. I, pp. 100–101. According to G. Blunes (op.cit., *De Antofagasta…*, pp. 690–691), the Chileans lost 516 killed and 179 wounded, while the Peruvians had 236 killed and 261 wounded. The ratio of the Chilean killed to wounded is also meaningful. In revenge for the massacre at Germain, the Peruvians were finishing off the wounded and were reluctant to take prisoners.

The battle of Tarapaca.

9. *Capture* of the gunboat *Pilcomayo*

Following the capture of Pisagua, the Chilean fleet concentrated its efforts on securing its new prize and on providing enough reinforcements and supplies to the army assembled at Tarapaca. The Chileans became so preoccupied with this task that, for some time, the Peruvian side had enough freedom to send reinforcements, armaments and supplies to Arica, which consequently allowed Daza's troops to be rearmed before his unsuccessful expedition to help Buendia. In the middle of November the main forces were joined by Rear Admiral Riveros along with the ironclad *Blanco Encalada*. Riveros decided it was necessary to intensify actions against the Peruvian coast to hinder the flow of supplies to Arica and ordered preparations to attack that harbour, which had already become the next natural target of the Chilean offensive.

On November 17, in the early afternoon, the *Blanco Encalada* left Pisagua and headed north to penetrate the Peruvian coast as far as the harbour of Islay. She reached her destination at dawn of the following day but, because the port of Islay was empty, turned south sailing along the coast. Around 06.00 the Chilean ironclad passed Mollendo (where no Peruvian ships were spotted). About 50 minutes later lookouts aboard the ironclad spotted three ships moving from the south. The encounter took place in the vicinity of Pacui Bay. The ships turned out to be the Peruvian corvette *Union*, the gunboat *Pilcomayo* and the transport *Chalaco* which, after delivering supplies and reinforcements to Arica, had left the harbour at night.

After spotting the ironclad, the Peruvian ships bid a hasty retreat. Riveros, being aware of the speed advantage of the corvette and considering the transport *Chalaco* to be of lesser value than the *Pilcomayo*, decided to concentrate his efforts on the latter. Consequently, he did not notice the fact that the *Chalaco* broke away from the Peruvian convoy, followed, at about 11.00, by the *Union* that first turned back towards the shore and, after gaining some distance from the *Blanco Encalada*, headed north. The Chilean ironclad was slowly gaining on the Peruvian gunboat, the only target that remained in front of her. Around 14.15, when the distance between the ships was about 5 kilometres, the *Pilcomayo* opened fire on the ironclad. This time the Peruvians were very accurate and, despite the long range, managed to score two hits on the Chilean ship. However, the Peruvian rounds bounced off of the *Blanco Encalada*'s armour causing no damage. Riveros, paying no attention to the enemy fire, continued his chase. When,

The Peruvian gunboat Pilcomayo.

85

The entrance of the Peruvian gunboat Pilcomayo *into the harbour of Valparaiso, following her capture on November 18, 1879.*

at 15.00, the distance between the ships was 4.2 kilometres, the *Blanco Encalada* fired her guns. The first round hit the top of the gunboat's mast, the second one hit the water close to the ship's side, right in front of her bow. The explosion peppered the Peruvian ship with shrapnel.

The accuracy of Chilean fire had an immediate effect on the Peruvian crew. The commanding officer of the *Pilcomayo*, Commander Antonio de la Guerra, having consulted his officers, decided to destroy his ship in order to prevent unnecessary casualties during a futile retreat. Two lifeboats were launched immediately, manned by the crew who had set fire to the bow section of the gunboat.

Because the abandoned gunboat was still flying the Peruvian colours, the ship continued to be fired upon by the ironclad for almost an hour. The Chileans ceased fire at about 16.20, when they approached the immobilized gunboat and saw surrender signals made by the Peruvian seamen from the lifeboats. A boarding party was immediately dispatched to the Peruvian ship and began extinguishing the fire. However, this was only possible when the ironclad approached the side of the gunboat and used her powerful pumps to aid the fire-fighting efforts on the *Pilcomayo*, which succeeded after two hours. In the meantime, a large breach in the bow section just above the waterline was patched. Not until then were the 167 men (two of whom had been wounded during the engagement) of the Peruvian crew taken aboard the *Blanco Encalada*. The ironclad took the captured gunboat in tow and, on the same day, the ships reached Pisagua[1]. After the most essential repairs, the *Pilcomayo* was towed to Iquique on November 20, and then to Valparaiso where she underwent a general overhaul which made her fit to enter service in the Chilean navy.

1   *Boletin…*, op.cit., pp. 517–518; *Voina mezhdu…*, part. 10, "Morskoi Sbornik" No. 4/1880, pp. 17–19 (Riveros' report).

10. Change of leadership in Peru and Bolivia

Military defeats resulted in the escalation of discontent in Peru and Bolivia. Consequently, both Prado and Daza became concerned with the loyalty of high officials left at the rear, which affected their plans.

On November 28, quite unexpectedly, president Prado boarded a ship at Arica and headed back to Callao, leaving command of all forces in the province to Rear Admiral Lizardo Montero. According to official assurances, his goal was to organize reinforcements and to appease the mood in the capital. The Peruvian president reached his destination on December 2, and arrived at Lima on the following day. At that time, the atmosphere in the capital of Peru had already been tense. There were riots and protests in the streets. To bring back order, Prado dismissed his ministers and took action to form a new government. However, before this happened, on December 18 he left the country aboard a British steamer taking his personal luggage and a large sum in gold from the national treasury. He left his powers in the hands of Vice-President Luis de la Puerta. Officially, Prado claimed he was going to Europe to purchase armaments and ships in order to turn the tide of the war at sea. It is difficult to guess the real motives that drove the Peruvian president. Even if he acted in good faith (which seems quite probable), the political effect of Prado's departure was catastrophic and lowered the general mood of the country in a considerable way. In that situation an outbreak of hostilities was imminent. On December 21, a rebellion was initiated by Prado's political opponent Nicolas Pierola, who had gained the support of the Lima garrison. During heavy clashes, troops fighting for de la Puerta dislodged the rebel forces from Lima. Pierola pulled back to Callao where he had always had supporters. He was well received there and began preparations to take over the capital by force.

Vice President Luis de la Puerta, to whom President Prado handed over the authority before fleeing the country.

Consequently, Peru stood on the verge of civil war. The situation was even worse with the Chileans occupying the southern provinces! To avoid bloodshed and facing a Chilean threat, de la Puerta resigned for the sake of the country and, on December 23, Pierola arrived in Lima as the new president of Peru. Immediately thereafter, motivating his actions by the threat to the country, on December 27 he changed the constitution which dissolved the parliament and substituted it with a puppet State Council, thus granting him enormous power. He used this to immediately pronounce his predecessor a traitor and deprive him of his citizenship. The new president refrained from repressions against Prado's supporters and limited his actions to changes in leadership of the reserve army stationed at Arequipa, appointing Colonel Segundo Leiva, his trusted man, as its new commander. Pierola did not dismiss his old political opponent and Prado's associate, Rear Admiral Montero, who commanded the Peruvian forces in Arica and Tacna. He also took action to mobilize more troops and rearm the reserve army as well as the units commanded by Montero. As a result, the effects of the coup d'etat in Peru were not very harmful and the situation became relatively calm (although distrust between different political fractions remained[1]).

Military defeats also resulted in increased discontent in Bolivia. President Daza's reputation suffered after a failed attempt to come to the rescue of Buendia that ended with the disgraceful retreat from Ca-

---

1   For example, Montero and his commanders complained that their units received less supplies and weapons. On the other hand, due to the fact that Montero's army could only be supplied by sea in the face of Chilean naval superiority, delivering provisions in large quantities was not possible. Thus, the fact that Leiva's army received more armament and supplies was quite understandable.

Above: Nicolas Pierola, the new President of Peru.

Above, right: General Narciso Campero, who became the President of Bolivia after Daza's removal from power.

marones. As a result of those actions, Daza's officers began contemplating a coup against the president. On December 27, in Daza's absence at Tacna (the Bolivian president had left on a train to Arica to meet Montero), the rebels managed to execute a coup d'etat, arrest commanders supporting Daza and seize control over the army at Tacna. When Hilaron Daza learned about those events, he headed to Molendo and then to Arequipa with the intention to return to La Paz and organize counteractions. However, after his arrival, it turned out that a rebellion had also broken out at the capital and his opponents were in control of the entire country. The president gave up all hope and, shortly after returning to Mollendo, boarded the first British ship that entered the harbour, went to Panama and then emigrated to Europe.

In the meantime, on January 2, at La Paz, a group of local officials decided to give all power to General Campero, who was the only one in the country backed by a force of as many as 2,500 soldiers. Campero, who initially had few political ambitions, on January 19 officially took office at Oruro. He decided to keep all alliance agreements and continue the war at the Peruvian's side (Daza had probably been contemplating making a separate peace with the Chileans) taking actions to organize a new army. However, the general mood in Bolivia did not support continuation of the war. Bolivians had already reconciled themselves with the loss of the *costa* and further military actions were considered unnecessary. This was reflected in the morale of the mobilized troops as well as in society's willingness to support the war effort.

Riots in the streets of Lima. Pierola's supporters fighting against those of the previous government.

11. Landing operations at Pacocha Bay and the battle of Tacna

After the Chileans had captured the province of Tarapaca, they gained a foothold for further attacks to seize control over the provinces of Arica and Tacna. The Allied forces concentrated in the region comprised about 12–13,000 troops that formed the 1. Southern Army (about 2,000 Peruvians in Arica and 9–10,000 Peruvian and Bolivian soldiers in the area of Tacna) commanded by Rear Admiral Montero and the 2. Southern Army in the area of Arequipa under the command of Colonel Leyva with over 3,000 Peruvian troops. For the planned operation, the Chileans concentrated a total of over 14,000 men in Pisagua and Iquique (excluding 3,000 freshly mustered troops and soldiers tasked with maintaining order in the captured provinces)[1].

Because the Chilean command considered direct attack against Arica to be too hazardous, they made the decision to blockade the harbour and later deploy troops farther north to begin the offensive on Tacna. After the defeat of the Peruvian-Bolivian 1. Army, Arica was to be attacked from the land. On November 28, the Chilean fleet began the blockade of Arica with the corvette *Chacabuco* and the gunboats *Magallanes* and the *Covadonga*. Simultaneously, the corvette *O'Higgins* initiated patrol oper-

1   B. W. Farcau, op.cit., pp. 131–134; B. Vicuña Mackenna, *Guerra del Pacifico. Historia de la campaña de Tacna y Arica 1879–1880*, Santiago de Chile 1881, p. 173; B. Vicuña Mackenna, *Guerra del Pacifico. Historia de la campaña de Lima 1880–1881*, Santiago de Chile 1881, p. 10.

Chilean navy anchored in the Pisagua roadstead, awaiting the embarkation of troops.

The Chilean Minister of War and the Navy Rafael Sotomayor Baeza. He died of natural causes during the campaign, shortly before the battle of Tacna.

Battle in the hills of Los Angeles.

ations along the coast north of Arica up to Ilo. At the beginning of December, the ironclad *Almirante Cochrane* (that had completed an overhaul in Valparaiso) appeared at Arica to relieve the corvette *Chacabuco*, which began the blockade of Ilo. This allowed the *O'Higgins* to concentrate her efforts on the blockade of Mollendo[2], rendering all harbours in the area of future operations inoperable. This was crucial as, after the blockade of Arica, the Peruvians began transporting supplies and reinforcements for Montero's army through Ilo and farther on by land, on mules. These tasks were also assigned to the corvette *Union* which, using her speed advantage, was a much more difficult catch for the enemy than the transports used by the Peruvians. On one occasion, on December 17, she left Callao, two days later delivered large quantities of weapons, ammunition and supplies to Ilo and despite encountering the corvette *O'Higgins* near Mollendo on December 20, returned safely to Callao.

Simultaneously, a taskforce commanded by Rear Admiral Riveros comprising the ironclad *Blanco Encalada* and armed transports *Loa* and *Amazonas* was deployed to the north. Its task was to intercept armament and supply transports for Peruvian units being formed in the area of Lima, which were to arrive at Callao from Panama. To achieve this, the *Blanco Encalada* and the *Loa* began patrolling the region north of Callao. The *Amazonas* headed to Lobos de Afuerta and then to Tumbes. There they were informed by passengers of a passing British ship of the Peruvian torpedo boat *Alay* sailing under the Hawaiian flag. The torpedo boat was delivered on October 24 from the USA to Colon aboard the British ship *Ailsa* and then, in the next two days, transported by rail via the Isthmus of Panama to Panama. Then, on November 29, she sailed to Callao on her own[3]. According to information obtained by the Chileans she was near the coast of Ecuador. The commanding officer of the *Amazonas*, Commander Thomson, began search operations and, on December 23, encountered *Alay* in the Ecuadorian harbour of Ballenitas. The *Alay* was captured without a fight (the torpedo boat was temporarily immo-

2   At the end of December *O'Higgins* was relieved by the ironclad *Huascar* that, after an overhaul in Valparaiso concluded on December 8, entered service in the Chilean fleet and was deployed for actions in the north, B. Vicuña Mackenna, op.cit., … Tacna y Arica, p. 347.

3   F. A. Acuña, op.cit., pp. 177–179; F. A. Machuca, op.cit., vol. II, Valparaiso 1928, pp. 63, 72.

The Chilean-Peruvian skirmish at Locumba.

bilized due to a shortage of coal)[4]. The *Amazonas* took the captured ship in tow and joined the taskforce on December 24, at Paita.

The capture of the *Alay* turned out to be the only success of Riveros' taskforce in the north. The admiral did not manage to intercept the transport *Rimac*, carrying a cargo of supplies and weapons, and decided to turn back to Pisagua.

When the Chilean command learned about supplies and armament being delivered via Ilo to the Allied army concentrated at Tacna, they made the decision to attack the harbour. Moreover, Commander Oscar Viel of the corvette *Chacabuco* discovered that it had little to no protection. As a result, on December 29, an infantry battalion (about 550 men) boarded the transport *Copiapó* at Pisagua and, escorted by the corvette *O'Higgins*, seized the above-mentioned harbour on the next day without a fight. The surprise attack allowed the Chileans to also capture two fully operational steam locomotives with a set of wagons at the local train station. Colonel Aristides Martinez, commander of the landing operation, took advantage of the situation and decided to raid Moquegua and again surprised the Peruvians. The city was taken almost without a fight. The victorious Chileans discovered large supplies of alcohol which resulted in a total collapse in discipline leading to rape and pillaging. Not being able to keep order among his men, in face of an approaching Peruvian counter-attack, Martinez quickly embarked his soldiers back onto the railway wagons and, on January 1, returned to Ilo. On the next day, after destroying everything that could be of use to the Peruvian army, his unit boarded the *Copiapó* and headed to Pisagua[5].

The raid on Ilo was only a partial Chilean success, however, it proved that it was a good place to land the main army forces and initiate an offensive towards Tacna. Preparations for the operation were concluded in the middle of February. Between February 21 and 24, over 10,000 soldiers and 850 mules were loaded onto 14 transports (the corvette *Abtao*, the steamers *Amazonas*, *Loa*, *Itata*, *Copiapó*, *Limari*, *Lamar*, *Matias Cousiño*, *Santa Lucia*, *Angamos*, *Tolten*, the sailing ships *Giuseppe Muzzi*, *Elvira Alvarez* and *Umberto I*). On February 25, they arrived at the Pacocha Bay and landed near Ilo. The convoy was escorted by the ironclads *Blanco Encalada* and *Almirante Cochrane*[6].

The main problem for the Chileans during their preparation for the operation was lack of transports. They were forced to include 3 sailing ships in the convoy. They were towed by the steam transports. Soldiers were also carried

General Manuel Baquedano, the Chilean army commander at the battle of Tacna.

4   F. A. Acuña, op.cit., pp. 174–183; G. Blunes, *Guerra del Pacifico. De Tarapaca a Lima*, Valparaiso 1914, p. 103.

5   *Boletin...*, op.cit., pp. 540–542, 544–545; G. Blunes, op.cit., *De Tarapaca ...*, pp. 65–69.

6   *Boletin...*, op.cit., pp. 576–578; G. Blunes, op.cit., *De Tarapaca ...*, pp. 114–115; A. Curtis, op.cit., vol. II, p. 5; B. Vicuña Mackenna, op.cit., *...Tacna y Arica*, p. 322.

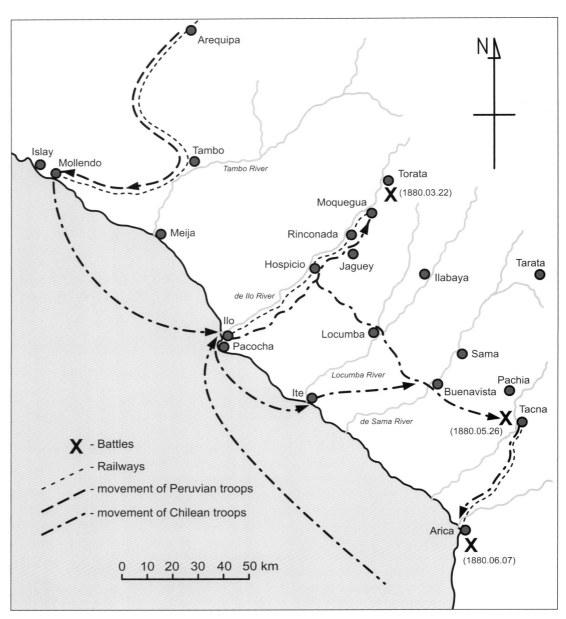

by both ironclads. There was no room for 4,000 troops who were left in Pisagua – they arrived at Ilo on March 8, aboard the transports *Amazonas*, *Loa*, *Itata* and *Matias Cousiño* that were sent back after the first landing operation had been concluded[7].

Due to the lack of transports, accumulating large quantities of supplies for the upcoming offensive had to take some time. In order not to waste time, the Chilean command decided to immediately send part of the 4. Division (about 2,000 men), that had landed as last, to capture the port of Mollendo. The force boarded the transports *Amazonas* and *Lamar*. Escorted by the ironclad *Blanco Encalada*, the troops arrived at their destination at night on March 8/9, and captured the city in the morning after a brief fight. One more time, insubordination of the soldiers ended with rape and pillaging. The Chilean officers somehow managed to restore order. When they learned about a Peruvian counter-attack coming from Arequipa, they decided not to engage in combat and evacuated Mollendo on March 11. The Chilean troops turned back to Ilo[8].

Meanwhile, Chilean intelligence informed their command that the Allies did not intend to attack them at Ilo (in fact the Allied forces were unable to do that). On March 10, 2,500 troops, commanded by General Manuel Baquedano, were sent to Moquegua. One thousand and four hundred Peruvians defending the city decided to pull back north to strong defensive positions at the hills of Los Angeles. On March 20, the Chileans took Moquegua without a fight. However, they did not stop there and, at night on March 21/22 they attacked the Peruvian positions, forcing the enemy to retreat to Torata and then towards Ilubaya. The clash at Los Angeles did not cause heavy casualties on either side. The Peruvians

---

7   A. Curtis, op.cit., vol. II, p. 6; B. Vicuña Mackenna, op.cit., ...*Tacna y Arica*, pp. 325, 400.

8   *Boletin...*, op.cit., pp. 602–603.

Admiral Lizardo Montero, the commander of the Peruvian forces at the battle of Tacna (the supreme command was in the hands of the Bolivian President Narciso Campero).

lost 100 men killed and 30 captured. The Chilean losses were smaller by half. The Chileans "cleared" their way for the offensive and, as a result, on April 8, their troops began gradually leaving Ilo and headed towards Moquegua along the railroad. Half way through, after arriving at Hospicio, they marched south-east towards the town of Locumba and then to Buenavista which was their concentration area. At that time, they had only one operational locomotive at their disposal (its main task was to transport supplies), soldiers marched on foot and the whole operation lasted quite a long time. To shorten the time of the troop concentration, 4. Division was transported by sea aboard the transports *Itata* and *Santa Lucia* to Ite at the mouth of the Locumba River where it landed on April 28, and, after a forced march, the troops reached Buenavista on May 3. The final concentration of the Chilean army in the area was concluded by May 11. The command of all forces was taken by General Baquedano, replacing General Escala who had been recalled to Santiago due to personal frictions. During the night of May 20/21, Rafael Sotomayor, Minister of War, died suddenly of natural causes which gave Baquedano full control over the entire Chilean army.

Meanwhile, on April 19, the new president of Bolivia, General Campero, arrived at Tacna with 1,500 reinforcements. He also took command of the combined Bolivian-Peruvian forces (Rear Admiral Montero was second in command)[9] and began preparations for a major engagement with the approaching Chilean army. On May 10, 10,500 Allied troops (including fewer than 5,000 Bolivians) with 17 cannons and 6 mitrailleuses, took up strong defensive positions west of Tacna. On May 26, they were attacked by the Chilean army with 13,400 men, 36 cannons and 4 mitrailleuses[10]. The battle began at about 09.00 and, although the fate

---

9   The change in command was consulted with President Pierola. Montero was one of Pierola's political opponents. After the change of leadership in Lima, he remained in command of the 1. Southern Army as Pierola feared that removing him from this position would cause confusion in the face of the approaching enemy. However, facing Montero's possible success, the possibility of taking command by Campero played into Pierola's hand.

10   A. Curtis, op.cit., vol. II, pp. 17–21; B. W. Farcau, op.cit., pp. 139–140. There is differing information concerning the strength of the armies fighting at Tacna. The Chilean sources have a natural tendency to overestimate the opposing forces (see.: G. Blunes, op.cit., *De Tarapaca ...*, pp. 308–309; B. Vicuña Mackenna, op.cit., *...Tacna y Arica*, pp. 1050–1054). However, taking into consideration that the Allied units were lacking in personnel, one should rather assume that the total number of men in Campero's army was between 10 and 11,000 (including 40–45% Bolivians).

Allied fortifications at Tacna.

of the battle was in the balance for a long time, finally, at 15.00, the Chileans managed to push the enemy from his positions. This success came at a high cost as the victors lost 470 men killed and about 1,450 wounded (a total of over 1,900). The Allies lost 3,500 men killed and wounded (half of whom were Bolivians) and 300 soldiers captured[11]. To make matters worse, after the battle, the remains of the Bolivian army commanded by Campero returned to their country, withdrawing from further operations (it was the Bolivians' last contribution to the war), the surviving Peruvian troops became partly scattered and, as a result, Montero was later not able to bring back more than a thousand soldiers to Arequipa.

---

11 *Boletin…*, op.cit., pp. 681–683; A. Curtis, op.cit., vol. II, pp. 24–25; B. W. Farcau, op.cit., p. 142; F. A. Machuca, op.cit., vol. II, pp. 241, 243; B. Vicuña Mackenna, op.cit., …*Tacna y Arica*, pp. 1084–1085. There is differing information concerning losses in the battle of Tacna, but according to most sources the Chileans lost from 1.8 to 2,200 men killed and wounded, the Allies 3,5–4,000.

Battle of Tacna.

12. The blockade and fall of Arica

The victory at Tacna practically sealed the fate of Arica, although its garrison was strong enough to put up resistance for some time. At the beginning of the war Arica was an unfortified city (although construction of fortifications began during the war with Spain in 1866, the undertaking was soon aborted), its strategic position made President Prado choose it as his headquarters and a transshipment point of troops and supplies for the southern army that was being formed. After being quite strongly fortified, it became an important foothold for the Peruvians.

In 1879, the town had about 3,000 inhabitants. It was situated in the foot of the 200 meters high hill of Morro located on the shore. Its slopes were very steep on three sides which made access to the top possible only from the east. North of the city, at the mouth of the Azapa River, the Peruvians placed three coastal batteries: San Jose, Santa Rosa and Dos de Mayo, manned by a total of 75–80 artillerymen, forming a group called Fuertes del Norte. From the northernmost San Jose battery up to the fortifications defending the eastern access point to the hill of Morro, there was a 1.4-1.5 metre tall and almost 3 kilometres long wall strengthened with sandbags, which protected the entrance to the city from the north. From the east, access to the top of the Morro was defended by two forts: from the north-east Fort Ciudadela and Fort Este from the south which formed a defence line called Fuertes del Este with a garrison of almost 120 artillerymen. Right behind them, on a small hill, there was another earthen fort, Cerro Gordo, which constituted the second line of defence. The central point of the Peruvian fortifications was the top of the Morro with Fort Alta connected into one defensive system, with Fort Baja on its eastern side. Both forts comprised a fortification system called Fuertes del Morro, manned by about 150 artillerymen. Most of Arica's artillerymen were seamen from the ironclad *Independencia*, lost by the Peruvians at the battle of Iquique. Apart from them, the commanding officer of the Arica garrison,

Peruvian troops in the parade grounds at Arica.

Colonel Francisco Bolognesi, had five more infantry battalions, two of which (about 600 men) were stationed in the city itself and manned the defensive wall from the San Jose battery to Ciudadela, two battalions (a total of 470 men) were stationed at Ciudadela, another battalion (430 men) was stationed at Fort Este. An additional element of Arica's defences from the sea was the monitor *Manco Capac* (Commander Jose Sanchez Lagomarsino) and the torpedo boat *Alianza* armed with spar torpedoes, with crews of 127 men[1]. The city was connected with Tacna by rail.

Table No 2: Armament of the Arica forts

Battery	229 mm ML Vavasseur	203 mm ML Parrot	163 mm ML Parrot	163 mm ML Blakely	162 mm ML Blakely-Varouz
Fuertes del Norte					
San Jose	-	2	-	-	-
Santa Rosa	1	-	-	-	-
Dos de Mayo	1	-	-	-	-
Fuertes del Este					
Ciudadela	-	-	2	-	1
Este	-	-	-	2	1
Fuertes del Morro					
Alta	1	-	2	-	-
Baja	-	-	-	-	4
Total	3	2	4	2	6

Based on: *Boletin...*, op.cit., p. 748; A. Curtis, op.cit., vol. II, p. 28–29; B. W. Farcau, op.cit., p. 144.

Despite the fact that the Peruvians made a lot of effort to turn Arica into a fortress, its fortifications left much to be desired. The town's primary role was to be a naval base, therefore coastal defences were built first. Indeed, the fortification system from the sea was satisfactory. However, the land fortifications were very poor, especially those protecting the city. Access to the city was protected only by a long wall made of sandbags which posed no obstacle to attackers (the Fuertes del Norte batteries were not prepared for all-round defence). Colonel Bolognesi, who was in charge of the city defences, had one big concern – the strength of the Arica garrison. To man all the positions defending access to the city and those protecting the Morro (despite some shortcomings, the latter were more effective), he needed

---

1   The monitor *Manco Capac* was towed by the steamer *Talisman*, accompanied by the transport *Oroya* from Callao to Arica at the beginning of September 1879 – on September 1, the ships left Callao and arrived at their destination on September 7 (A. Curtis, op.cit., vol. I, p. 68; T. B. M. Mason, op.cit., p. 38). The torpedo boat *Alianza* was transported to Arica aboard the corvette *Union* in March 1880 – she left Callao on March 12 and was delivered on March 17 (F. A. Acuña, op.cit., pp. 234, 347).

Arica, view from the north at the Morro.

Arica, view of the town from the Morro.

The Peruvian battery Alta del Morro.

4–5,000 men. Actually, his forces were half that size. In that situation, his decision to man all positions seems to have been a mistake – it would have been more sensible to concentrate all forces at the Morro which was the main point of defence.

Because of Arica's role as the main supply harbour for Rear Admiral Montero's Southern Army, soon after taking Pisagua, on November 28, the Chileans began the city's blockade. It was initiated by the corvette *Chacabuco* and the gunboats *Magallanes* and *Covadonga*. At the beginning of December, the first ship was replaced by the ironclad *Almirante Cochrane*. She did not spend much time at Arica and was deployed north to intercept Peruvian transport sailing from Panama to Callao. Then she was sent to Valparaiso for a short overhaul. The blockade of Arica was entirely dependent on the two gunboats. The operation was uneventful as the Chilean ships had too little strength to undertake any actions against the Peruvians and their strong coastal batteries.

The situation changed with the beginning of the landing operation at Ilo, at the end of February 1880. The *Cochrane*, that had already joined the squadron, was redeployed to support the operation

A 9-inch (229 mm) Vavasseur gun of the Alta del Morro battery (the photograph was taken after the fall of Arica).

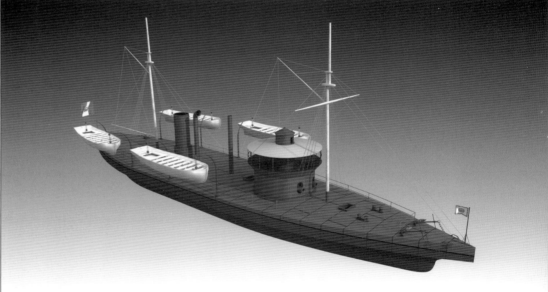

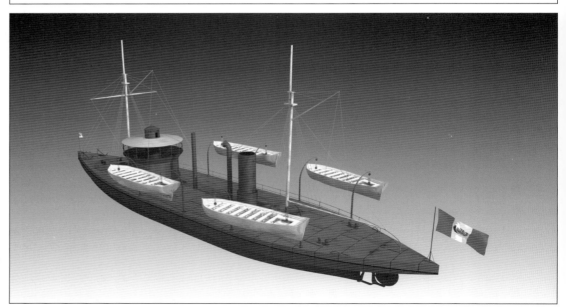

The Peruvian monitor Manco Capac. (Mario Merino)

along with the ironclad *Blanco Encalada*. The main forces were joined by the *Huascar* that had been operating off Mollendo. Despite undergoing an overhaul at Valparaiso, the ship was not as efficient as it had been under the Peruvian flag – the makeshift repairs to the power plant only allowed the ship to reach a speed of 8 knots, which was by ⅓ less than it used to be during her Peruvian service. As far as the Chileans were concerned, this was a minor issue – they needed the ship only for the blockade operation and to fire on enemy positions on land. Therefore, high speed was not a necessity[2].

After joining the main forces, Rear Admiral Rivieros dispatched the *Huascar* to reinforce the blockade of Arica. He gave the command to Commander Manuel Thomson (the previous commanding officer of the transport *Amazonas*), who was aggressive and displayed initiative in all his actions. The new commanding officer of the ironclad was to take command of all the ships in the blockade.

The *Huascar* arrived off Arica on February 25. Already on the next day, in the morning hours, Thomson decided to conduct a combat reconnaissance of the coastal batteries. As a result, a 50-minute artillery battle ensued between the batteries of Fuertes del Norte and Alta on one side and the *Huascar* and the gunboat *Magallanes* on the other. At 09.20, the clash was over. The *Huascar* was hit three times but, fortunately for the Chileans, she sustained no damage.

In the morning of February 27, the Chileans spotted a train leaving Arica station (the first section of the railway, up to the Azufre River, ran along the coast). In order to stop this train, Thomson decided to engage it so he entered the roadstead, coming within range of the Peruvian coastal battery. It immediately opened fire and, shortly after that, *Huascar* was hit by a heavy round which caused substantial damage, killing 7 and wounding 9 seamen. Simultaneously, the Peruvian monitor *Manco Capac* headed towards the Chilean ironclad. Commander Thomson decided to ram the enemy, but he then noticed the torpedo boat *Alianza*, accompanying the monitor, so he broke off his attack. The Peruvian torpedo boat soon turned back but the *Manco Capac* was still in pursuit, ready to engage the *Huascar*. Consequently, the distance between the Peruvian ship and the shore increased and the Chilean commander decided to take advantage of that fact. The *Huascar* made a turn and, using her speed and manoeuvrability, came between the Peruvian monitor and Arica, cutting off the enemy's escape route. However, Thomson underestimated his opponent and made a cardinal mistake by decreasing the distance between the two ships[3]. As a result, when, after 14.00, his ship closed to less than 200 metres to the enemy, the Peruvians managed to score a direct hit on the *Huascar*. A heavy, 450-pound projectile broke the foremast and destroyed the conning tower, killing the Chilean commander. The broken mast jammed the turret rendering the ironclad unable to fight, so Lt. Velvarde, who took command after Thomson's death, had no choice but to withdraw from the engagement, which ended after 15.30. The Chileans lost 8 men killed and 17 wounded, the *Huascar* sustained heavy damage[4].

The damage rendered the *Huascar* inoperable for only one day. On February 29, the ironclads resumed engaging the Peruvian positions on land (this time from a greater distance) accompanied by the transport *Angamos* armed with a modern, long range, 203 mm Armstrong breech-loader. During the next few days, up to March 6, the Chileans bombarded the Peruvian positions (the

Captain Jose Sanchez Lagomarsino, the commanding officer of the monitor Manco Capac.

Colonel Francisco Bolognesi, the Peruvian commander of the Arica garrison (in a photograph taken in the 1860s).

---

2 Wood G.L., Somervell P., Maber J., *The Ironclad Turret Ship "Huascar"*, part 2, "Warship" No. 38, vol. X (1986), p. 92.

3 *Manco Capac* was armed with obsolete but powerful 15-inch (381mm), smoothbore guns that fired round, 450-pdr projectiles. Their range was inferior to that of rifled guns. They were also less accurate. However, due to the weight of their projectiles, they was still very dangerous at close range

4 *Boletin...*, op.cit., pp. 584–586, 607; *Voina mezhdu...*, part. 11, "Morskoi Sbornik" No. 5/1880, pp. 2–3; B. Vicuña Mackenna, op.cit., *...Tacna y Arica*, pp. 388–390, 397. During the battle, the Peruvians fired a total of 250 rounds (193 from Morro, 40 from the northern batteries, 17 were fired by *Manco Capac*), the Chileans fired 184 rounds (*Huascar* – 116, including thirty-five 254 mm rounds and *Magallanes* – 68)., B. Vicuña Mackenna, op.cit., *...Tacna y Arica*, pp. 394–395, 398; F. A. Machuca, op.cit., vol. II, pp. 66–67.

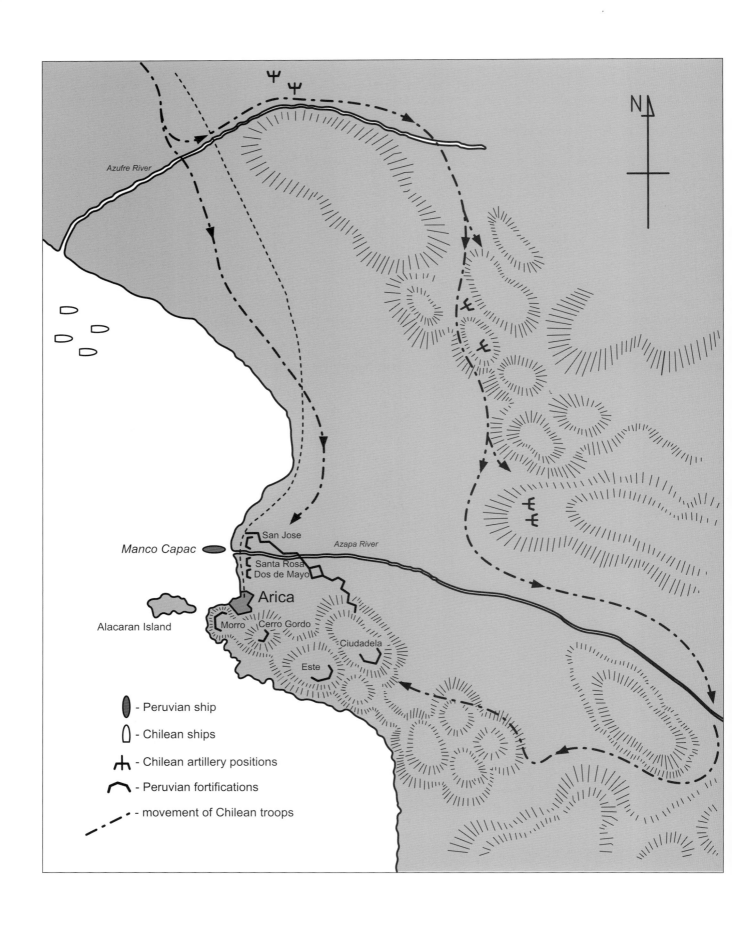

Azufre River

N

Manco Capac

San Jose

Azapa River

Santa Rosa
Dos de Mayo

Arica

Alacaran Island

Morro

Cerro Gordo

Ciudadela

Este

- Peruvian ship

- Chilean ships

- Chilean artillery positions

- Peruvian fortifications

- movement of Chilean troops

The capture of Arica.

Angamos from a distance of 6 kilometres, well outside the range of the Peruvian coastal artillery) caus-ing heavy casualties in the city and harbour[5].

Meanwhile, taking advantage of the Chilean forces' engagement in the landing operation at Ilo, the corvette *Union* left Callao on March 11 with a cargo of large quantities of weapons and supplies for the army at Tacna. Initially, the Peruvian commander Cpt. Villavicencio intended to deliver the entire cargo to Quilca to be later transported by land, however, he learned from the passengers of a passing British ship that Arica was, at that time, blockaded only by the gunboat *Covadonga* (the *Blanco Encalada* and the *Angamos* provided cover for the landing operation off Mollendo). The Peruvian commander decided to break the blockade of Arica and deliver all the weapons and supplies to this harbour. He managed to do that without any problems at night on March 16/17. On the following day the *Covadonga* was joined by the *Huascar* and the transport *Matias Cousiño*. The commanding officer of the *Huascar*, Commander Carlos Condell, immediately sent the transport *Matias Cousiño* to Rear Admiral Riveros to inform him of the *Union*'s presence at Arica. At the same time he began bombarding the port from a distance of 3.5 kilometres, aiming mainly at the Peruvian corvette. Soon, the *Blanco Encalada* and the *Angamos* arrived at Arica. The former took position north of the town, cutting off the *Union*'s escape route towards Callao. Both ships began firing at the harbour, at a distance of 2.7 to 3 km, targeting mainly the Peruvian corvette.

Battle of Arica, fought on February 27, 1880, between the Chilean ironclad Huas-car *and the Peruvian monitor* Manco Capac *supported by coastal batteries.*

---

5   The *Huascar* fired a total of 76 rounds (the largest number on February 29 – 39) and *Angamos* 60 (the largest number also on February 29 – 19). Because the Chileans fired mostly from outside the range of the Peruvian artillery, Arica defenders fired only 11 rounds (at *Huascar*; the batteries at the Morro – 9 and the northern batteries – 2, mostly on February 29) B. Vicuña Mackenna, op.cit., …*Tacna y Arica*, pp. 394–395.

Another illustration of the February 27th engagement. Warships of neutral states, the Italian frigate Gari-baldi *and the French aviso* Chasseur, *can be seen in the foreground.*

101

Commander Manuel Thompson, the commanding officer of the monitor Huascar. *He was killed on February 27, 1880, during the engagement off Arica.*

Despite the barrage, the Peruvians continued unloading the supplies. Chilean fire was not very accurate but the *Union* was hit by two rounds causing some damage (one of them damaged the funnel, the other one exploded on the deck – one Peruvian sailor was killed and seven were wounded). The damage was not very serious and, about 16.00, taking advantage of a lull in the barrage, Cpt. Villavicencio left Arica and headed south at full speed which completely surprised the Chileans. The *Amazonas* was the only ship to give chase after the *Union*, but she did not succeed and the Peruvian corvette was able to run the blockade and return to Callao on March 22[6].

After this incident, the Chileans did not undertake any major operations at Arica. In the meantime, General Baquedano's army defeated the Allies at Tacna, which made Arica his next target. Baquedano was forced to detach occupying forces and units to provide security in the face of the Peruvian concentration at Arequipa, so the only troops he was able to send against Arica were Colonel Pedro Lagos's group that comprised about 4,800 men and 4 artillery batteries (three batteries of field artillery and one of mountain artillery)[7]. Up to June 4, his units were transported by rail near Arica and, on the following day, began taking positions north and north-east of the city. The day after, Chilean negotiators presented the defenders with a capitulation proposal. After it was rejected, at 11.00 Colonel Lagos ordered his artillery to open fire on the enemy positions. At 13.00 the ships joined the barrage. The Chilean batteries were countered by the Peruvian guns from Fuerta del Este and Fuerta del Norte. The artillery duel was won by the Peruvians who silenced the Chilean batteries and forced them to change positions[8].

Shelling of the Peruvian positions was resumed on the next day, but this time, the ships imposing the blockade also joined the bombardment: the ironclad *Almirante Cochrane*, the gunboats *Magallanes* and *Covadonga* and the armed transport *Loa*. The ironclad began shelling the city and the positions at Fuerta del Norte after closing in to the shore to about one kilometre, the gunboats fired at the city and the Morro from a distance of about 2.2 kilometres. The *Loa* took position 7 kilometres from the shore. The duel between the Peruvian artillery and the Chilean ships lasted until 16.00. During that time, the Chilean ships fired a total of 80 rounds at the Peruvian positions causing heavy casualties in the city. The Peruvians fired a total of 74 rounds scoring a hit on the ironclad *Almirante Cochrane* and two hits on the gunboat *Covadonga*. While the damage to the gunboat was not serious, a heavy round that hit

---

6   *Boletin...*, op.cit., pp. 608, 611, 659; *Voina mezhdu...*, part. 12, "Morskoi Sbornik" No. 6/1880, pp. 4–6; B. Vicuña Mackenna, op.cit., *...Tacna y Arica*, pp. 721–723. During the entire engagement, the Peruvians fired a total of 135 rounds (Fuertes del Moro – 92, Fuertes del Norte – 21, the monitor *Manco Capac* – 4, the corvette *Union* – 18), the Chileans fired 84 rounds (including 48 fired by the *Huascar*; mainly at the *Union*).

7   A. Curtis, op.cit., vol. II, p. 30.

8   B. Vicuña Mackenna, op.cit., *...Tacna y Arica*, p. 1129. On that day, the Peruvians fired a total of 71 rounds (Morro – 40, northern batteries – 21, Este battery – 5 and *Manco Capac* – 5), the Chileans fired 272 times (land artillery – 186, *Almirante Cochrane* – 19, *Magallanes* – 28, *Covadonga* – 27 and *Loa* – 12).

The harbour of Arica on March 17, 1880. The corvette Union *can be seen in the centre, which managed to boldly rupture the blockade at night, delivering weapons and supplies to the besieged fortress.*

the ironclad went through an open gun port inside the ship and went off, initiating the explosion of two propellant charges in an ammunition storage room for one of the 229 mm guns. Twenty seven Chilean seamen were wounded (7 of them later died of their wounds) and the ship was heavily damaged. After the barrage, Colonel Lagos again sent negotiators to Arica with capitulation demands and again the defenders rejected them.

At night, in secrecy, Lagos redeployed 2,700 troops east of Arica. In the morning they took positions for attack at the foot of the hill, no farther than 300–400 metres from the forts of Ciudadela and Este. Simultaneously, positions north of the city were taken by another regiment supported by the entire Chilean cavalry (a total of 900 infantry and up to 500 cavalrymen) who were ordered to execute a synchronized attack against the Peruvian positions at Fuertes del Norte and then the city itself. Peruvian prisoners testified that the defenders had powerful fougasses installed in front of their positions[9] and the Chilean commander intended to use the element of surprise to prevent the enemy from exploding them. Indeed, the attack from the east that began at dawn of June 7, surprising the defenders but the first Chilean assault was repelled. Soon, the Chilean troops launched another attack and, despite the discharging of one of the mines by the Peruvians which caused heavy casualties among the attackers[10], they gradually pushed the enemy to the top of the Morro. The remaining 400 defenders assembled at the top of the hill where a dramatic fight ensued. Colonel Bolognesi was killed in action along with almost all the Peruvian soldiers fighting at his side[11].

The fall of the Morro resulted in the capitulation of all the units defending the city by 09.00. The monitor *Manco Capac* was scuttled at 08.42 and her crew taken prisoner by the transport *Itata*. The torpedo boat *Alianza* took her chance and tried to escape north along the shore. She was spotted by the Chilean ships and, after a long pursuit, forced to run ashore by the steamers *Loa* and *Toro* in vicinity of Punta de

Captain Manuel Villavicencio, the commanding officer of the corvette Union, *who managed to rupture the blockade of Arica.*

9   On June 4, while blowing up the bridge over the Azufre River, the Chileans captured the Peruvian engineer who had installed these weapons.

10   The Chilean soldiers who deemed the fact as "dishonourable" were so furious that, during the attack on the Morro, they did not take prisoners and killed the wounded en masse.

11   *Boletin...*, op.cit., pp. 722–723; Cpt. Juan Guillermo Moore, former commander of the *Independencia*, was also killed on top of the Morro.

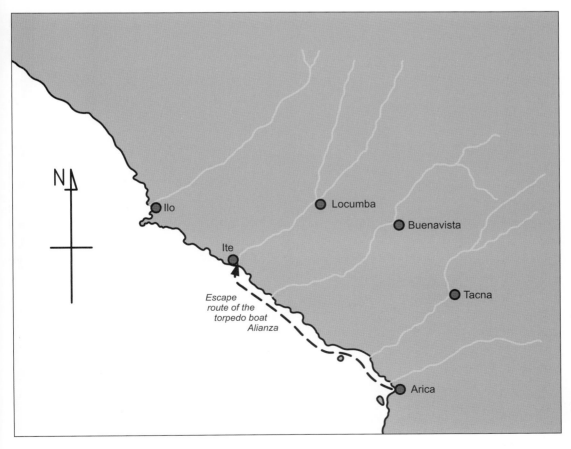

The attempted escape of the torpedo boat Alianza *from Arica.*

Coles near Ite (the torpedo boat's power plant malfunctioned). Her wreck was blown up by her crew who then tried to reach Moquegua by land. They did not succeed and were soon taken prisoner[12].

The capture of Arica came at a cost of over 450 men killed and wounded. The Peruvians lost at least 700 killed (some sources claim the casualties among the defenders were as high as 900), 900 men (including over a hundred wounded) became prisoners of war[13]. Taking control over this strategically important harbour, sometimes called the "Gibraltar of South America", was undoubtedly a huge success that made it possible for the Chileans to realize their minimum plan formed before entering the war.

---

12 F. A. Acuña, op.cit., pp. 358–359; *Boletin…*, op.cit., pp. 669–672, 674, 697–699; *Voina mezhdu…*, part. 15, "Morskoi Sbornik" No. 9/1880, p. 3.

13 A. Curtis, op.cit., vol. II, p. 33; C. R. Markham, op.cit., p. 207; B. Vicuña Mackenna, op.cit., *…Tacna y Arica*, pp. 1158, 1160. G. Bulnes (op.cit., *De Tarapaca …*, p. 388) and D. Barros Arana (op.cit., vol. II, p. 11) claim that the number of Peruvian POWs was as high as 1,328 but this number seems exaggerated. Due to a high number of missing in action, not all of whom were killed, Peruvian losses are difficult to estimate. Several dozen civilians were also killed during the attack or afterwards, when the Chileans soldiers pillaged the city.

The Assault on Arica.

Final fight atop the Morro.

The Morro after the battle.

*Battery San Jose following
the fall of Arica.*

105

13. Blockade of Callao

Callao, as the main base of the Peruvian navy and a transshipment point for all war materiel purchased abroad, had been a thorn in the Chilean side since the beginning of the war. However, during the period of the military operations in the south of the country, the Chilean navy was needed to support them, thus a blockade of that harbour was out of the question – the Chileans did not have enough ships to cope with such an undertaking. It was only made possible after the victory at Tacna which practically settled the outcome of the campaign in the south. Some of the ships could then be used to perform other tasks than supporting the Chilean army and blockading ports that were used to supply Montero's army. At that time, Arica was still held by the Peruvians, but only a portion of the Chilean navy was needed to execute its blockade. The rest could be deployed to initiate a blockade of the most important Peruvian harbour.

The last Peruvian ship to leave Callao before the blockade was established was the transport *Oroya* which, at the beginning of April, delivered large supplies of weapons and a battalion of infantry (about 500 soldiers) to Islay (the transport was meant to reinforce the army at Arequipa). Then she sailed farther south to Tocopilla where, on April 7, she captured a small Chilean steam launch and, on April 9, returned with her prize to Callao. On the same night, the blockade of the port began[1].

---

1   *Voina mezhdu...*, part. 12, "Morskoi Sbornik" No. 6/1880, pp. 6-7. During that raid the *Oroya* tried to capture a small steamer *Taltal*, however, she managed to take refuge in the port, where the Peruvian ship was unable to reach her.

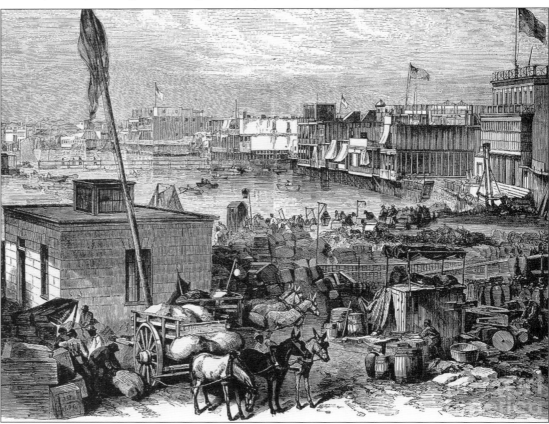

Evacuation of foreign citizens from Callao, following the Chilean proclamation of the blockade of the harbour.

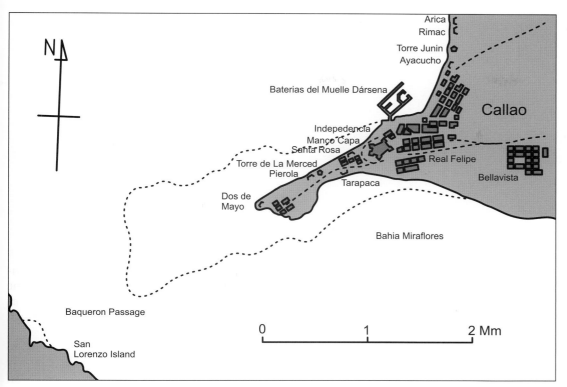

Fortifications of Callao.

The Chilean command made the decision to impose a blockade on Callao right after the main forces began their march towards Tacna. On April 9, Rear Admiral Riveros' group departed from Ilo and headed to the Peruvian harbour. The task force comprised the ironclads *Blanco Encalada* and *Huascar*, the gunboat *Pilcomayo*, the armed transport *Angamos*, and the torpedo boats *Guacolda* and *Janequeo*. The *Matias Cousiño* performed the role of a collier. According to the plan, *Huascar* and the torpedo boats were to sail ahead of the main force and arrive at Callao before dawn to allow the torpedo boats to use their spar torpedoes against the last Peruvian ship that was a threat to Chilean shipping, the corvette *Union*. After the attack, the blockade of the harbour was to be imposed.

However, as it usually happens, not everything went according to the Chilean plans. While towing the torpedo boats, the *Guacolda*'s boilers malfunctioned and the *Huascar* left the ship behind to be taken care of by the main force. *Huascar* and *Janequeo* continued on. In the dark, the ironclad lost her way

A 20-inch (1,000-pdr) Dahlgren of the Dos de Mayo battery (La Punta).

A 20-inch (1,000-pdr) Rodman gun of the Dos de Mayo battery (La Punta). Along with the similar Dahlgren piece, these were the largest smoothbore guns ever manufactured.

and arrived at Callao after dawn. Meanwhile, Riveros' group managed to find the *Guacolda* and, after the necessary repairs, the whole group arrived at Callao early enough to commence the attack. While approaching the harbour in darkness, the *Guacolda* hit a small fishing boat, breaking one of her spars with a torpedo fitted to its end. When she attacked the *Union*, it turned out the Peruvian corvette was surrounded by a boom. To breach the barrier, it was necessary to use a torpedo but the Chilean warship had only one (the other one had been lost along with the broken spar). The ship used her weapon to break the obstacle protecting the Peruvian corvette and, with no more mines, had to abort the attack and withdraw[2].

In the morning of April 10, at about 10.00, Rear Admiral Riveros sent negotiators to Callao to inform the Peruvians that the Chilean navy was going to impose a blockade on April 14 and all neutral ships were ordered to leave the harbour within 8 days from that date[3].

---

2   *Voina mezhdu...*, part. 13, "Morskoi Sbornik" No. 7/1880, pp. 3-4.
3   W. L. Clowes, op.cit., p.104.

An 11-inch (279 mm) Blakely gun of the Santa Rosa battery.

Callao was undoubtedly the most heavily fortified Peruvian harbour and also one of the strongest naval bases in all South America. On its western, outermost promontory of La Punta, there was the Dos de Mayo battery armed with two gigantic 1,000-pound, smoothbore guns (Dahlgren and Rodman) with a very good field of fire in almost all directions – towards the open sea, the Boqueron Strait and Miraflores Bay. Farther north, in the middle of the peninsula, there were two batteries – Zepita (later called Pierola) and Torre de La Merced. The former was just a makeshift battery protected by sandbags, armed with two heavy, smoothbore Rodman guns. The latter, built before 1866, was a brick construction with a rotating turret with two 254 mm, Armstrong muzzle-loader guns. East of the battery, on the other side of the peninsula, there was another makeshift battery – Tarapaca (its construction was completed in May), initially armed, like the Zepita, with two heavy, smoothbore Rodman guns (one of them was replaced by a rifled, 229 mm, Vavasseur muzzle-loader). Unlike the other batteries, whose field of fire was directed towards the sea, the latter was trained on Miraflores Bay. The brick fort of Santa Rosa was positioned at the base of the peninsula. Its armament comprised two rifled, 279 mm, Blakely muzzle-loader guns, also trained at the sea. The 21 de Diciembre battery was nearby. It was armed with 6 old 32-pdr guns (they were of no combat value in 1880). Behind the batteries, there was the five-bastion fortress of Real Felipe, built in the 16th century but modernized several times. The fortress had two towers – Manco Capac and Independencia. The former was armed with two rifled Vavasseur guns and the latter with two Blakely guns identical to those of the Santa Rosa battery. At the foot of the fortress lay another line of fortifications with six batteries (Maipu, Provisional, Zepita, Abtao, Pichincha and Independencia) armed with old smoothbore 32-pdr guns which, in 1880, were of no military value; in fact, they were not manned and should not be taken into consideration when discussing the Peruvian fortifications.

The harbour of Callao was protected by a pier where, in spring of 1880, more batteries were placed (17 de Marzo, Elias Aguirre and two others). Their total armament comprised one rifled Vavasseur gun, 3 heavy and two smaller Rodman and Dahlgren smoothbore guns (the number of Rodman and Dahlgren guns increased to 5 during the blockade, as in October one of the 166-pdr guns was moved to the fortification line at Miraflores) and two obsolete 32-pdr guns. Three other batteries were positioned to the north, on the other side of the city – Ayacucho, Junin and Rimac (it was later renamed to Pacocha). The Arica battery was still under construction. The first one was placed in a brick fort and comprised a 279 mm Blakely gun and a heavy Rodman smoothbore gun. The second was a turreted battery similar to Torre de La Merced with identical armament. The third was a makeshift battery protected by sandbags, armed with 2 heavy Rodman guns. The Arica battery was nearby, still under construction. It was to be similarly armed. The construction work was concluded by November.

Table No 3: Armament of the forts of Callao

Battery	279 mm ML Blakely	254 mm ML Armstrong	229 mm ML Vavasseur	1000-pdr (508 mm) SB	450-pdr (381 mm) SB	166-pdr (279 mm) SB
Southern group						
Dos de Mayo (La Punta)	-	-	-	2	-	-
Pierola (Zepita)	-	-	-	-	2	-
Torre de La Merced	-	2	-	-	-	-
Tarapaca	-	-	1	-	1	-
Santa Rosa	2	-	-	-	-	-
Central group (castle and pier; excluding obsolete batteries armed with 32-pdr smoothbore guns)						
Manco Capac	-	-	2	-	-	-
Independencia	2→1	-	-	-	0→1	-
Baterías del Muelle Dársena (molo)	-	-	1	-	3→5	2→1
Northern group						
Ayacucho	1	-	-	-	1	-
Torre Junin	-	2	-	-	-	-
Pacocha (Rimac)	-	-	-	-	2	-
Arica	-	-	-	-	2	-
Total						
	5→4	4	4	2	11→14	2→1

Based on: F. A. Acuña, *Las Fuerzas Sutiles y la defensa de costa durante la Guerra del Pacífico*, Lima 2001, pp. 200, 266–269, 314, 319–320, 375–376; D. Barros Arana, op.cit., vol. II, pp. 53–54; *Boletín...*, op.cit., p. 49; A. Curtis, op.cit., vol. II, pp. 35–36; B. W. Farcau, op.cit., p. 144.

Pier battery. The photo taken after the fall of Callao.

A 15-inch (450-pdr) Rodman gun of the Tarapaca battery.

Overall, excluding the obsolete 32-pdr smoothbore guns with no military value, all batteries protecting Callao were initially armed with a total number of 28 and later, at the end of the blockade, 29 heavy guns. However, most of them were smoothbore guns with range and accuracy inferior to those of rifled guns. But the clash at Arica between the *Huascar* and the monitor *Manco Capac* proved the guns to be quite effective. Moreover, two of them, the gigantic 1000-pounders, were the biggest smoothbore guns in the world with tremendous firepower. However, during long range combat, only the heavy Blakely, Armstrong and Vavasseur guns were of real value[4].

4   W. L. Clowes, op.cit., pp.111–112; A. Curtis, op.cit., vol. II, pp. 35–36; T. B. M. Mason, op.cit., pp. 57–58.

Fortress of Real Filipe with the low artillery turrets Manco Capac and Independencia.

A supplement for the coastal fortifications of Callao were the ships stationed in the harbour – the monitor *Atahualpa* armed with 2 heavy 15-inch Dahlgren guns (identical to those of the *Manco Capac*), the corvette *Union*, the torpedo boat *Republica* (of the same class as the *Alianza*, destroyed near Arica) and 7 steam launches (*Independencia, Lima, Urcos, Resguardia, Capitania, Tocopilla* and *Arno*) armed with light guns, mitrailleuses and spar torpedoes[5]. Access to the harbour was also protected by mine barriers. However, they were placed too close to the shore to make a difference. The Peruvians also had drifting mines which were used several times during the blockade but with no effect.

April 22 was the deadline set by the Chileans for all neutral countries' ships to leave Callao. That is when they decided to execute the first bombardment of the city. In the morning, at about 04.00, the gunboat *Pilcomayo* chased away the Peruvian steam launches patrolling the roadstead and, at 13.00, she took position facing the northern batteries, the *Huascar* and the *Angamos* positioned themselves in front of the harbour and the ironclad *Blanco Encalada* faced the southern batteries. Half an hour later, the Chilean ships opened fire from a distance of 4.5 to 6.3 kilometres (later joined by the armed transport *Loa* firing from over 7 km). Their main target was the ships in the harbour but several rounds hit buildings in the city and the train station (probably by accident). Up to 16.50, the Chileans fired 170 rounds and scored hits on the corvette *Union*, the transports *Rimac, Chalaco* and *Talisman* and the training ship *Marañon* (apart from the latter, the ships did not sustain any substantial damage). The Peruvians countered the barrage with 17 guns of the coastal batteries (all guns of the northern and central groups excluding the 279 mm smoothbore guns on the pier) and those of the *Union* and the *Atahualpa*. It soon turned out that the range of the smoothbore guns was too short so the only guns engaging the enemy were those of the Manco Capac, Independencia, Ayacucho and Junin batteries along with the *Union*. During the three-hour engagement the Peruvians fired 127 rounds (including 78 from the *Union*), scoring no hits[6].

From that moment on, the Chilean ships began the blockade of Callao. Their main anchorage was the area behind the unfortified island of San Lorenzo where they also organized temporary depots and workshops. During daytime, the Chilean ships would remain in sight of the harbour and spend the nights at anchor while the smaller vessels, mainly torpedo boats (which proved to be very useful during the blockade) patrolled the area off Callao[7]. This was caused by the threat from the Peruvian armed steam launches and from drifting mines. Already on April 15, lookouts on the *Huascar* spotted such

---

5   F. A. Acuña, op.cit., pp. 272–274, 294; A. Curtis, op.cit., vol. II, p. 36. The Peruvians also mobilized the steam launch *Callao* which was not armed and so used only for auxiliary tasks.

6   *Boletin…*, op.cit., pp. 629–630; W. L. Clowes, op.cit., pp.115–116; A. Curtis, op.cit., vol. II, pp. 35–36; T. B. M. Mason, op.cit., pp. 58–59; *Voina mezhdu…*, part. 13, "Morskoi Sbornik" No. 7/1880, p. 4.

7   At Callao, the Chileans had a total of 5 torpedo boats, *Janequeo, Guacolda* (former Peruvian *Alay*), *Fresia* (from June), *Tucapel* and *Colo-Colo* (both from September), R. Markham, op.cit., pp.188–189.

The harbour of Callao.

The bombardment of Callao, April 22, 1880.

a mine. It was destroyed by the ship's guns. On May 7, the *Amazonas* spotted another two mines. One of them was destroyed with mitrailleuse fire from the torpedo boat *Guacolda* and the other exploded during an attempt to tow it to the shore[8].

For employing the drifting mines, Rear Admiral Riveros decided to retaliate and ordered another bombardment of Callao on May 10. On that day, at 13.25, the Chilean ships left the anchorage at San Lorenzo and took their positions. At 13.32, the ironclad *Huascar* began engaging targets on land at a range of 4.5 km. Other Chilean ships joined the fight: at 13.35 the corvette *O'Higgins*, at 13.37 the *Pilcomayo*, at 13.44 the *Amazonas*, at 13.49 the ironclad *Blanco Encalada* and then the *Angamos* (she fired from a distance of 8 km). The *Huascar*, *Pilcomayo*, *Amazonas* and *Angamos* concentrated their fire on the harbour, the *O'Higgins* entered the Boqueron Strait and engaged the battery of Dos de Mayo, the *Blanco Encalada* initially fired at the harbour, but later shifted her fire to the Dos de Mayo battery, shelling it from the north[9]. The bombardment of the Peruvian positions lasted until 18.00, however, the flagship *Blanco Encalada* was the first one to withdraw from the fight, at 16.45. The Chileans fired

---

8   A. Curtis, op.cit., vol. II, p. 36; W. F. Sater, Andean Tragedy: Fighting the War of the Pacific 1879–1884, Lincoln-London 2007, p. 162. As it later turned out, they were Peruvian-made mines with 300-pound explosive charges and a chemical fuse.

9   W. L. Clowes, op.cit., p. 117.

mainly from a range of 3 to 4 kilometres. After 16.00, *Huascar* shortened the distance to 2.7 km (flooding her ballast tanks which decreased the height of her freeboard to a mere several dozen centimetres, making her a hard target for the Peruvian artillerymen). The corvette *O'Higgins* shelled the Dos de Mayo battery from the Boqueron Strait at a range of 4-5 kilometres[10].

The majority of the Chilean rounds reached the area of the harbour, however, there were not many direct hits on the Peruvian ships or the pier battery. The corvette *Union* sustained minor damage (she caught fire which was soon put out)[11].The *Saucy Jack*, the ship that had been captured by Grau, was hit and sunk. The *O'Higgins* fired very accurately and, being out of range of the targeted battery, caused some damage, forcing its crew to abandon their positions. The majority of Peruvian rounds fired at the enemy fell short of their targets. The only ship hit was the *Huascar*, struck three times but with no major damage. During the barrage, the Chileans fired a total of 418 rounds and the Peruvians 152. A dozen or so Chilean rounds hit the city causing damage and civilian casualties (at least 2 people were killed and 30 wounded)[12].

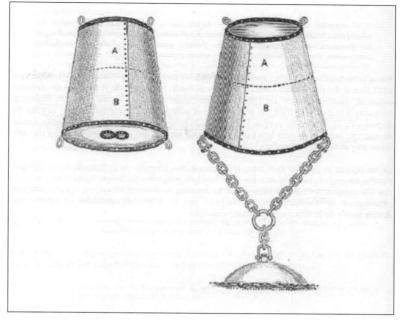

One of the moored contact mines used by the Peruvians in the defences of Callao.

---

10 F. A. Acuña, op.cit., pp. 320–323.

11 To protect the corvette *Union* from Chilean fire, on the north side, the Peruvians constructed a wall of sandbags on the pier which "caught" rounds aimed at the corvette. They also put sandbags on the deck and superstructure which proved to be quite an effective protection. G. de Lisle, *Royal Navy & the Peruvian-Chilean War 1879–1881*, p. 97; Madan, op.cit., p. 708.

12 B. Vicuña Mackenna, op.cit., ...Lima, pp. 88–90. The Chilean ships fired the following amount of ammunition: *Blanco Encalada* – 8, *Huascar* – 145 (including thirty-three 254 mm rounds), *O'Higgins* – 100, *Pilcomayo* – 108, *Amazonas* – 25, *Angamos* – 32. The Peruvian round count was as follows: Dos de Mayo – 20, Terra de La Merced – 7, Santa Rosa – 2, Manco Capac – 6, Independencia – 5, Ayacucho – 10, Junin – 12, Rimac – 24 (a total of 86) rounds; the ships: *Union* – 31, *Talisman* – 31, *Rimac* – 1, *Oroya* – 1, *Limena* – 1, *Atahualpa* – 1., *Boletin...*, op.cit., p. 652–653; *Voina mezhdu...*, part. 14, "Morskoi Sbornik" No. 8/1880, pp. 6-10.

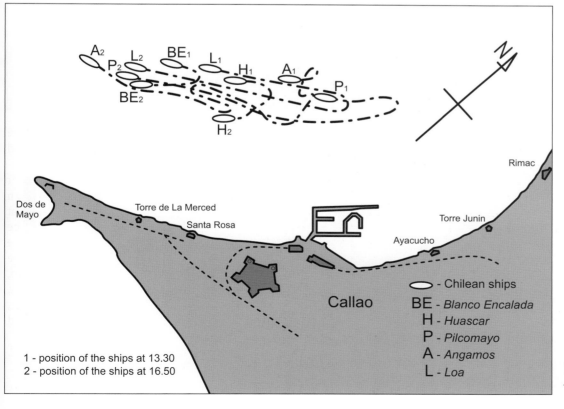

1 - position of the ships at 13.30
2 - position of the ships at 16.50

- Chilean ships
BE - *Blanco Encalada*
H - *Huascar*
P - *Pilcomayo*
A - *Angamos*
L - *Loa*

The bombardment of Callao – April 22, 1880

A Herreshoff torpedo boat. The Peruvians ordered three of those but collected only two (Alianza and Republica; the latter operated at Callao).

Between subsequent bombardments of the Peruvian positions, the Chilean ships only patrolled the area around Callao keeping out of range of the Peruvian artillery. At night, in fear of mines and attacks by Peruvian launches armed with spar torpedoes, the roadstead of the Peruvian harbour was patrolled by the Chilean torpedo boats that usually operated in pairs. The Peruvian light forces were also very active, systematically entering the roadstead and patrolling the area in front of the harbour. Consequently, during the first two weeks of the blockade, there were at least four engagements (on May 11,14, 19 and 24) between the Chilean torpedo boats and the Peruvian armed launches[13]. These encounters were usually brief and ended with an ineffective exchange of fire.

At night on May 24/25, the Chilean torpedo boats *Janequeo* and *Guacolda* departed for another patrol. At the same time (at about 22.40 hours), the Peruvian steam launches *Independencia*, *Resguardia* and *Callao* left the harbour to lay mines in the roadstead – two moored contact mines were carried by the *Callao*, the other ships comprised her escort. The two groups encountered each other at about 02.00, over 6 km from the harbour. In the darkness, the Chilean torpedo boats spotted the *Independencia* which was attacked by the *Janequeo*. The Peruvians were not surprised and opened fire at the enemy with a gun mounted on board the launch. When the Chilean torpedo boat approached the *Independencia* at a small distance and both ships almost touched, the commanding officer of the launch, Ensign Jose Gálvez, along with another crew member, threw a 30-pound explosive charge aboard the *Janequeo*, which was later exploded by Gálvez with a shot from a handgun. A huge explosion ripped the

---

13 F. A. Acuña, op.cit., pp. 308–309; J. A. Bedoya, N. W. Mitiuckow, *Bitwa 25 maja 1880 roku – pierwsze starcie torpedowców?*, „Okręty Wojenne" Nr 4/2008, pp. 5-6.

The nocturnal battle of torpedo boats on May 24/25, 1880. The author made a mistake and drew the Chilean torpedo boat as one of the Herreshoff class ships.

114

A model of the Chilean torpedo boat Janequeo. It probably shows the second ship of that name. The first one built for Italy and purchased by the Chileans, which was sunk in May 1880 at Callao, looked slightly different.

hull of the Chilean torpedo boat apart but also seriously damaged the stern of the Peruvian launch[14]. As a result, the torpedo boat sank within five minutes with the loss of 2 men, the *Independencia* stayed afloat for another 15 minutes. The Peruvian ship's losses included 3 seamen killed and 6 wounded. Her wounded commanding officer along with 6 other seamen were picked up by the *Guacolda* and became prisoners of war (the wounded Gálvez was later delivered to the Peruvians in a courtesy gesture). Right after picking up the survivors, the Chilean torpedo boat came into a short combat contact with the Peruvian launches *Arno* and *Urcos*, which, at the sound of the fight, had left the harbour. Then, the Chilean ship retreated towards the island of San Lorenzo[15].

Two days later, two Peruvian launches attempted to locate the wreckage of the *Janequeo*, sunk in shallow waters, however they were chased away by the *Huascar*, which then, at about 10.40, approached to 1.3 km of the shore and engaged the enemy coastal batteries. After 20 minutes, she was supported by the *Angamos* that took position 7 km to the shore and joined the barrage. The shelling did not last long and soon (11.30), the Chilean ironclad withdrew after firing 14 rounds (during that time, the Peruvians fired 86 times), the *Angamos* ceased firing at 12.12 having fired 8 rounds[16]. In the evening, the Peruvians made another attempt to approach the wreck of the *Janequeo* but their efforts were hampered by fire

---

14 Madan, op.cit., p. 706. According to some Chilean sources the *Janequeo* simultaneously fired her spar mine under the *Independencia*'s stern, however, it seem unlikely. Probably, the only explosion came from the charge dropped aboard the Chilean torpedo boat and its blast damaged the Peruvian launch, which did not manage to move away to a safe distance.

15 F. A. Acuña, op.cit., pp. 324–338; J. A. Bedoya, N. W. Mitiuckow, op.cit., pp. 6–11; *Boletin...*, op.cit., pp. 654–656; *Voina mezhdu...*, part. 15, "Morskoi Sbornik" No. 9/1880, pp. 3-4.

16 *Voina mezhdu...*, part. 15, "Morskoi Sbornik" No. 9/1880, pp. 5-6.

A steam launch similar to the Chilean torpedo boat Guacolda (ex. Peruvian Alay).

The blockade of Callao.

from the *Angamos*. Finally, to prevent the *Janequeo* from falling into Peruvian hands (she was at a depth of 7-8 meters), the ship was destroyed at night on May 29/30 by a large explosive charge placed on the wreck by a diver from the torpedo boat *Guacolda*[17].

The *Guacolda*'s actions drew out three Peruvian launches from the harbour which forced the Chilean torpedo boat to retreat and triggered a reaction from Riveros' squadron blockading the port. Consequently, the gunboat *Pilcomayo*, moving in to help the *Guacolda*, at 06.40 began firing at the pier and the ships anchored at the harbour from a range of 5.7-6 km. Shortly thereafter, at about 6.50, the gunboat was joined by the *Angamos* and 10 minutes later by the *Huascar*, that took position 6-6.4 km from the shore. The Chilean ships fired from a range far exceeding that of the Peruvian coastal artillery, so the defenders deployed the monitor *Atahualpa* to a position about a kilometre from the tip of the pier, however, with no effect. The attackers remained unpunished. The shelling (up until 09.05 the Chileans fired 99 rounds, the Peruvians 48), despite the long range, caused some damage. The Chilean rounds sank the training ship *Tumbes*, a hulk with 700 tons of coal and hit the *Union*[18]. Later, on August 30 (between 10.30 and 11.35), August 31 (between 12.45 and 15.30) and September 1 (between 10.40 and 12.40) harassing fire on Callao was executed by the Chilean transport *Angamos*, that, on September 1, scored a hit on the corvette *Union* and sank one of the hulks[19].

At the beginning of June, the Chilean forces in Callao were joined by several ships that, up till then, had been blockading Arica. Riveros' group was reinforced by the corvette *Abtao*, the armed transport *Loa*[20]

17 W. L. Clowes, op.cit., pp.119; A. Curtis, op.cit., vol. II, p. 37; T. B. M. Mason, op.cit., p. 61; G. de Lisle, op.cit., p. 106. However, J. A. Bedoya, N. W. Mitiuckow claim this event took place at night on June 7/8 (op.cit., p. 11).

18 The amount of ammunition expended by the Chilean ships was as follows: *Huascar* – 25, *Pilcomayo* – 62 and *Angamos* – 12 rounds. On the Peruvian side, the pier battery fired 40 rounds, the Dos de Mayo battery – 4, Ayacucho – 2, Terra del Mercem – 2, the monitor *Atahualpa* fired 1 round., *Voina mezhdu...*, part. 15, "Morskoi Sbornik" No. 9/1880, pp. 7-8.

19 In the following days *Angamos* fired 6, 25 and 19 of her 203 mm rounds at Callao., *Boletin...*, op.cit., pp. 766–767.

20 On June 22, the transport *Loa* delivered 510 wounded Peruvian soldiers from Tacna and Arica, who were transported to land in a courtesy gesture., D. Barros Arana, op.cit., vol II., Santaiago 1881, p. 9; B. Vicuña Mackenna, op.cit., ...Lima, p. 176.

The Chilean transport Angamos. Armed with a modern, long range 203 mm Armstrong breech-loader, she proved useful during the blockade of Callao.

The Chilean gunboat Covadonga.

and the torpedo boat *Fresia* and soon thereafter by the corvette *Chacabuco* and the gunboat *Covadonga*. The last two ships were immediately deployed for patrol operations along the Peruvian coast north of Callao. Simultaneously, up until October, the corvette *O'Higgins* (twice) and the transport *Angamos* (three times) took advantage of lulls in operations at Callao and executed patrols to the north, to intercept any ships carrying contraband from Panama to Peru. However, their actions brought no results.

The transport *Loa*'s service at Callao was not a long one. On July 3, during an afternoon patrol, the ship spotted a small sailing ship drifting to the north. At the sight of the approaching Chilean ship, her three-men crew abandoned ship and, unharassed, safely reached the shore in a small boat. At that time, the *Loa* intercepted the drifting sailing ship and the crew tied her to the side of the transport. The Chileans found large quantities of fresh fruit and vegetables aboard the Peruvian ship, which was a precious booty for the seamen who had been at sea for a long time, and wanted to transfer the cargo aboard their ship. As soon as the Chilean seamen boarded the Peruvian ship, a huge explosion sank *Loa* along with 118 officers and seamen of her 181-men crew (63 men were rescued by the warships of neutral countries that happened to be nearby: the British *Thetis*, the American *Alaska*, the Italian *Garibaldi* and the French *Decres*)[21].

On August 30, 31 and September 1, harassing fire on Callao was executed from a range of 7 km by the Chilean transport *Angamos* which, on September 1 scored two hits on the corvette *Union*[22]. The *Angamos* fired on Callao again on September 3. At the sight of the Chilean ship, three launches, the *Urcos*, *Lima* and *Arno* left the harbour with the clear intent to attack the enemy. They tried to approach the *Angamos*, firing at her with their light guns, which forced the Chilean ship to increase its distance making her fire less accurate. After "playing" for several hours, the Chileans (the *Angamos* was reinforced by the corvette *O'Higgins*) managed to hit and damage the *Lima* which turned back to Callao escorted by the two other ships. All three managed to reach the harbour but when the *Lima*'s crew anchored their ship behind the transport *Oroya*, a heavy Chilean round went through the hull of the latter (causing no major damage) and hit the launch killing two of her crew members and sending her to the bottom[23].

On September 13, the Chileans suffered another loss when the gunboat *Covadonga* was sunk in similar circumstances to the *Loa*. On that day, the Chilean ship was patrolling the area off the port of Chancay, 78 km north of Lima. The *Covadonga* spotted a small sailing ship, in fact a sailing boat. A boarding party was dispatched immediately. The boat was abandoned by her crew and, since no suspicious cargo was discovered, the gunboat's commanding officer, Lt. Cdr. Pablo de Ferrari, gave the order to tie her to the *Covadonga*'s side. While performing this task, a huge explosion sank the gunboat along

21 G. Bulnes, op.cit., *De Tarapaca* ..., p. 541; A. Curtis, op.cit., vol. II, p. 38; C. R. Markham, op.cit., p. 210; W. F. Sater, op.cit., p. 164; *Voina mezhdu*..., part. 15, "Morskoi Sbornik" No. 9/1880, pp. 9-10. F. A. Machuca (op. cit., vol. III, Valparaiso 1929, p. 71) claims that the transport had one more crewman and therefore her losses were 119.

22 *Voina mezhdu*..., part. 16, "Morskoi Sbornik" No. 11/1880, p. 12. On August 30 *Angamos* fired 6 rounds, on the next day 25.

23 Ibidem, p. 13. Later, *Lima*'s hull was salvaged with the intent to return the ship to service, however, after the fall of the port of Lima, the overhaul was not completed and, for the second time, the launch was scuttled on January 17, 1881, this time by the Peruvians themselves. (F. A. Acuña, op.cit., pp. 519–520). On September 3, *Angamos* fired 19 heavy rounds (F. A. Machuca, op.cit., vol. III, p. 73).

The Chilean torpedo boats Janequeo (2nd) and Glaura (the photo taken in the 1890s).

with 73 crew members (including the commander) – only 64 survived, including 49 who were taken prisoners and 15 who escaped on a boat later found by the *Pilcomayo*[24].

The sinking of the *Loa* and the *Covadonga* were not the only cases of the use of booby-trapped ships by the Peruvians. In October, the transport *Toltén* encountered a similar vessel. The Chilean commander, aware of the recent events, did not even attempt to search the boat but opened fire at her, detonating the explosives hidden on board[25].

The use of booby-trapped boats at Callao caused outrage among the Chileans who considered such a way of conducting warfare as "dishonourable". Consequently, after the sinking of the *Cavadonga*, Riveros demanded turning the corvette *Union* and the transport *Rimac* over to the Chileans as compensation. Had the Peruvians refused to comply, he threatened to fire upon the nearby towns. The Chilean admiral's demands were obviously rejected. On September 22, the ironclad *Almirante Cochrane* shelled Chorrillos (she fired a total of 84 rounds but only 13 hit their target), the *Blanco Encalada* bombarded Ancón with 152 rounds, the gunboat *Pilcomayo* targeted Chancay and fired one hundred rounds. Only the gunboat managed to set the town afire causing heavy losses; neither of the ironclads managed to inflict major damage[26].

In October, the Chileans began preparations to redeploy their army's main forces to the north and, at the beginning of November, several ships were sent back to Arica as an escort for the planned expedition. The ships that remained at Callao were: the ironclad *Huascar*, corvette *Chacabuco*, the gunboat *Pilcomayo*, the armed steamers *Lautaro* and *Toro*, the transport *Angamos* and 4 torpedo boats: the *Guacolda* and the *Fresia* and the freshly arrived *Colocolo* and *Tucapel*. Command of the forces was given to the commanding officer of the corvette *Chacabuco*, Commander Ocar Viel.

During the operation, one of the ironclad *Huascar*'s 254 mm guns malfunctioned. As a result, her muzzle-loader guns were replaced by modern, 203 mm, Armstrong breech-loader guns (identical to those that had been earlier mounted on the transport *Agamos*). The guns were tested on November 3 by firing several rounds at the Peruvian harbour[27]. Bombarding the harbour became incidental since most of the Chilean ships were operating as escorts for troops deployed to attack the Peruvian capital. The ships blockading Callao limited their actions to observation of the harbour and sporadic operations against light Peruvian forces that were still being active.

In the morning of December 6, on the Callao roadstead, there was an encounter between Chilean torpedo boats and a group of Peruvian launches the *Arno*, *Urcos*, *Capitania* and *Resguardia*.

24 *Boletin...*, op.cit., pp. 727–728; Madan, op.cit., p. 708; C. R. Markham, op.cit., pp. 211–212; *Voina mezhdu...*, part. 17, "Morskoi Sbornik" No. 12/1880, pp. 9-10.

25 W. F. Sater, op.cit., p. 166.

26 *Boletin...*, op.cit., pp. 806–807; A. Curtis, op.cit., vol. II, p. 39; C. R. Markham, op.cit., pp. 213–214. B. Vicuña Mackenna, op.cit., ...Lima, pp. 205–206.

27 Madan, op.cit., p. 709; F. A. Machuca, op.cit., pp. 216, 224; T. B. M. Mason, op.cit., p. 67. For the Chileans, the 203 mm guns aboard the *Huascar* were not as useful as the similar gun mounted on the transport *Angamos*. The gun ports on the *Huascar* allowed for elevation of only 9.5 degrees, which decreased their range to 6.5 km. The *Angamos*, with her gun elevated to more than 15 degrees, was able to fire at targets on land from distances of more than 8 km while staying out of range of the Peruvian artillery.

Because the clash took place relatively close to the harbour, the Chilean ships came in range of the coastal guns and the corvette *Union*. Despite the action of the *Huascar*, which immediately came to the rescue, the torpedo boat *Fresia* was hit in the stern by a round, probably fired by the *Arno* (at that time, she was armed with a 120 mm muzzle-loader) that heavily damaged the ship killing 2 seamen and wounding 1. Although the other ships managed to tow her out of the range of the Peruvian artillery (the engagement ended about 07.15), the gravely damaged ship sank on the shore of the island of San Lorenzo[28]. Fortunately for the Chileans, the torpedo boat sank in shallow water, not far from the shore (at a depth of several meters) and a week later was recovered and, after an overhaul, returned to service. However, she did not participate in any further military operations.

Between September 9 and 11, the transport *Angamos* continued shelling the harbour in order to draw the Peruvians' attention from the prepared landing operation. Despite the fact that the harassing bombardment was executed from long range, the Chileans managed to hit the corvette *Union*, which was their main target, once on the first day and three times on the second. However, on the third day, the *Angamos*'s modern 203 mm Armstrong breach-loader malfunctioned when fired, broke off from its mount and fell into the sea, killing one and wounding three crew members. Before it happened, the Peruvian monitor *Atahualpa*, accompanied by the launches *Arno* and *Urcas*, had left Callao and moved to a position 2 km from the pier. The *Huascar*, *Chacabuco*, *Pilcomayo*, *Toro* and *Lautaro* joined the fight. The long range fire exchange was ineffective and it ended after the *Atahualpa* returned to the harbour[29].

The last episode of the naval operations at Callao was an unsuccessful torpedo attack executed by the Peruvian torpedo boat *Republica* on January 3, 1881. To achieve the element of surprise, the Peruvians had transported the ship and two Lay torpedoes in secret by rail to Ancón, a harbour 15 miles north of Callao. The *Republica* was launched at night and headed out, towing a torpedo on each of her sides, with the intention to attack the Chilean ironclads. However, in the darkness she was not able to locate them and, at dawn, she was spotted by the corvette *O'Higgins* and one of the Chilean torpedo boats. With no chance of escape, the Peruvians cut loose the torpedoes, which sank, and ran their ship ashore. The wreck was then shelled and destroyed by the corvette *O'Higgins*[30].

---

28 F. A. Acuña, op.cit., pp. 524–525; F. A. Machuca, op.cit., pp. 219–220; C. R. Markham, op.cit., p. 219. During this engagement, the *Huascar* fired 15 rounds including ten 203 mm and five 120 mm rounds, while the *Arno* fired thirty 120 mm ones. Small numbers of projectiles was also fired at the Chilean ships by the Peruvian coastal batteries.

29 *Boletin...*, op.cit., p. 907. During the engagement, besides 7 rounds fired by the *Angamos*, the *Huascar* fired 16 rounds, *Chacabuco* – 5, *Pilcomayo* – 52 and *Toro* – 16. On the Peruvian side the *Atahualpa* fired 9 times, *Arno* – 10, *Urcos* – 3, 5 rounds were fired by the coastal batteries (F. A. Acuña, op.cit., p. 544).

30 F. A. Acuña, op.cit., pp. 560–567; Madan, op.cit., p. 711.

The Chilean torpedo boat Colo Colo, which operated off Callao in the final phase of the siege. Small torpedo boats proved useful in blockade operations.

14. Lynch expedition

Commander Patricio Lynch, the commander of the expedition which wreaked havoc on the northern coast of Peru.

Soon after the capture of Arica, the military governor of occupied Tarapaca, Commander Patricio Lynch, presented President Pinto with a proposal to raid the northern coast of Peru which had not yet been touched by the war. This was to inflict more losses on the Peruvian side and make a statement of Chilean supremacy, thus breaking the Peruvian's will to resist.

On one hand, the proposal was accepted by the Chilean president, but on the other, he expressed his concerns over international repercussions of the attack. Pinto feared that, during the operation, the property of foreign citizens and companies would suffer, triggering their governments' protests. The last thing the Chilean government wanted, especially when their military operations were taking a favourable turn, was the intervention of foreign countries. Finally, the Chilean authorities accepted Lynch's plan, with the condition that all operations would be limited to that part of the coast up to Paita in the north, his troops would not move inland farther than 30 km, taking no unnecessary risks and trying not to inflict any damage to foreign property. The operation was to be executed by over 2,100 troops (5 battalions) with 3 artillery pieces from General Baquedano's army depot. They were to be transported by the transports *Itata* and *Copiapó* escorted by the corvette *Chacabuco*. Lynch was appointed the commander of all forces (although he was a navy officer, he had some experience commanding land forces). He was also assigned a government commissar, Daniel Carresco Albabo, whose task was to supervise the operation from the "political" side[1].

At the beginning of September, Lynch's troops boarded the transports at Arica and, on September 10, landed at Chimbote. There, Lynch destroyed railway material warehouses and demanded a contribution of 100,000 soles from local hacienda owners. Simultaneously, President Pierola, having learned of the Chilean troops' landings, issued a telegram to local authorities that forbade any payments to the enemy. Thus, Lynch's demands were rejected. Consequently, the Chilean soldiers began systematically destroying the haciendas, moving from the north towards Virú. Fortunately, Lynch managed to maintain discipline among his men and there was almost no uncontrolled looting or rapes which, so far, had been very common with the Chilean troops.

During the destruction of the haciendas in the area of Chimbote, the corvette *O'Higgins* entered the port with information about large supplies of ammunition for the Peruvian army, that had been delivered to Supe, about 130 miles south. Immediately, Lynch dispatched an infantry battalion. The unit reached the harbour on September 14, but found no munitions as it had already been transported inland by the Peruvians. As a result, the Chileans demanded contributions and, after a refusal, destroyed local haciendas. Two days later they returned to Chimbote.

On September 17, Lynch's forces were transported from Chimbote north to Paita. On their way, they destroyed guano loading stations on the islands of Lobos da Afuerta and reached their destination two days later. In Paita, the Chileans managed to intercept a transport of banknotes, delivered by the British ship *Islay*, printed for the Peruvian government in the USA with a total value of 7.29 million soles and postage stamps worth 370,000 soles[2]. As contribution from the local authorities, the Chileans collected about 10,000 soles in silver. From Paita, Lynch's troops headed to Eten and arrived there on September

---

1   B. Vicuña Mackenna, op.cit., ...Lima, pp. 231–232.

2   D. Barros Arana, op.cit., vol. II, p. 111; *Voina mezhdu...*, part. 17, "Morskoi Sbornik" No. 12/1880, p. 11. It is worth mentioning that real value of banknote sol was far less than that of silver sol. At that time, banknote sol was worth no more that 10 centesimos in silver (at the end of the year its value decreased to 7 centesimos).

24. In the town, the Chileans collected a contribution from a local railway company despite the fact that it was owned by foreigners (which later triggered diplomatic protests). Additionally, local hacienda owners were also demanded to pay a contribution and, after they refused, their property was destroyed. Systematically, the Chilean units were moving north to Chiclayo (which was reached on September 27) and south towards Trujillo, via Pueblo Nuevo, Pacasmayo to Chocope (which was reached on October 5). Soon thereafter, Lynch received orders to abort the operation as a large operation to capture the capital of Peru, Lima, was being prepared. The troops under his command began withdrawing and concentrated at Malabrigo on October 24. They boarded transport ships and, by November 10, all troops partaking in the expedition returned to Arica[3].

Lynch's raid did not break the Peruvians' will to resist, however, it caused huge material losses estimated at 4.2 to 4.7 million soles (excluding the captured banknotes) which decreased the Peruvian defensive potential[4]. The operation also impaired the Peruvians' trust in President Pierola, who was unable to provide security for his citizens. Moreover, during his operations, Lynch liberated Chinese coolies working at haciendas, who were treated as slaves by the Peruvians, and employed them for auxiliary tasks[5]. This had further repercussions for the Peruvians as the Chinese working for them expressed Chilean sympathies and often collaborated with the enemy (later, Chinese volunteers formed a battalion that fought alongside the Chilean army). Lynch's successful and effective raid became leverage for his career. In rank of Colonel, Lynch commanded Chilean units that participated in battles of Chorillos and Miraflores.

---

3   *Boletin...*, op.cit., pp. 832–835.

4   Ibidem, p. 839; W. F. Sater, op.cit., p. 166. Moreover, Lynch's troops collected over 127,000 soles as contribution and requisitioned large amounts of goods (mainly sugar and rice).

5   As a young man, Lynch served in the British Navy, where he earned his stripes, and participated in the first Opium War, which allowed him to learn basic Chinese.

Officers of the Chilean 1.Regiment "Buin", which provided the largest contingent of troops for the Lynch expedition.

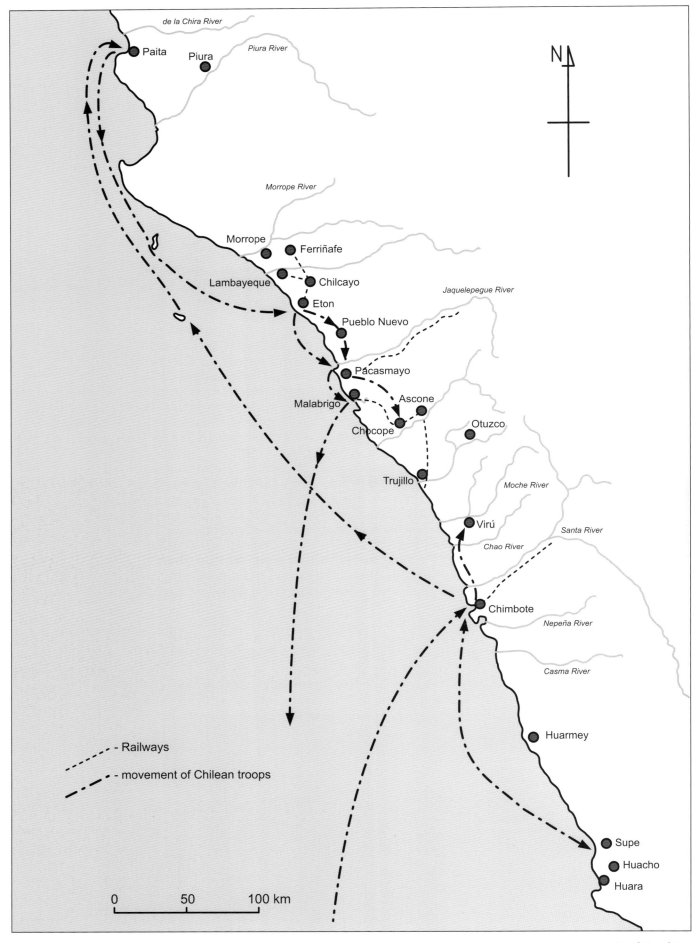

de la Chira River

Paita
Piura

Piura River

Morrope River

Morrope
Ferriñafe
Lambayeque
Chilcayo
Eton
Pueblo Nuevo

Jaquelepegue River

Pacasmayo
Malabrigo
Ascone
Chocope
Otuzco

Trujillo
Moche River

Virú
Santa River
Chao River

Chimbote
Nepeña River

Casma River

Huarmey

Supe
Huacho
Huara

- - - - - Railways

— · — · — movement of Chilean troops

0   50   100 km

N

Lynch Expedition.

15. Battles of Chorillos and Miraflores and the fall of Lima

The Chilean-Peruvian-Bolivian war raised quite a high level of interest in the world, especially in Great Britain as that country maintained trade contacts with Chile and Peru and hoped the conflict would soon be over. The British Prime Minister, William Gladstone, contemplated a joined military intervention along with France, Germany and Italy, however, due to Bismarck's reluctant attitude towards the idea, this never materialized. Moreover, the United States opposed the idea of European countries being involved in the conflict. The US also wanted the war to end quickly as its government feared that Chile would grow in power which, in turn, would weaken the American position in that part of the continent. When, after the defeat at Tacna and the fall of Arica, Peru and Bolivia were ready to accept American mediation, the United States proposed their arbitration during peace talks. It was accepted by all sides of the conflict (although with some objections on the part of Chile) and, on November 22, 1880, the peace talks began on board the American corvette *Lackawanna*, which was anchored at Arica.

Differences in opinion appeared right after the beginning of negotiations. The Chileans immediately stated they would not give up the Bolivian *costa* (the province of Antofagasta), nor the Peruvian Tarapaca – an area rich with deposits of saltpetre, guano and copper. They also demanded all Chilean citizens' property, confiscated by the Peruvian or the Bolivian authorities, to be returned or compensat-

The Chilean 1. Artillery Regiment awaiting embarkation aboard the transports at Arica.

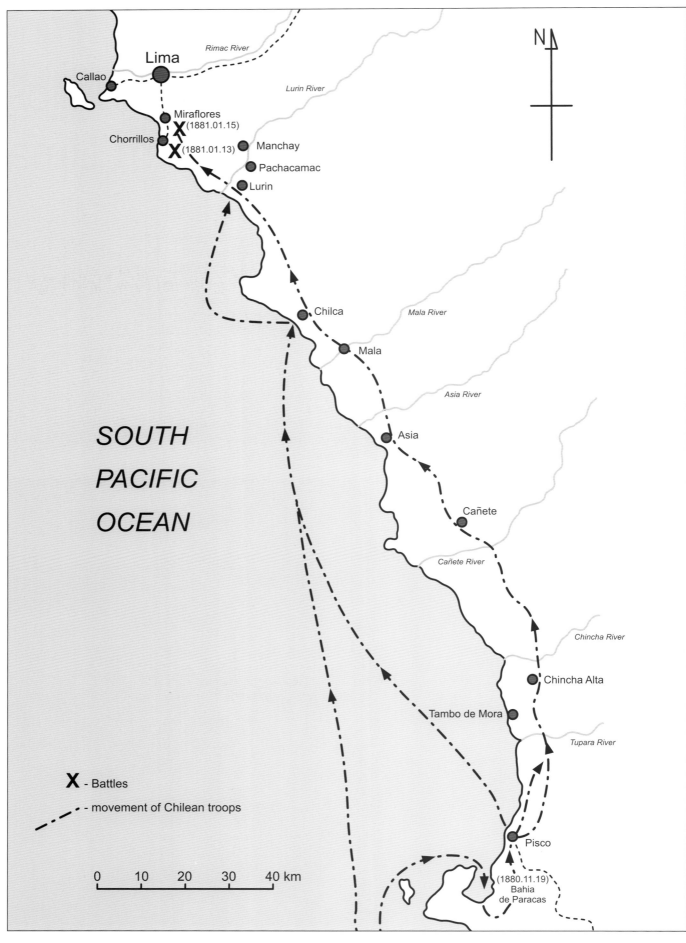

Callao

Lima

Rimac River

Lurin River

Miraflores
X (1881.01.15)

Chorrillos
X (1881.01.13)

Manchay

Pachacamac

Lurin

Chilca

Mala River

Mala

Asia River

Asia

Cañete

Cañete River

SOUTH

PACIFIC

OCEAN

Chincha River

Chincha Alta

Tambo de Mora

Tupara River

X - Battles

- movement of Chilean troops

0   10   20   30   40 km

Pisco

(1880.11.19)
Bahia
de Paracas

Lima Campaign.

ed for. The Allies were to be obliged to return the steamer *Rimac*, pay a contribution of 20 million sols and not to fortify Arica. Until the payment was fulfilled, Chilean forces would occupy Tacna, Arica and Moquegua as a form of pledge or security.

Soldiers of the Chilean 5. Regiment "Santiago" at Arica.

These demands met strong opposition on the Peruvian side. Although the Bolivians had already accepted the loss of Antofagasta, the Peruvians would not even think about giving up Tarapaca. They also had objections concerning other Chilean demands. Consequently, on November 27, after five days of negotiations, the talks were broken off. It meant the hostilities would continue, which opened the possibility for the Chileans to invade the central part of Peru and to attack its capital[1].

The Chileans began preparations for the attack on Lima at the beginning of October, gradually concentrating their forces at Arica which was to become their base for the invasion. Up until the beginning of November, almost 30,000 soldiers and large quantities of supplies were amassed there (some of the troops constituted the occupation forces of the province). The main disadvantage for the Chileans was an insufficient number of pack and draught animals to transport supplies for such a large army. Moreover, they lacked transport ships to transfer the troops by sea. Consequently, some sailing ships were commandeered. They were to be towed by steamers, thus supplementing the transport fleet. In face of the Chilean's total supremacy at sea (the only threat to the Chilean convoys was the Peruvian corvette *Union* but she was still blockaded at Callao) it was an acceptable operation, however, the towed sailing ships limited the Chilean convoys' speed. It was still impossible to deploy all its forces near Lima simultaneously – the operation had to be executed in several stages.

Another issue was the choice of a landing area. With the insufficient number of transport ships and not being able to transfer all troops simultaneously, the Chilean command feared a Peruvian attack. Thus, the landing zone could not be too close to Lima where the main Peruvian forces were concentrated.

On November 14, the transports at Arica began embarking the first batch of troops – General Villagran's 1. Division with 9,000 men, 20 artillery pieces and over 1,600 horses and mules. Soon, a convoy comprising 14 transports left the harbour (7 steamers with 7 sailing ships in tow: *Limari – Excelsior, Lamar – Julia, Itata – Norfolk, Carlos Roberto – Orcero, Santa Lucia – 21 de Mayo, Copiapó – Inspector* and *Angamos – Umberto I*) accompanied by the corvettes *O'Higgins* and *Chacabuco* (which also carried equipment belonging to an artillery regiment assigned to Villagran's division)[2]. On November 19, the

1   C. R. Markham, op.cit., p. 224–227.

2   *Boletin...*, op.cit., pp. 870–871; A. Curtis, op.cit., vol. II, pp. 44–45.

Chilean transports in the Arica roadstead.

The Chilean landing at Curuyacu.

The Chilean troops on the shores of Curuyacu.

Chorillos. The hill of the Morro Solar can be seen in the distance.

Destroyed Chorillos patrolled by the Chilean soldiers.

127

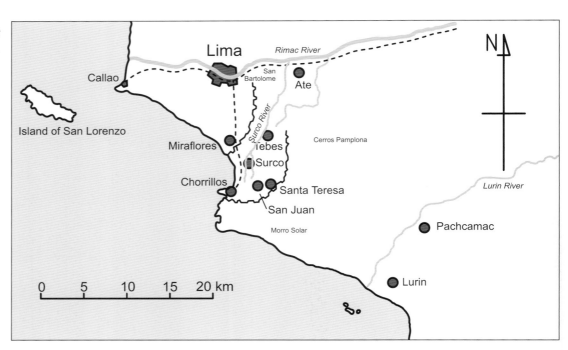

convoy reached the area of Pisco. Soldiers and equipment were disembarked in the bay of de Paracas, several kilometres south of the city. There were no major Peruvian forces in the vicinity so the Chilean troops, without any problems, took Pisco and Ica, located farther inland. Before the debarkation of men and equipment was completed, another convoy had left Arica on November 27, comprising 3 steamers towing 3 sailing ships (*Huanay – Dordrecht*, *Chile – Elvira Alvarez* and *Matias Cousiño – Elena*), escorted by the corvette *Abtao* and the gunboat *Magallanes*. The convoy carried the 2. Brigade of the 2. Division with about 3,300 troops[3]. It arrived at Pisco without any problems on December 2.

The troops that had landed at Pisco were far away from Lima. It was necessary to redeploy them 300 km north to the Peruvian capital. Time was of the essence and the Chilean command made the decision to dispatch General Villagran's 1. Division by land, while the freshly-arrived 2. Division was to be transferred to the concentration point at Lurin by sea, along with the rest of the forces still stationed at Arica, awaiting their turn to be transported.

3   A. Curtis, op.cit., vol. II, p. 45.

128

The battlefield at Chorillos.

The embarkation of over 11,600 Chilean soldiers was executed on December 10 and, on the same day, a convoy comprising 10 steamers towing 11 sailing ships (*Chile – Uumberto I, Paita – Julia, Copiapó – Norfolk, Limari – Excelsior, Santa Lucia – Juana, Pisagua – Avestruz, Bernard Castle – Lota, Lamar – Orcero, Matias Cousiño – Murzi, Amazonas – Wilhelm* and the sailing ship *Otto* towed by the corvette *O'Higgins*), escorted by the ironclads *Blanco Encalada* and *Almirante Cochrane* and the corvette *O'Higgins*, departed from Arica[4]. On December 9, it arrived at Pisco where the 2. Brigade boarded the transports and, on the same day, headed farther north. The convoy arrived at the Curayaco Bay near Chilca on December 22. Troops of the 3. Division and the 1. Brigade of the 2. Division were disembarked.

4   *Boletin…*, op.cit., pp. 884, 930.

Battle of Miraflores.

Battle of Miraflores – fighting at Chorillos.

The 2. Brigade of the 2. Division landed two days later at Lurin along with heavy equipment while units of the 1. Division were approaching by land, from Pisco. During the next few days, all the Chilean forces, over 24,000 men, concentrated in the area of Lurin[5].

Meanwhile, the Peruvians were making intensive preparations to defend their capital city. Pierola announced general conscription of all men of 18 to 50 years of age. There were 240,000 of them in Peru,

---

5   Ibidem, pp. 884, 930.

A view of Lima from the hill of San Christobal, captured by the Chileans.

The Chilean troops marching into Lima.

however, it was impossible to conscript such a large number of men. What is more, a system of military exemption was introduced, which allowed conscription no more than 19–20,000 men (that was also the number of weapons available in military depots) under the presidential decree[6]. Along with units already in service, this made about 30,000 troops stationed around Lima and Callao. With these forces at his disposal President Pierola decided to adopt a defensive strategy and face the Chileans in positions located on the outskirts of Lima. The first line of defence was a 15 km long line of fortifications along the mountain ridge from the town of Chorillos, in fact they stretched from the hills of Morro Solar to the south, through San Juan, up to the hills of Cerros Pamplona to the north-east. It was manned by a total of 20,500 men with 56 field guns and as many fixed guns (including many obsolete smoothbore ones). Those were not all the Peruvian forces because 5 battalions (about 2,000 men) protected the capital from the north in case of an enemy diversion, 3,000 constituted the Callao garrison and another 5–6,000 (mainly poorly trained conscripts and units formed of sailors) took positions in the city itself and on the second line of defence, weaker than the first one, made up of 10 redoubts connected by light field fortifications stretching for about 12 km from the town of Miraflores on the shore to the hills of San Bartolome.

Up until January 12, 1881, the Chilean troops took positions facing the first line of the Peruvian defences and began their attack on the next day[7]. The Chilean attack was supported from the sea by the ironclads *Blanco Encalada*, *Almirante Cochrane*, the corvette *O'Higgins* and the gunboat *Pilcomayo*. After a fierce fight, the Chilean troops managed to break through the Peruvian defences in the centre and on their right flank and gradually push them out of the other positions. The battle ended at 14.30 with a Chilean victory. The success came at a cost of 797 men killed in action and 2,522 wounded. The Peruvian losses were much higher – about 4,000 men killed and wounded and up to 2,500 captured[8]. What was worse, part of the Peruvian forces scattered and Pierola was able to concentrate not more than 10,500–11,000 soldiers with 80 cannons of different patterns at the second line of defence.

On January 15, the Chileans began to storm the second line of the Peruvian defences[9]. The attack began after 11.00 and, despite fierce resistance matching that of the battle of Chorillos, General Baquadeno's forces defeated the Peruvians. Once more, a huge role in breaking through the defences in the coastal sector (in the area of the Alfonso Ugarte redoubt) was played by the Chilean navy. The *Blanco Encalada*, *Huascar*, *O'Higgins*, *Pilcomayo* and *Toro*, actively participated in shelling the Peruvian positions, causing heavy casualties[10]. During the battle of Miraflores the Peruvians lost 3,200 men killed

---

6   B. Vicuña Mackenna, op.cit., ...Lima, pp. 60–61.

7   According to official Chilean reports, over 19,000 soldiers participated in the battle (ibidem, p. 941).

8   *Boletin...*, op.cit., p. 991; A. Curtis, op.cit., vol. II, pp. 60–62.

9   To attack the Peruvian fortifications at Miraflores the Chileans deployed about 13,000 troops, op.cit., p. 970.

10   The Chilean ships fired a total of 357 rounds (*Blanco Encalada* – 40, *Huascar* – 107, *O'Higgins* – 93, *Pilcomayo* – 101 and *Toro* – 16)., B. Vicuña Mackenna, op.cit., ...Lima, pp. 473–474.

and wounded, however, losses on the Chilean side were also high (502 killed and 1,622 wounded)[11]. The victory opened the way to the Peruvian capital and practically decided the fate of the war.

For the Peruvians, the battles at Chorillos and Miraflores were a real disaster. Their army ceased to exist. Demoralized groups of soldiers, withdrawing towards the capital, began robbing stores and houses. They were soon joined by the scum of society. The spreading chaos and anarchy forced foreign diplomats residing in Lima and a group of the capital's inhabitants to put pressure on General Baquedano to capture the city as soon as possible and restore order. On January 16, the Chilean commander accepted the official capitulation of Lima and, on the following day, his troops entered the capital of Peru.

Simultaneously, the garrison at Callao began destroying the coastal fortifications and the remaining warships of the Peruvian navy bases in the harbour[12]. The guns and coastal fortifications were blown up with dynamite. The corvette *Union* and the monitor *Atahualpa* were taken to the roadstead and set on fire – eventually, the corvette drifted toward the shore and sank in shallow waters, the monitor exploded after the fire reached her magazines. The transports *Limena*, *Oroya*, *Chalaco*, *Rimac* and *Talisman* along with some of the armed launches were also sunk[13]. Only several small ships managed to run the blockade and reach Chancay, Ancón and Huacho. This was the end of the naval operations of the Chilean-Peruvian war.

---

11 *Boletin…*, op.cit., p. 991. In both battles the Chileans lost 1,299 men killed and 4,144 wounded which is also confirmed by C. R. Markham (op.cit., p. 260). The Peruvian losses were estimated by the Chileans at about 6,000 men killed (which seems to be an exaggerated number), 3,000 wounded and 3,000 captured (*Boletin…*, op.cit., s. 970).

12 The ships were unable to leave the harbour because, right after the battle of Miraflores, on January 15, Rear-Admiral Riveros sent the ironclad *Huascar*, the corvette *O'Higgins* and the gunboat *Pilcomayo* back to Callao., Rodriguez Asti J., El hudimento de la corbeta Union de la Escuadra peruana el 17 de enero de 1881, "Revista de Marina" No 1/2018, p. 15.

13 Ibidem, p. 18–20; G. Bulnes, op.cit., *De Tarapaca …*, pp. 696–697. The *Arno* and *Capitania* made a successful attempt to escape, the former to Chancay, the latter probably to Ancón (F. A. Acuña, op.cit., p. 585).

Destruction of the Peruvian squadron at Callao. The corvette Union *is burning in the foreground. The monitor* Atahualpa *explodes in the background.*

16. Military operations following the fall of Lima and the end of the war

The capture of Lima and Callao by the Chileans put an end to naval operations, but it did not end the war. President Pierola withdrew deep into the *sierra*, to Ayacucho and formed a new government there, while individual officers made attempts to recreate the army. Admiral Lizardo Montero soon assumed command of the group at Arequipa (former 2. Southern Army) with 5–6,000 troops. In the central part of the country, in the area of Mantucana and Chosica, General Andres Adelino Cáceres created another army of not more than 3,000 soldiers supported by numerous native guerrillas, which blocked the occupying forces from moving into the *sierra*. In the north, in the area of Cajamarca, yet another army was formed by General Miguel Iglesias, who was the Minister of War in Pierola's government.

Pierola's refusal to begin peace negotiations made the Chileans establish a new Peruvian government which would be more acquiescent and willing to accept the annexation of Tarapaca and end the war. That is why, in February 1881, the Chileans called a convention of notables from the *costa*, mainly the wealthy *haciendados*, to appoint a new government. With the approval of the Chilean occupation authorities, the assembly chose Francisco Garcia Calderon to be the new president. On May 12, he established a new government at Magdalena near Lima.

Calderon's new government had practically no power and had been created mainly to present the Chileans with a political body to sign a peace treaty with. The Chileans thought the freshly appointed Peruvian President would yield to their demands and give up Tarapaca, but they were dearly disappointed. Calderon refused to give up any Peruvian territory. Therefore, in September, the Chileans arrested and imprisoned him. However, before this happened, he had appointed his deputies – Lizardo Montero and Andres Adelino Cáceres. The former accepted his nomination at the beginning of October, thus renouncing his allegiance to Pierola. Cáceres withheld from accepting the position offered to him by Calderon, but, on November 24, he also mutinied against Pierola and followed Iglesias who had done so earlier, at the beginning of November. Having lost all his support, Nicolás de Piérola had no choice but to resign from

Left: Francisco Garcia Calderon, anointed by the Chileans to serve as the President of Peru. He refused to sign the peace treaty, in September 1881, in which he would cede the southern provinces to Chile, and therefore, he was imprisoned.

Right: Lizardo Montero. The commander of the Peruvian forces at Arequipa, appointed Vice President by Calderon. Following the arrest of the latter and the flight of Pierola, he became the President in the autumn of 1881.

his office, at the end of November, and leave Peru. Soon thereafter, the three revolting leaders concluded an agreement in Arequipa acknowledging Francisco Garcia Calderon, imprisoned by the Chileans, as the president, with Montero and Cáceres, appointed by him, as vice presidents. Montero, as the senior vice president, was to take office during Calderon's absence and act in his stead (de facto taking the position as president of Peru).

The coalition of the three generals and creation of the new government triggered the Chilean's response. In January 1882, they began a large offensive from Lima to defeat the Peruvians, especially Cáceres's forces. The main attack was directed towards Tarma, Huancayo and then Izuchaca, Despite deploying quite a large force (over 5,000 troops), the campaign did not bring significant success (the Peruvians avoided big confrontations and utilized hit-and-run tactics). The losses that the Chileans suffered, due to combat and illness, exceeded 10% of their troops taking part in the operation.

The campaign of 1882, also called the *Campaña de la Breña*, once more proved that a military solution to the conflict was very difficult for the Chileans. On the other hand, military operations executed with increasing atrocities caused huge losses among the Peruvians and ravaged their economy. Local mutinies among the Chinese coolies, black workers on the coast and natives in the *sierra*, caused chaos inside the country. In face of the increasing disorder and destruction, on August 31, 1882, Miguel Iglesias, commanding the Peruvian forces in the north of the country, announced the proclamation *grito de Montána*, renouncing his allegiance to the government in Arequipa and postulating a quick conclusion of peace. Soon thereafter, in October 1882, Iglesias was appointed president of Peru during a Congress he had called himself. His postulates of immediate peace negotiations gave him support of the Chilean government, who presented him with authority over the northern coast.

To support Iglesias in his conflict with Montero and Cáceres, in April 1882, the Chileans launched another offensive deeper into Peruvian territory. It began with an attack from Lima towards Tarna. Then the Chilean forces headed north towards Pasco, Huanuco and Yungay to engage Cáceres's main forces. However, Cáceres would utilize the same tactics as during the previous year and withdrew northwards to avoid major confrontation. On July 5, at Huamachuco, he encountered a Chilean detachment that had left Trujillo in May and was heading into the *sierra*. Convinced of his superior numbers, Cáceres decided to attack the enemy. During the battle of July 10, his forces suffered a decisive defeat and Cáceres himself barely fled with his life to Ayacucho, chased by Chilean patrols. Soon, another Chilean offensive from Tacna (2,200) and from Ilo (3,000) headed towards Arequipa where Montero was stationed with his army. Both Chilean columns joined at Moquegua, however, before they reached Arequipa, the city inhabitants, who had had enough of the war, followed by the poorly paid Peruvian soldiers, rebelled against their authorities and, on October 29, surrendered Arequipa to the Chileans without a fight. Montero attempted to pacify the mutineers, but failed and was forced to flee to Bolivia.

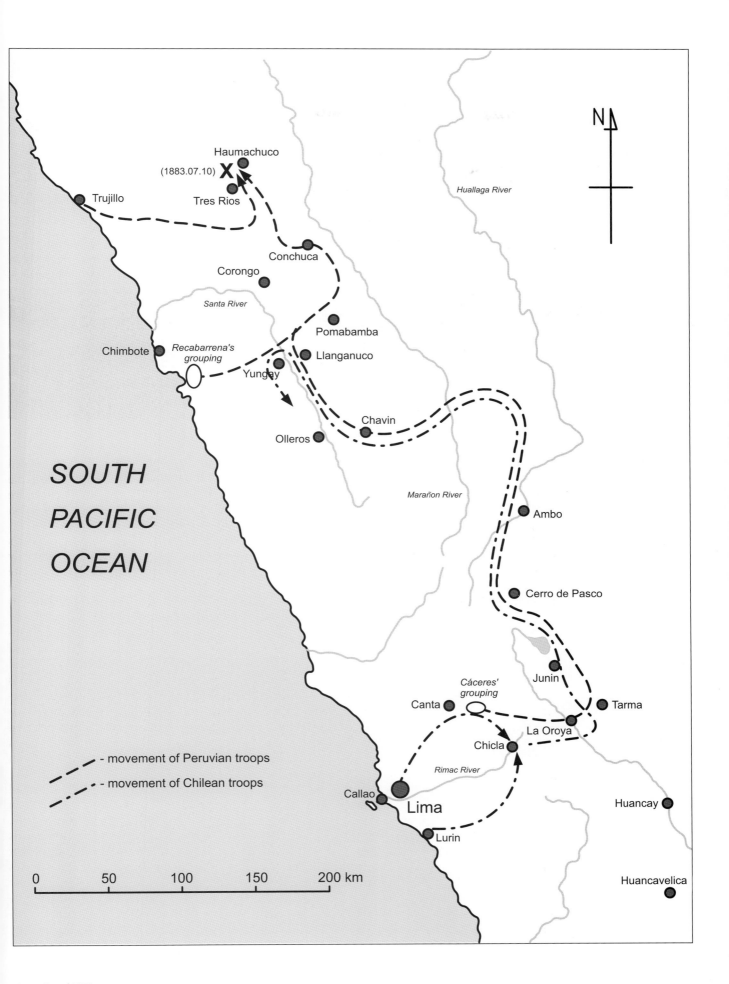

Haumachuco

(1883.07.10) X

Tres Rios

Trujillo

Conchuca

Corongo

Santa River

Pomabamba

Chimbote   *Recabarrena's grouping*

Llanganuco

Yungay

Chavin

Olleros

SOUTH PACIFIC OCEAN

Marañon River

Huallaga River

N

Ambo

Cerro de Pasco

Junin

Cáceres' grouping

Canta

Tarma

La Oroya

Chicla

Rimac River

Callao

Lima

Lurin

Huancay

Huancavelica

- - - - movement of Peruvian troops

-·-·- movement of Chilean troops

0   50   100   150   200 km

Campaign of 1883.

After the Chileans left Arequipa in September 1884, the city was again occupied by Cáceres. However, in the meantime, on September 20, 1883, Iglesias signed a peace treaty with the Chileans at Ancón. According to this document, Peru lost Tarapaca and accepted a 10-year occupation of Tacna and Arica. After that time, the provinces would conduct a plebiscite to decide their dependency[1]. Peru also agreed to pay compensation to Chilean citizens for losses they suffered during the war. The Chileans could mine one million tons of guano, however, half of the profit was to be transferred to the creditors of Peru.

After signing the peace treaty, the Chileans began evacuation of their forces from Peruvian territory which was concluded in October. Meanwhile a civil war was raging between Iglesias and Cáceres and their supporters. Although the latter accepted the treaty at Ancón in June 1884, the conflict went on until the end of 1885 when, on December 1, Cáceres's forces launched a surprise attack on Lima and forced their opponent to leave office. On June 5, 1886, Cáceres officially became the president of Peru which ended the turmoil.

For the Chileans, the end of the war with Peru did not mean the conclusion of the conflict with Bolivia. Although, since the battle of Tacna, the Bolivians had not participated in military operations, the countries were still in a state of war and something had to be done about that. There were two conflicting options both in Peru and Bolivia – to sign a peace treaty as soon as possible or to continue the war. Naturally, after the treaty at Ancón, the majority of Bolivians opted for the peace solution as it had become clear that their country was not able to stand alone against Chile. Negotiations began and, on April 20, 1884, at Valparaiso, a treaty was signed between Chile and Bolivia which left Chile in control of the Bolivian *costa*. Its fate was finally sealed by a Chilean-Bolivian peace treaty signed at Santiago on October 20, 1904. According to this document, the Bolivian coast was to be taken by Chile, which in return would pay compensation to the Bolivians and allow them to use transit facilities at Antagofasta and Arica.

---

1   Due to lack of agreement concerning terms and organization of the plebiscite, the case of dependency of Arica and Tacna was not decided until 1929 when, with help of US mediators, a compromise was reached and Tacna returned to Peru and Arica became part of Chile.

The Chilean soldiers of the "Esmeralda" Regiment during a training exercise.

17. Naval operations on Lake Titicaca

Lake Titicaca had always played a crucial role as a transport route that connected Peru and Bolivia. Since the beginning of the 1870s, the Peruvians had had two 140-ton steamers *Yavari* and *Yapura*, which had been used to transport goods and people[1]. After the beginning of the war, the steamers were used to transport troops, weapons and supplies. Their role increased after the fall of Lima when units fighting inland, especially Montero's group, were only able to be supplied from Bolivian territory. Their role was so important that, after seizing the province of Arequipa, the Chileans decided to transfer the torpedo boat *Colocolo* to Lake Titicaca to prevent any further operations of the steamers. This was done at the end of 1883, by transporting the disassembled torpedo boat from Mollendo to the port of Puno which had already been taken by the Chileans.

The *Colocolo* entered service the same year and she succeeded in hampering the operations of both steamers by blockading them in Chililaya where they were soon captured by Chilean troops. However, their success was insignificant as, in August 1884, the Chileans evacuated their forces from Arequipa along with the torpedo boat *Colocolo* which was disassembled and transported to the coast. The Peruvian steamers were handed over to their previous owners and later they returned to their service on the lake[2].

---

1   Both steamers were ordered from Great Britain in 1861. Their construction was concluded a year later. They were shipped in parts by sea to Arica, then by railroad to Tacna and farther on, transported by mules to the harbour of Puno at lake Titicaca. There, they were assembled – *Yavari* entered service in 1870, *Yapura* in 1873., C. Méndez Notari, A Naval Operation on Lake Titicaca, "Warship International" No 1/2013, pp. 79–80.

2   In the mid 1980's the wreckage of the steamer *Yavari* was found and, after restoration, she has been a museum-ship since 1987.

The ironclad Huascar *(present day photograph). Since 1952 the ships has been commissioned as a memorial ship.*

The artillery turret of the ironclad Huascar (present day photograph). The ship is armed with 203 mm Armstrong breech-loaders, which were mounted by the Chileans after the battle of Angamos.

One of the original 10-inch (254 mm) Armstrong rifled muzzle-loaders, which were mounted aboard the ironclad Huascar (present day photograph).

The harbour of Callao prepared for the reception of Rear Admiral Grau's ashes, which had been exhumed in July 1889.

A 9-inch (279 mm) Dahlgren smoothbore gun discovered during the archaeological excavation of the former Peruvian positions at Chorillos.

18. Outcome of the war

The Chilean-Peruvian-Bolivian war was one of the biggest conflicts fought in South America in the 19th century. The scale of operations, military effort measured by financial expenditures, material and human losses on all sides were enormous. The conflict's political significance altered the borders set after the fall of the Spanish colonial empire. Political ramifications of the conflict can be felt even today, over 130 years after the war.

The war consolidated the position of Chile as a local power, increased the country's prestige, enlarged its territory with the Bolivian *costa* and the province of Tarapaca (later, also Arica) – areas rich with mineral resources which strengthened the Chilean economy and became a strong stimulus for its development. Consequently, Chile's budgetary revenues in 1885 were as high as 35 million pesos (40% more than before the war). In 1888, they increased to 39 million, which was almost twice as much as before the war. All this happened despite the huge costs that Chile had suffered while conducting military operations and later during occupation of the Peruvian *costa*[1]. Although the country's public debt increased to 87.3 million pesos in 1885, it began to decrease during the following years (especially the foreign debt) and, in 1888, it dropped to 82.5 million pesos[2]. It proved that Chile handled the war effort well, and the conflict itself, although costly, brought the country substantial economic gains.

The war's economic balance for Peru was much different. The country's economy suffered a huge loss when provinces rich with resources were taken over by Chile. Moreover, military operations were conducted almost entirely on Peruvian soil, causing destruction hard to estimate. Consequently, not only did Peru lose its saltpetre deposits but the war also decreased the country's sugar industry potential which, before the war, had constituted over ¼ of Peruvian exports. Losses suffered by the Peruvian economy are best presented by the country's budget after the war – in 1878, its treasury budget was about 11 million soles and, in 1884, it dropped to a mere 6.2 million soles. It had not reached its pre-war level until 1896, when the income was 10.7 million soles with expenditures exceeding 11 million[3]. The Peruvian economy was hugely affected by the country's public debt which did not increase significantly during the war (in 1884 it was 50 million pound sterling), but with lower budgetary revenues, it became an issue. Consequently, Cáceres's government signed an agreement with a company representing the creditors of Peru (the Peruvian Corporation Ltd. based in London). According to this document, in return for cancellation of the debt, the company would gain 66 years of freedom to use Peruvian ports, all customs income, the right to mine 3 million tons of guano and money that was to be paid to the creditors of Peru by the Chileans on grounds of their right to mine a million tons of guano which had been established by the peace treaty[4]. The agreement did not solve the issue of the entire debt but only the foreign one which was 31.5 million pounds. The problem of domestic debt was partly solved by issuing banknote sols with a face value of 14 million pounds, however, they soon devalued and, after 1884, they were worth merely 4-5 centavos. This "paper inflation" caused other issues and did not make the country's economic situation any better. However, it is safe to say that, despite huge difficulties, Peru coped well with the economic results of the war, although its costs were enormous and hampered the country's development for many years.

Paradoxically, the war did not affect the Bolivian economy in the least. Indeed, the country lost the coast, but it did not cause significant economic perturbations. The government lost its income from

---

1   At the end of April 1882, official war expenditures were 23.3 million pesos but the amount was certainly understated. Total cost of the war, including occupation of the Peruvian territory are estimated at, at least, 80 million pesos, however, a large portion of the costs was financed with contributions and confiscations in the occupied Peruvian territories (up to 35.5 million), the rest with current income (10 million), loans and other sources., R. Gonzales Amaral, op.cit., pp. 35–36.

2   *The Statesmen's Year-Book...*, vol. XXVII (1890), op.cit., p. 403.

3   Ibidem, pp. 807–808.

4   *Dzieje Ameryki Łacińskiej...*, op.cit., p. 132.

minerals mined at Antagofasta but the primitive Bolivian economy handled the loss well. In a sense, seizing the *costa* by the Chileans had a positive long term outcome. Chile invested in communications infrastructure in their new territories and, after signing the relevant treaties with Bolivia, facilitated export of Bolivian goods – copper, silver and, from the 1890's, tin which became an export "hit" that boosted the country's development. In result, the Bolivian treasury income, despite losing the coast, decreased only slightly and soon returned to its level from before the war.

The Chilean-Peruvian-Bolivian war put a heavy financial burden on its participants, however, human casualties were the most painful. By European standards, where conflicts fought during that time involved much larger forces, the losses were not very significant, but for South American societies with populations between 2 to 3 million, the number of casualties was huge and raised high emotions. The victory for the Chileans came at a cost of 3,500 people who were killed or died of wounds or illnesses (including 400 seamen). At least 9,000 soldiers were wounded in action or became ill. For the majority of them, it resulted in permanent disability. Those were huge losses for the Chilean society, however, the Peruvians suffered even more casualties. It is estimated that during the war almost 10,000 Peruvian soldiers and guerrillas fighting in the second phase of the conflict were killed or died of wounds. Another 10,000, or more, were heavily wounded or became ill. These losses do not include civilian casualties. All military operations took place on Peruvian soil and it is certain that civilian casualties far exceeded losses suffered by the Peruvian army and later by the guerrillas. In captured areas, the Chilean troops often robbed and raped and after the fall of Lima, when military operations moved farther inland, the fighting became very brutal, which mostly affected the civilians. The Peruvian population suffered huge losses during several riots and purges which took place in the areas captured by the Chileans (mainly during the Chinese and black workers' mutinies and retaliatory ethnic cleansings of Chinese populations in the cities) and deep in the *sierra*, where native people's uprisings, although intended to fight the Chilean occupiers, often affected the Peruvian Creole population. Taking into account victims of epidemics, it is possible that tens of thousands civilians lost their lives.

The Bolivians suffered the smallest losses. It is estimated that during the war (which for the Bolivians lasted until the Battle of Tacna) less than a thousand soldiers were killed and about 2,200–2,300 were wounded or became seriously ill.

The Chilean-Peruvian-Bolivian war was observed by military strategists all over the world with great interest. The conflict was important for development of the art of war, especially naval operations. It proved the strategic importance of fleets in naval conflicts like this one. Although all sides of the war were bordered by land, the Atacama Desert did not allow large numbers of troops to be transported by land. Thus, to be able to deploy troops over long distances, it was crucial to achieve supremacy at sea. That is why the first phase of the war was limited to naval operations which affected its further course.

With the victory at sea the Chileans achieved operational freedom and gained the initiative. As a result, without significant superiority in land forces, they were able to deploy their troops to strategic locations and achieve local dominance. On the other hand, the Peruvians, not being able to predict the places that were to be attacked, were forced to scatter their forces to occupy all key positions. Consequently, during all the major land battles, the Chileans had more troops and were able to achieve victories over a tough and equal opponent.

Great interest was raised by the commerce war fought by the Peruvians from May to October 1879. Undoubtedly, Rear Admiral Grau achieved huge success blocking the Chilean invasion against Peru for six months with only two fully fledged ships: the ironclad *Huascar* and the corvette *Union*. His actions have been analysed numerous times and later became an example of proper commerce operations to engage superior enemy forces and seize strategic initiative. The operations ended after the battle of Angamos, when the Chileans captured the *Huascar*. Although defeated, Grau left his mark on the concept of a commerce war.

In the field of naval combat tactics, artillery demonstrated its importance. Wartime experience proved big, smoothbore guns to be obsolete. The Peruvians had a large number of such artillery pieces in their coastal batteries and on two monitors bought from the USA. The clash at Arica on February 27, 1880, showed that big, smoothbore guns were still dangerous in the right circumstances, however, their short range and accuracy inferior to that of rifled guns made their effectiveness very low and so the conclusions were clear – their time had passed. On the other hand, modern breach-loaders used in the war passed their test with flying colours. During the war, the Chileans purchased three 203 mm Armstrong and several 152 mm guns from Great Britain. Their effectiveness outclassed all older models in long range engagements.

During the combat operations, the Peruvians and the Chileans utilized torpedo boats on a large scale. The Peruvians had only two ships of that type, the others were armed steam launches, but the Chileans deployed at least 6 torpedo boats which were very effective in the so called "little war" fought during blockades of harbours (especially Callao). It is interesting to note that it was during this conflict when, on May 25, 1880, the first nocturnal torpedo boat engagement in history took place which resulted in sinking of the Chilean *Janequeo* and the Peruvian launch *Independencia*. It is interesting that neither the Chilean, nor the Peruvian torpedo boats had self-propelled torpedoes but were armed only with spar torpedoes. Self-propelled torpedoes were deployed in several attacks but with no significant success. Shortly before the fall of Lima, the Peruvian torpedo boat *Republica* attempted to launch her two self-propelled Lay torpedoes, towed on her sides, however, the attack was unsuccessful and the ship was lost. The Lay torpedo (the Peruvians purchased a total of 10) was used in combat on August 27/28, during the attack by the ironclad *Huascar* against the Chilean ships anchored at Antagofasta. A torpedo launched at the corvette *Abtao* turned back and headed towards the *Huascar* which was miraculously not hit by her own weapon. After such an unfortunate experience, Rear Admiral Grau and other Peruvian commanders became very sceptical towards this kind of armament. Moreover, the launching procedure was rather complicated and difficult in combat conditions which limited the possibilities to utilize the weapon. Consequently, the Chilean-Peruvian war was bad publicity for the Lay torpedo, and soon the easier to operate and more effective Whitehead self-propelled torpedoes became more popular[5].

The Peruvians also devoted much attention to the use of mines. On land, they utilized weapons such as fougasses – explosive charges buried outside defensive positions, fired by an electric impulse. At sea, during the defence of Callao, the Peruvians utilized several types of mines, purchased abroad or made domestically, however, they played a minor role in the operations. Contact mines were placed too close to harbours and in insufficient numbers to have a major impact on the outcome of a battle. Drifting mines of domestic production were used several times at the beginning of the blockade and made an impression on the Chileans, however, they were not an effective weapon. Mines were replaced by booby-trapped ships – small sailing ships or boats with hidden explosive charges, usually with an inertia fuse that would ignite during a cargo inspection carried out by an unaware enemy. Such booby-trapped ships caused the sinking of two Chilean ships, the transport *Loa* and the gunboat *Covadonga*. The Peruvians launched at least three of those "hellish machines". This type of weapon was effective only if the enemy was surprised. Having lost two ships, the Chileans became more cautious, making further attempts to utilize the booby-trapped ships ineffective.

Overall, the naval operations of the war brought interesting experiences which, although with no significant influence on the art of naval warfare, were observed with great interest and recorded thoroughly.

---

5   The *Huascar* had already encountered the new torpedo during an engagement with the British frigate *Shah* in the roadstead of the harbour of Ilo on May 29, 1877 (the *Huascar*, taken over by mutineers, was deemed a pirate ship and was then attacked by the frigate *Shah* and the accompanying corvette *Amethyst*). During the engagement, which ended with the Peruvian ironclad being damaged, the Whitehead system self-propelled torpedo was used in combat for the first time. The weapon was launched by the British frigate but missed its target.

19. Appendices

Appendix 1

CHILEAN AND PERUVIAN NAVY LIST

The list includes the warships that were commissioned, completed or purchased during the war, including transports along with some special purpose types (including the chartered ones). Vessels which were completely obsolete and therefore did not take part in military operations, as well as those employed for auxiliary duties or in reserve are not included.

The list includes ironclad warships (with side armour) divided into broadside ironclads (with artillery carried on a closed battery deck along their sides), turret ironclads (with artillery mounted in rotating turrets) and monitors (turret ironclads with low freeboard and limited seakeeping characteristics); corvettes (unarmoured warships with displacement above 1,000 tons and with an open battery deck); gunboats (gun ships with displacement below 1,000 tons); torpedo boats (small torpedo vessels armed with spar torpedoes, including armed steam launches); armed steamers (armed merchants used as auxiliary warships) and transports, as well as some auxiliaries.

Within each type, the ships are grouped according to classes – from the oldest to the newest. The list has been presented in a form of tables. The tactical-technical data includes:

The name of the class – given first in a separate line. In case of ironclads the same line includes information concerning the armour of a given class. The data contains thickness of the side armour (waterline armoured belt; however, shown in case of varied thickness armoured belt as the maximum thickness in the bow, midship and stern section), the deck armour, the artillery armour and the armoured conning tower. The thickness of the armour is given in the millimetres.

Below the individual columns contain the following information:

1) name of the ship,
2) name of the shipyard where built and its location,
3) year of launch and commission,
4) displacement – normal (i.e. including equipment compliant with effective regulations in particular navies),
5) dimensions – in the following order: length (between perpendiculars) x maximum beam x maximum draught at normal displacement. Dimensions in metres (rounded to 0.1 m),

6) induced machinery power (designed or achieved in service), If not known the nominal power is given (n),
7) maximum speed (achieved during trials). The speed is given in knots (nautical miles per hour).
8) artillery armament – given in formulas: number of guns x calibre (shell diameter) given in millimetres or in weight of the shot (in case of smoothbore ordnance) given in pounds and type of gun. In case of rifled ordnance barrel length in calibres is also provided (before the type of the gun). The following abbreviations are used: SB – smoothbore, ML – rifled muzzle-loader, BL – rifled breech-loader, MG – revolver guns or mitrailleuses. In case of torpedo boats the number of spar torpedoes carried aboard is given (mw).
9) Remarks column includes all additional information, mostly that concerning the ship's fate during the war (+ – sunk, = – heavily damaged, # – captured, s – scuttled, k – disaster, z – collision).

"?" at a given information means "probably", "supposably".

In case of transports and minor auxiliaries, they were arranged alphabetically in a row with only partial data given: name, year of completion, year of charter/acquisition, displacement or tonnage, maximum speed (not applicable to sailing ships), potential armament (as above), the most important information concerning the war fate.

Abbreviated shipyard names:

Carraca – Arsenal de la Carraca
Dennis – Dennis Brothers
Earle – Earle's Shipbuilding & Engineering Co.
Green – Richard & Henry Green Ltd.
Jollet – Jollet & Babin
Herreshoff – Herreshoff Manufacturing Co.
Laird – Laird Bros.
Pitcher – William & Henry Sotheby Pitcher
Rennie – G. Rennie & Sons
Samuda – Samuda Bros.
Swift – Alexander Swift & Co.
Wigram – Money Wigram & Sons
Yarrow – Yarrow & Co. Ltd.

Chile

Name	Builder	Launched/Completed	Displacement (t)	Dimensions (m)	Machinery (ihp)	Speed (kn)	Armament	Remarks
Ironclad warships								
Central battery ironclads								
"Almirante Cochrane" class								
Side armour: 114-229-114 mm (entire length of the hull); main battery armour: 203-152 mm (central battery); transverse bulkhead: 152 mm (bow & stern); conning tower: 76 mm								
Almirante Cochrane	Earle Hull	1874-75	3370	64 x 13.9 x 6.7	2960	12,7	6x229/15 ML, 1x95/14 BL, 1x76/18 BL, 2 MG	
Blanco Encalada		1875-76			3000			
Turret ironclads								
"Huascar" class								
Side armour: 51-114-51 mm (entire length of the hull); main battery armour: 203-140 mm (turret); armoured deck: 51 mm; conning tower: 76 mm								
Huascar	Laird Birkenhead	1865-80	1745	57.9 x 10.7 x 4.8	1650	12,3	2x254/15 ML→2x203/26 BL, 2x120/16 ML, 1x76/20 ML, 3MG	ex Peruvian *Huascar*, captured 8.10.79, at Punta Angamos
Unarmoured warships								
Corvettes								
"Esmeralda" class								
Esmeralda	Pitcher Northfleet	1855-56	854 (bm)	61 x 10.7 x 4.3	200 (n)	8	14x120/16 ML	+21.05.79, Iquique roadstead, *Huascar*
"Abtao" class								
Abtao	Dennis Glasgow	1863-67	1670	65.6 x 10.3 x 5.1	800	10	3x178/18 ML, 4x120/16 ML	ex CSS *Pampero*, purchased 1866
"O'Higgins" class								
O'Higgins	Green Blackwall, London	1865-68	1650	66.6 x 10.2 x 5.3	1200	12	3x178/18 ML, 2x163/16 ML, 4x120/16 ML	
Chacabuco		1866-68						
Gunboats								
"Covadonga" class								
Covadonga	Carraca Cadiz	1859-65	630	48.5 x 7.1 x 3.1	160 (n)	8	2x163/16 ML, 1x76/20 ML	+13.10.80, at Chancay, Peruvian booby trapped boat

Name	Builder	Launched/ Completed	Displacement (t)	Dimensions (m)	Machinery (ihp)	Speed (kn)	Armament	Remarks
"Magallanes" class								
Magallanes	Green Blackwall, London	1874-75	772	59.9 x 9.1 x 3.5	1040	11,5	1x178/18 ML, 1x160/16 ML, 1x95/14 BL	
"Pilcomayo" class								
Pilcomayo	Wigram Blackwall	1874-80	600	55.4 x 7.5 x 3.5	1080	10	2x152/26 BL (?), 2 MG	ex Peruvian *Pilcomayo*, captured 18.11.79 at Pacui
Torpedo boats								
"Vedette" class								
Vedette	Yarrow Poplar (London)	1879-79	10			16,5	1 MG, 2 mw	
"Colocolo" class								
Colocolo	Yarrow Poplar (London)	1880-80						
Tucapel		1880-80	5	14.6 x 2.4 x ?	60	12,5	1 MG, 2 mw	
"Guacolda" class								
Guacolda (1)	Des Vignes Chester	1879-79	30	24 x 3.7 x 1.7	40 (n)	18	1 MG, 2 mw	ex Peruvian *Alay*, captured. 23.12.79 at the coast of Ecuador while on the way to Callao; +5.04.81, at San Gallán in a storm
Italian class								
Janequeo (1)	Yarrow Poplar (London)	1879-80	30	26.8 x 3.7 x 1.5	400	18	1 MG, 3 mw	+25.05.80, Callao roadstead, Peruvian armed launch *Independencia*

Name	Builder	Launched/ Completed	Displacement (t)	Dimensions (m)	Machinery (ihp)	Speed (kn)	Armament	Remarks
"Glaura" class								
Glaura		1881-81						
Guale		1881-81						
Rucumilla	Yarrow Poplar (London)	1881-81	35	30.5 x 3.8 x 2.1	400	18	1 MG, 2 mw	
Tegualda		1881-81						
Janequeo (2)		1881-81						
Guacolda (2)		1881-81						+6.12.80, Callao roadstead, gunfire of the Peruvian *Arno*, later raised
"Fresia" class								
Fresia	Yarrow Poplar (London)	1880-80	25	26.2 x 3.8 x 1.5	400	18-19	1 MG, 2 mw	
Lauca		1881-81						
Quidora		1881-81						
Sidewheel avisos								
"Tolten" class								
Toltén	F. y G. Rennie (France)	1873-75	240	39 x 7.1 x 2.7	270	10	4x?	
Armed steamers								
Various classes (purchased 1879)								
Loa	John Reid & Co. Glasgow	1873-74	1657 GRT	88.2 x 12.2 x 5.9	320 (n)	12	2x152/26 BL (?)	Acquired 1879; +3.07.80, at Callao, Peruvian booby trapped boat
Amazonas	John Reid & Co. Glasgow	1874-79	2019	92 x 11.8 x ?	2400	13	1x152/26 BL	Purchased 1879
Angamos	James E. Scott Greenock	1876-79	1180	71.6 x 9.5 x 5	1480	14,5	1x203/26 BL, 1x76/18 BL, 1 MG	ex *Belle*, purchased 10.79
Various small classes (auxiliary gunboats)								

Gaviota (1875; 30 t; also a tugboat); *Lautaro* (1870, purchased 1879, 1880 ex *Princesa Luisa*; 120 t; 6 kn; 1x120/16 ML); *Rimaquito* (1875; 30 t; also a tugboat); *Toro* (1874, purchased 1879; 150 t; 8 kn; 1x120/16 ML)

Transports and auxiliaries

Name	Builder	Launched/ Completed	Displacement (t)	Dimensions (m)	Machinery (ihp)	Speed (kn)	Armament	Remarks

Various classes

Chile (1864, purchased 11.1880; 1672 t; 12 kn), *Isluga* (1850, ex Peruvian captured 1880); *Valdivia** (1865; 900 t);

Various classes (chartered 1879-1883)

Bernard Castle (1878, acquired 1879; 1673 t); *Carlos Roberto* (1872, acquired 1879; 1337 GRT; 12 kn; 4 guns); *Cousiño* (1870, acquired 1879; 1337 GRT; 8 kn); *Copiapó* (1870, acquired 1879; 643 GRT; acquired 1880; 650 GRT); *Huanay** (1864, acquired 1879; 336 GRT; 11 kn; returned 02.80); *Isidora de Cousiño* (1873, acquired 1880; 635 GRT); *Itata* (1873, acquired 1879; 1776 GRT; 12 kn); *Julia* (1850; acquired 1880; 1000 t); *Lamar* (1870; 1400 GRT; 10 kn; b=6.08.79, Caldera Bay, later raised and repaired.; k+after 14.07.80, missing); *Limari* (1869, acquired 1879; 967 GRT; 12 kn; returned 03.80); *Louis Cousiño* (1872; acquired 1880; 1890 GRT; 11 kn); Matias Cousiño (1859, acquired 1879; 877 GRT; 9 kn); Paquete de Maule (1866, acquired 1879; 313 GRT; 11 kn; returned 1880); Payta (1864, acquired 1880; 1344 GRT; returned 10.80); *Pisagua* (1868, acquired 1880; 1600 GRT; 9 kn; b+15.08.1882, Huanchaco); *Rimac* (1872, acquired 1879; 1805 GRT; 13 kn; 4 guns; #23.07.79 off Antofagasta, Peruvian *Huascar* and *Union*); *Santa Lucia* (1866?, acquired 1879; 350 t; z+ 08.79, Caldera Bay, Chilean TRS *Huanay*); 21 de Mayo (1880, chartered 1880; 400 t)

Various classes – sailing vessels (chartered 1879-1883)

Avestruz (1840, acquired 1880; 798 GRT); *Dordrech* (1850, acquired 1880; 835 t); *Elena* (1821, chartered 1880; 400 t); *Elvira Alvarez* (1847, acquired 1879; 943 t); *Excelsior* (1850, acquired 1880; 1000 t); *Inspector* (1860, acquired 1880; 1415 GRT; returned 12.80); *Juana* (1850, acquired 1880; 550 t); *Kate Kellock* (1864, acquired 1879; 1175 t); *Lota* (1866, acquired 1880; 1067 GRT); *Murzi Giuseppe* (1879?, chartered 1880; 1000 t); *Norfolk* (1856, acquired 1880; 1300 t); *Orcero* (1850?, acquired 1880; 400 t); *Umberto I* (1875, acquired 1880; 1098 GRT); *Wilhelm* (? ; acquired 1880)

* – sidewheeler

Name	Builder	Launched/ Completed	Displacement (t)	Dimensions (m)	Machinery (ihp)	Speed (kn)	Armament	Remarks
Ironclad warships								
Broadside battery ironclads								
"Independencia" class								
Side armour: 114 mm (entire length of the hull); main battery armour: 114 mm (broadside battery)								
Independencia	Samuda Poplar (Londyn)	1865-66	3500	65.5 x 13.6 x 6.6	2200	12	1x229/15 ML, 1x203/17 ML, 2x178/16 ML, 12x163/16 ML,	b=21.05.79, at Punta Gruesa, during the chase after the Chilean gunboat, s+21.05.79
Turret ironclads								
"Huascar" class								
Side armour: 51-114-51 mm (entire length of the hull); main battery armour: 203-140 mm (turret); armoured deck: 51 mm; conning tower: 76 mm								
Huascar	Laird Birkenhead	1865-66	1745	57.9 x 10.7 x 4.8	1650	12,3	2x254/15 ML, 2x120/16 ML, 1x76/20 ML, 1 MG	# 8.10.79, at Punta Angamos, Chilean ironclads *Alm. Cochrane* and *Blanco*; *Encalada* → Chilean *Huascar*
Monitors								
American "Canonicus" class								
Side armour: 127 mm (entire length of the hull); main battery armour: 254 mm (turret); armoured deck: 38 mm								
Atahualpa	Swift	1864-65	2100	68.5 x 13.2 x 3.8	320	8	2x450 SB	Purchased 1868, ex American *Catawba*; s+17.01.81, Callao
Manco Capac	Cincinnati	1864-65						Purchased 1868, ex American *Oneota*; s+7.06.80, Arica
Unarmoured warships								
Corvettes								
"Union" class								
Union	Jollet Nantes	1864-65	1827	67.1 x 9.2 x 5.5	400 (n)	13	2→0x163/20 ML, 12x162/15 ML, 1x107/23 ML	s+17.01.81, Callao
Gunboats								
"Pilcomayo" class								
Pilcomayo	Wigram Blackwall	1874-75	600	55.4 x 7.5 x 3,5	180 (n)	10	2x163/16 ML, 4x120/16 ML	#18.11.79, at Pacui, Chilean ironclad *Blanco Encalada* → Chilean *Pilcomayo*

Name	Builder	Launched/ Completed	Displacement (t)	Dimensions (m)	Machinery (ihp)	Speed (kn)	Armament	Remarks
Torpedo boats								
"Republica" class								
Republica	Herreshoff Bristol (Rhode Is.)	1879-79						+3.01.81, Ancud Bay, gunfire of the Chileans gunboats *Pilcomayo* and *Toro*
Alianza		1879-79	10	18 x 2.1 x 1.5	100	12,5	1 MG, 2 mw	s+ 7.06.80, north of Arica, following a failed attempt at breaking the blockade
?		1879-&						Not collected by the Peruvian side
"Alay" class								
Alay	Des Vignes Chester	1878-79	30	24 x 3.7 x 1.7	40 (n)	18	1 MG, 2 mw	# 24.12.79, Ballenita, Ecuador, while on her way to Callao → Chilean *Guacolda*

Various classes (armed steam launches and small tugs)

Arno; *Capitania*; *Independencia* (+25.05.80, Callao roadstead, in combat with the Chilean TB *Janequeo*); Lima (+3.09.80, Callao, gunfire of the Chilean armed transport *Angamos*; raised, s+17.01.81; Resguardia (s+17.01.81, Callao); Urcos (s+17.01.81, Callao); ? (# 14.08.79, at Pisagua, Chilean ironclad *Blanco Encalada*)

Armed steamers

Various classes (sidewheeler steamers)

Limeña (1865, purchased 1877; 1163 t; 12 kn; 2x120/16 ML→2x162/15 ML; s+17.01.81, Callao); Oroya (1873; 1597 t; 11.5 kn; 2x 120/16 ML; s+17.01.81, Callao)

Various classes (propeller steamers)

Chalaco (1863; 990 t; 12 kn.; 4x107/23 ML; s+17.01.81, Callao); *Rimac* (1872, ex Chilean *Rimac* zd. 23.07.79 at Antofagasta; 1805 t; 12.5 kn; 4x89/17 ML; s+17.01.81, Callao); Talismán (1871; 310 t; 12 kn; 4x76/20 ML; s+17.01.81, Callao)

Appendix 2

THE CHILEAN AND PERUVIAN NAVAL ARTILLERY

Chilean artillery

Nominal calibre (mm)	Actual calibre (mm)	Type	Barrel length (in calibres)	Barrel weight (t)	Riffled artillery Projectile weight (kg)	Muzzle velocity (m/s)	Range (km)/(elevation)	Designation
229	228.6	ML	15	12	116.1-113.4	432	4.7 / 10°	Armstrong 12-ton
203	203.2	BL	26		95.3	621	7.3 / 10°	Armstrong 8" Pattern E (?)
178	177.8	ML	18	7	52-50.8	427	5.4 / 15°	Armstrong 7-ton
163	162.6	ML	16	3.5	36.3-31.8	424-453	5 / 15°	Armstrong 70-pdr 69-cwt
160	160	ML	16	3.25	29.3	343	3.5 / 12°	Armstrong 64-pdr
152	152.4	BL	26	4	36.3	573	6.3 / 12°	Armstrong 6" BL (80-pdr)
120	120.65	ML	16	1.6	18.4	391	4.2 / 12°	Armstrong 40-pdr ML
120	120.65	BL	22	1.8	18.4	360	4.3 / 13°	Armstrong 40-pdr BL
95	95.25	BL	14	0.7	9.8	335	4 / 16°	Armstrong 20-pdr BL
76	76.2	ML	20	0.6	5.1	378	4.2 / 16°	Armstrong 12-pdr
76	76.2	BL	18	0.3	3.9	321	3.4 / 16°	Armstrong 9-pdr

Peruvian artillery

Nominal calibre (mm)	Actual calibre (mm)	Type	Barrel length (in calibres)	Barrel weight (t)	Projectile weight (kg)	Muzzle velocity (m/s)	Range (km)/(elevation)	Designation
Rifled artillery								
279	279.4	ML	14	13.6	272.4-204.3		3.4 / 7,5°	Blakely 450-pdr (11")
254	254	ML	15	12.2	133.8-131.5	414	4.7 / 12°	Armstrong 300-pdr (10")
229	228.6	ML	15	11.75	109-105.3		4.3 / 10°	Vavasseur 250-pdr
203	203.2	ML	17	7.4	67.6	385	2 / 5°	Parrot 150-pdr
178	177.8	ML	16	7.12	53-52	475	5.1 / 12°	Armstrong 7"
163	162.6	ML	20	4.41	45.4-36.3	394-440	6.7 / 25°	Parrot 100-pdr
163	162.6	ML	16	3.5	32.5-31.8	453	5 / 15°	Armstrong 70-pdr
162	161.9	ML	15	3.81	31.8-30			Voruz-Blakely 70-pdr
120	120.65	ML	16	1.6	18.4	391	4.2 / 12°	Armstrong 40-pdr ML
107	106.68	ML	23	1.61	13.2	380	6.1 / 25°	Parrot 30-pdr
89	89	ML	17	0.36	5.6			Blakely 12-pdr
76	76.2	ML	18	0.3	5.1	378	4.2 / 16°	Armstrong 12-pdr
Smoothbore artillery								
508 (20")	508	SB	12	52.3	486.3-340	435	7 / 25°	Rodman 20" SB (1000-pdr)
508 (20")	508	SB	11	45.4	486.3-340	417	5.6 / 25°	Dahlgren 20" SB (1000-pdr)
381 (15")	381	SB	13	22.6	199.6-181,5	440-455	4.5 / 25°	Rodman 15" SB (450-pdr)
381 (15")	381	SB	12	19.5	199.6-181.5	430-450	2 / 5°	Dahlgren 15" SB (450-pdr)
279 (11")	279.4	SB	15	7.2	84.4-75.3	405-430	3.1 / 15°	Dahlgren 11" SB

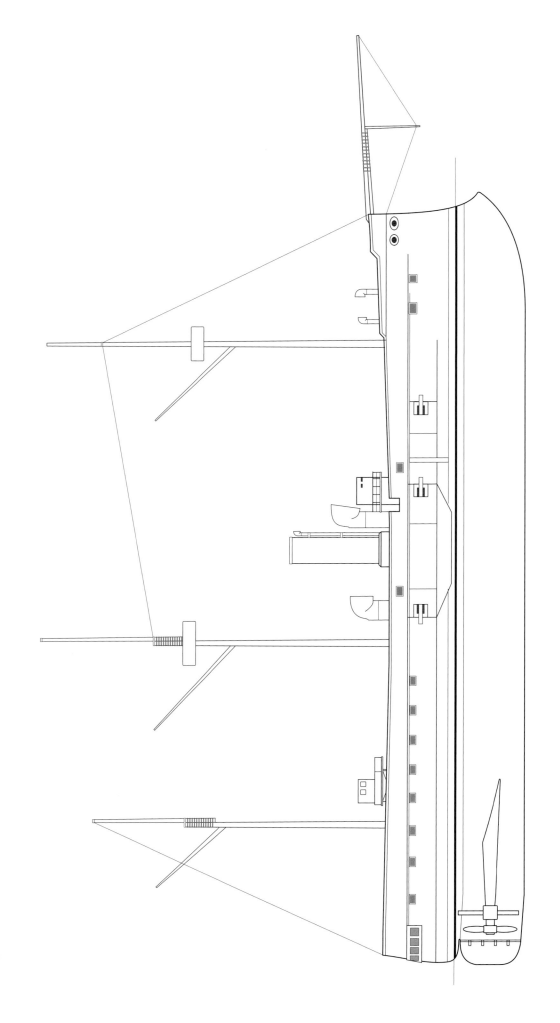

Almirante Cochrane

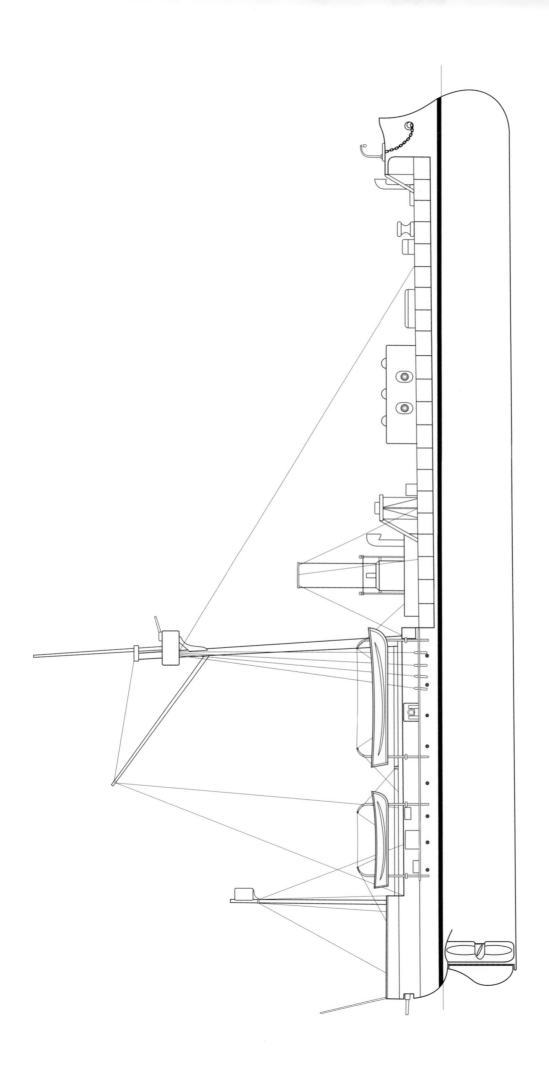

Huascar

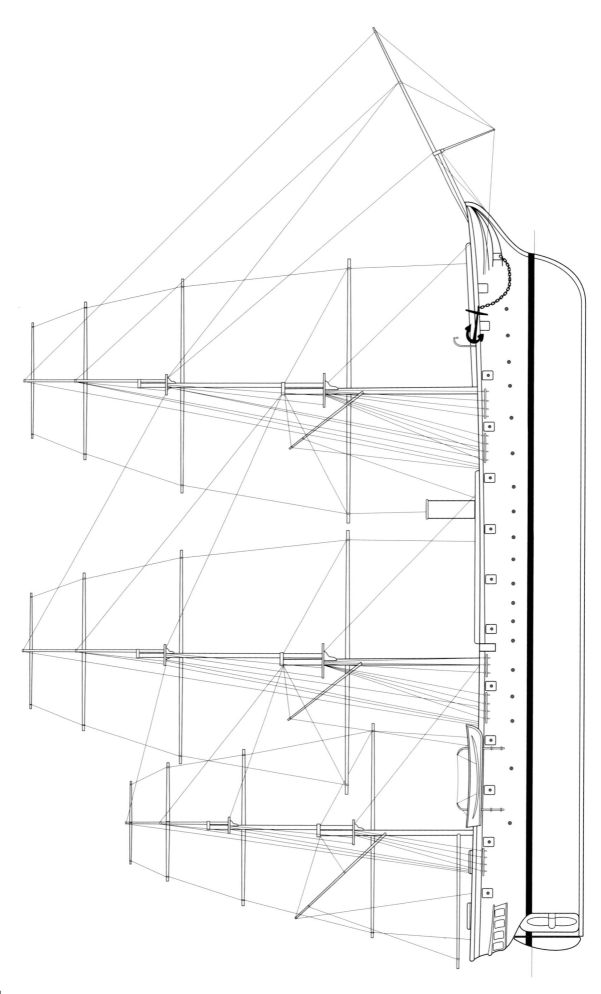

Esmeralda

Covadonga

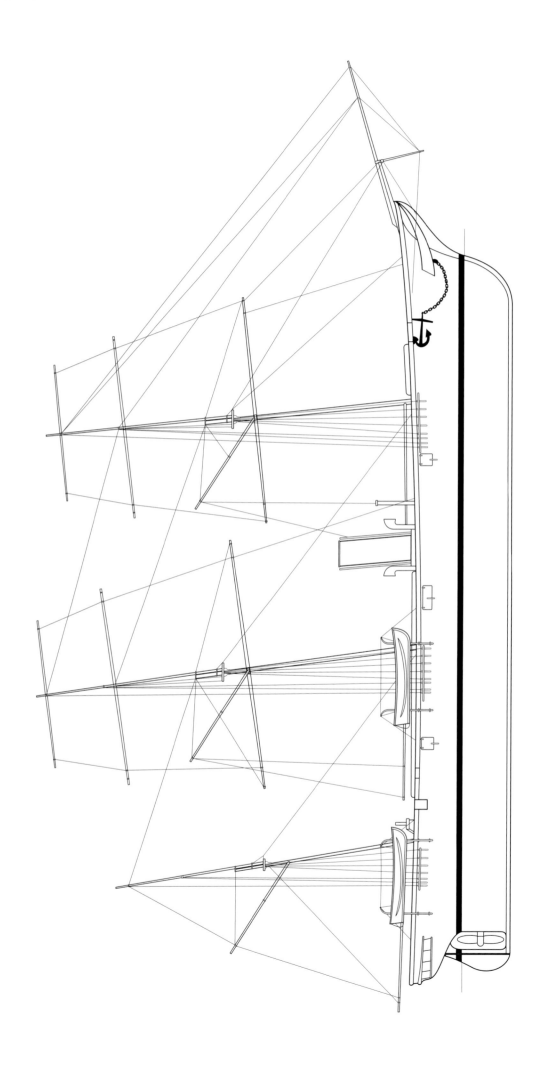

Pilcomayo

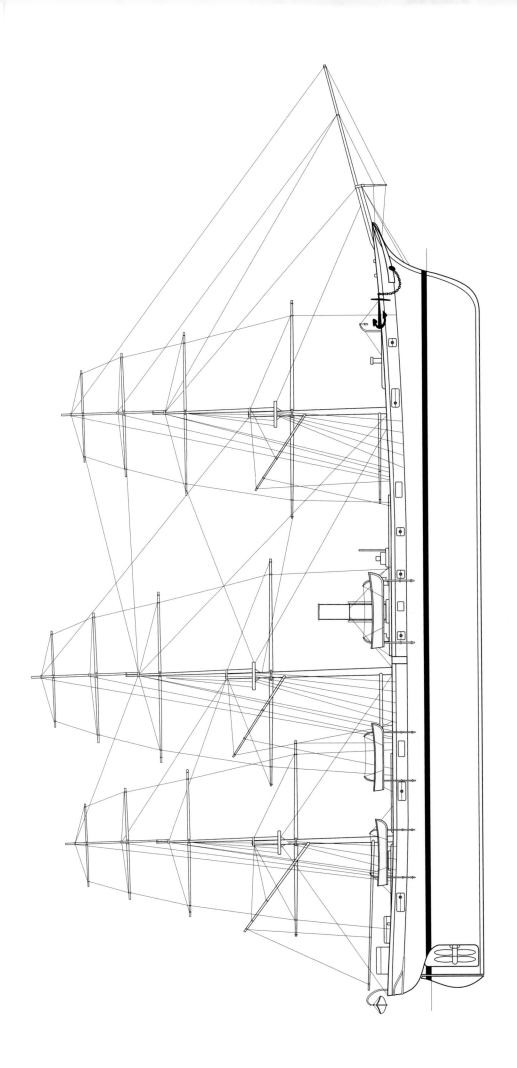

Union

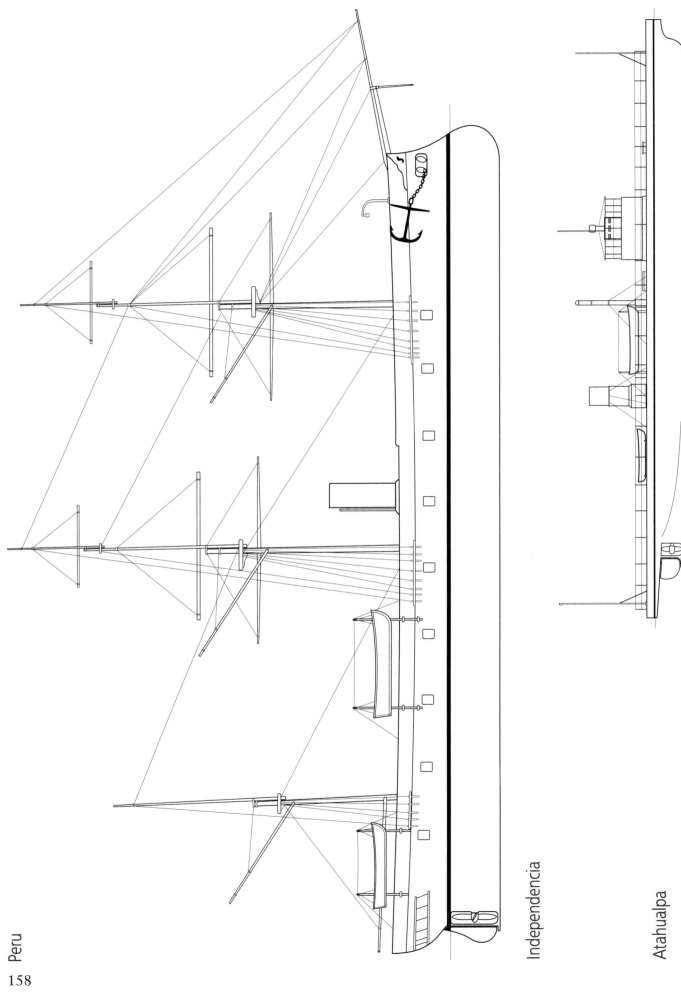

Peru

158

Independencia

Atahualpa

Bibliography

Published documents:

Boletin de la Guerra del Pacifico (red. A. Bello), Santiago 1979

Correspondencia Jeneral de la Comandancia Jeneral de la 1. Division Naval bajo el mando del contra-almirante don Miguel Grau, comendante del "Huascar", Santiago 1880

Memoria de Guerra i Marina presentada al Congresso Nacional de 1880, Santiago de Chile 1880

Riveros G., *Angamos*, Santiago 1882

Voina mezhdu yuzhno-amerikanskimi republikami Peru, Chili i Bolivya. Morskaya khronika. Part 1-17, "Morskoi Sbornik" No. 7–12/1879, 1–9/1880, 11–12/1880

Books & Articles:

Acuña, F., A., *Las Fuerzas Sutiles y la defensa de costa durante la Guerra del Pacífico*, Lima 2001

Amunategui, M., L., *El Diario de la Covadonga*, Santiago 1902

Barros, Arana, D., *Historia de la Guerra del Pacifico (1879–1880), vol. I-II*, Santiago 1880–1881

Bedoya, J., A., Mitiuckow, N., W., *Bitwa 25 maja 1880 roku – pierwsze starcie torpedowców?*, „Okręty Wojenne" Nr 4/2008

Benavides, Santos, A., *Historia Compendiada de la Guerra del Pacifico (1879–1884)*, Buenos Aires 1972

Boyd, R., N., *Chili: Sketches of Chili and the Chilians during the war 1879–1880*, London 1881

Brassey's, *Naval Annual 1886*, London 1886

Bulnes, G., *Chile and Peru. The causes of the War of 1879*, Santiago de Chile 1920

Blunes, G., *Guerra del Pacifico. De Antofagasta a Tarapaca*, Valparaiso 1911

Blunes, G., *Guerra del Pacifico. De Tarapaca a Lima*, Valparaiso 1914

Blunes, G., *Guerra del Pacifico. Ocupacion del Peru – La Paz*, Valparaiso 1919

The Capture of the "Huascar", "Engineering" 12.12.1879, 5.03.1880

Carnet de L'Officier de Marine, 8ᵉ Année – 1886, Paris 1886

Chabaud-Arnault, C., *Istoriya voennykh flotov*, St. Peterburg 1896

Characteristics of Principal Foreign Ships of War, prepared for the Board on Fortification, etc., in the Office of Naval Intelligence, Bureau of Navigation, Navy Department, 1885

Clowes, W., L., *Four Modern Naval Campaigns.*, London 1902

Clowes, W., L., *The Ram, in Action and Accident.*, JRUSI vol. XXXVIII (1894)

Conway's All the World's Fighting Ships 1860–1905., London 1979

Crawford, K., R., Mitiukov, N., W., *Identification of the Parameters of Naval Artillery*, Prague 2013

Cruz, E., A., *The Grand Araucanian Wars (1541- 1883) in the Kingdom of Chile*, 2010

Curtis, A., *To the Last Cartridge. The story of the War of the Pacific 1879–1884, vol. I-II*, West Chester 2007

Custance, R., *The Ship of the Line in Battle*, Edinburgh-London 1912

De La Motte du Portail C., *La Guerra maritime entre le Péru et la Chili*, "Revue Maritime et Coloniale" part 1-4, vol. 65–67 (1880), 71 (1881)

Dzieje Ameryki Łacińskiej, vol. II: 1870/1880–1929 (red. R. Mroziewicz, R. Stemplowski), Warszawa 1979

Durassier, H., *Coup d'ceil sur la guerre chilo-péruvienne*, "Revue Maritime et Coloniale" vol. 68 (1881)

Esposito, G., *Armies of the War of Pacific 1879–1883, Chile, Peru & Bolivia*, Osprey Publishing Ltd., 2016

Esposito, G., Garcia Pinto, A., *The War of the Pacific*, Winged Hussar Publishing 2018

Farcau, B., W., *The Ten Cent War. Chile, Peru and Bolivia in the War of Pacific, 1879–1884*, Westport, Conn. 2000

Farret, E., *Étude sur les combats livrés sur mer de 1860 a 1880, part 2*, "Revue Maritime et Coloniale" vol. 70 (1881)

Fokieiew, K., F., *Woienno-morskoie isskustwo parowogo flota wo wtoroj połowinie XIX w.*, Pietrodworiec 1962

Fuentes, Bush, M., *Captura del Escuadrón de Carabineros de Yungay, cautiverio en la Peru y posterior canje*, "Cauderno de Historia Militar" No 10 (2014)

Garcia, y, Garcia, D., A., *Apuntamientos sobre la fregta blindada „Independencia"*, Lima 1866

Gonzales, Amaral, R., *La artilleria en la Guerra del Pacifico, Academia de Historia Militar*, Santiago de Chile 2013

Gozdawa-Gołębiowski, J., *Od wojny krymskiej do bałkańskiej.*, Gdańsk 1985

Grant, S., A., *The Herreshoff Spar Torpedo Boats of 1878–1880.*, "Warship International" No. 3/1977

Greene, J., Massignani, A., *Ironclads at War. The Origin and Development of the Armored Warships, 1854–1891.*, Pensylvania 1998

Guerre chilo-péruvienne, "L'Année Maritime" 1880–1881 (vol. V-VI)

Guerre du Pacifique, "L'Année Maritime" 1879 (vol. IV)

Hancock, A., U., *A History of Chile*, Chicago, 1893

Higginson, F., J., *Naval Battles in the Century*, London-Edinburgh 1906

Historia del Ejercito de Chile, vol. IV-VII, Santiago de Chile 1985

Historia ilustrada de la Guerra del Pacifico (1879–1884)., Santiago de Chile 1979

Katorin, Y., F., Yurin, I., V., *Peruvian monitors of American Origin*, "International Naval Journal", Vol. (2), № 2 (2013)

King, J., W., *Warships and Navies of the World 1880*, Boston 1881

Lisle, G., de, *Royal Navy & the Peruvian-Chilean War 1879–1881*, Brnsley 2008

Little, I., C., *The Naval Campaign in the War of the Pacific 1879–1884*, "Scientia Militaria, South African Journal of Military Studies" vol 24 (1994), Nr 1

Lopez, J., *Historia de la Guerra del Guano y la Salitre*, Lima 1980

Lopez, J., E., *Mis Recuerdos de la Guerra del Pacifico de 1879*, Santaiago de Chile 1910

Machuca, F., A., *Las Cuatro Campañas de La Guerra del Pacífico, vol. I-III*, Valparaiso 1926–1929

Madan, *Incidents of the War between Chili and Peru, 1879–80.*, JRUSI vol. XXV (1882)

Markham, C., R., *A History of Peru*, Chicago 1892

Markham, C., R., *The War between Chile and Peru 1879–1882.*, London-Edinburgh 1882

Marley, D., F., *Wars of the Americas. A Chronology of Armed Conflict in the Western Hemisphere*, Santa Barbara, Cal. 2008

Mason, T., B., M., *The War on the Pacific Coast of South America between Chile and the Allied Republic of Peru and Bolivia, 1879–81*, ONI War Series No II, Washington 1883

Méndez, Notari, C., *A Naval Operation on Lake Titicaca.*, "Warship International" No. 1/2013

McCray, D., A., *Eternal ramifications of the War of the Pacific*, University of Florida 2005

Mitrofanov, A., *Monitor Huáscar pod dwoma banderami*, "Okręty Wojenne" Nr 1/2002

Molinare, N., *La campaña a Lima. Batallas de Chorrilos y Miraflores.*, "Cauderno de Historia Militar" No 10 (2014)

The monitor "Huascar"..., WI Nr 1/1993

Olender, P., *Niezwykłe losy pancernika Huascar.*, MSiO Nr 2/1998

Paz, Soldan, M., F., *Narracion Historica de la Guerra de Chile contra el Peru y Bolivia*, Buenos Aires 1884

Pietrow, M., A., *Obzor gławniejszich kampanji i srażienji parowogo fłota w swjazi s ewoluciej woienno-morskogo iskusstwa.*, Leningrad 1927

Pojen, G., *Znachene morskoi artylerii v srazhenyakh poslednyago vremeni.*, St. Petersburg 1888

Rawson, E., K., *Twenty Famous Naval Battles, vol. II*, New York 1899

Rodriguez, Asti, J., *El hudimento de la corbeta Union de la Escuadra peruana el 17 de enero de 1881*, "Revista de Marina" No 1/2018

Sater, W., F., *Andean Tragedy. Fighting the War of the Pacific, 1879–1884*, Lincoln-London 2007

Scheina, R., L., *Latin America. A Naval History 1810–1987.*, Annapolis 1987

Shippen, E., *Naval Battles, Ancient and Modern*, Philadelphia 1883

Shippen, E., *Naval Battles of the World*, Havernhill, Mass. 1898

Silverston, P., H., *Warships of the Civil War Navies*, Annapolis, Mar. 1989

South American Navies, "Engineering" 4.07.1879

The Statesmen's Year-Book. Statistical and Historical Annual of the States of the Civilised World for the year 1878–1883 (vol. XV-XX; red. F. Martin), London 1878–1883

Steam, *Steel and Shellfire. The Steam Warship 1815–1905.*, London 1992

Stenzel, A., *Istoriya voyny na morye.*, vol. V, Petrograd 1916

Uribe, y, Orrego, L., *Los Combates Navales en la Guerra del Pacifico 1879–1881.*, Valparaiso 1886

Varigny, Ch., de, *La Guerra del Pacifico*, Santiago de Chile, 1922

Very, E., W., *Navies of the World*, New York 1880

Vicuña, Mackenna, B., *Guerra del Pacifico. Historia de la campaña de Tarapaca, vol. I-II*, Santiago de Chile 1880

Vicuña, Mackenna, B., *Guerra del Pacifico. Historia de la campaña de Tacna y Arica 1879–1880*, Santiago de Chile 1881

Vicuña, Mackenna, B., *Guerra del Pacifico. Historia de la campaña de Lima 1880–1881*, Santiago de Chile 1881

Warner, W., E., *Warships of the Chincha Island Wars (1864–1866). Spain's Last Imperial Adventure*, Middletown 2015

Wieczorkiewicz, P., P., *Historia wojen morskich. Wiek pary (vol. II).*, Londyn 1995

Williams, Rebolledo, J., *Guerra del Pacifico. Operaciones de la Escuadra Chiliena*, Valparaiso 1882

Wilson, H., W., *Battleships in Action. vol. I*, London 1926

Wilson, H., W., *Ironclads in Action. vol. I-II*, London 1896

Wood, G., L., Somervell, P., Maber, J., *The Ironclad Turret Ship "Huascar". part 1-2*, "Warship" Nr 37–38

Sources of illustrations:

Graphic

Illustrated London News

La Ilustracion Española y America,

Le Monde Illustré,

Historia ilustrada de la Guerra del Pacifico (1879–1884)., Santiago de Chile 1979

Canal YouTube „Morskie opowieści"

Author's own collection